The History of Swedish Economic Thought

Routledge History of Economic Thought Series

A History of Australian Economic Thought
Peter Groenewegen and Bruce McFarlane

A History of Japanese Economic Thought
Tessa Morris-Suzuki

The History of Swedish Economic Thought

Edited by Bo Sandelin

London and New York

First published 1991
by Routledge
11 New Fetter Lane, London EC4P 4EE

Simultaneously published in the USA and Canada
by Routledge
a division of Routledge, Chapman and Hall, Inc.
29 West 35th Street, New York, NY 10001

© 1991 Bo Sandelin

Typeset by Leaper & Gard Ltd, Bristol, England
Printed and bound in Great Britain by
Biddles Ltd, Guildford and King's Lynn

British Library Cataloguing in Publication Data
The History of Swedish Economic Thought.
  1. Sweden. Economics. Theories, history
  I. Sandelin, Bo
  330.1

  ISBN 0-415-02130-8

Library of Congress Cataloging in Publication Data
The History of Swedish Economic Thought / edited by Bo Sandelin.
        p.   cm. – (Routledge History of Economic Thought Series)
     Includes bibliographical references.
     ISBN 0-415-02130-8
        1. Economics–Sweden–History.   I. Sandelin, Bo, 1942–
  II. Series.
  HB116.5.A2H57   1990
  330′.09485–dc20
                                                                    89-77035
                                                                         CIP

HB
116.5
A2
H57
1990

Contents

1 **Introduction**
   Bo Sandelin University of Göteborg   1

2 **Before economics**
   Johan Lönnroth University of Göteborg   11

3 **David Davidson: the transition to neoclassical
   economics**
   Carl G. Uhr University of California, Riverside   44

4 **Knut Wicksell, neoclassicist and iconoclast**
   Carl G. Uhr   76

5 **Gustav Cassel, popularizer and enigmatic Walrasian**
   Lars Magnusson University of Uppsala   122

6 **Eli F. Heckscher: the economic historian as economist**
   Rolf G.H. Henriksson University of Stockholm   141

7 **The Stockholm school and the development of
   dynamic method**
   Björn Hansson University of Lund   168

8 **Beyond the Stockholm school**
   Bo Sandelin   214

   References   225
   Index   239

Chapter one

Introduction

Bo Sandelin

To write the history of economic thought is an arduous mission, even if it is confined to the evolution of thought in a single country. Generally no single person can master all the texts and all the epochs that he should. This means that a sole author who takes upon himself such a task must either have excessive erudition and genius – which have been granted to but a few persons in our trade – or must to a large extent rely on secondary sources and judgements. In the latter case, a great deal of courage is required.

This is one reason why this book is not one man's work. Five specialists in different aspects of the history of Swedish economic thought contribute in areas where they are experts. One cannot, however, deny that there are risks involved in such an approach, and not only the risk of lacking formal uniformity in the presentation.

In the words of S. Tood Lowry:

> our methodology and our notions of what is important, our paradigms and our research programs, keep changing from generation to generation, both in evolutionary and revolutionary transitions. This would lead us to believe that the study of the history of thought is one of the best possible antidotes for intellectual ossification. Economic thought should be as dynamic and responsive to the challenges of the economy as are cultural and natural forces. (1987: 5)

It is not a unique idea that the history of economic thought should focus on *change*.[1] This was, for instance, expressly a leading principle for Heimer Björkqvist (1986) when he wrote his large-scale work on the history of economic thought in Finland, which partly coincides with that in Sweden, as Finland was a part of Sweden until 1809. The intimated risk in a multi-author book like ours is that the link between different stages will be suppressed, i.e. that the book will give a number of snapshots while concealing the dynamics in the evolution of thought. It is for the reader to determine whether we have obtained a reasonable trade-off between expertise in single epochs and exposition of change between epochs.

Before economics

The next chapter, by Johan Lönnroth, differs from the subsequent chapters by extending over two millennia, ending at the end of the nineteenth century, when modern economics, represented by Davidson and Wicksell, took over. However, for lack of written sources there is not much to say about the first millennium.

The provincial laws, *landskapslagarna*, were written down from the beginning of the thirteenth century and indicate a change from extended to nuclear family relations as a basis for inheritance rights and maintenance obligations, and from the promotion of the economic interests of relatives to the interests of the Church and the king.

Another kind of economic text began to circulate among educated landowners early in the sixteenth century: husbandry literature with practical advice on sowing, beekeeping, brewing, etc. Economic literature, as we interpret the term nowadays, did not appear until the seventeenth century, when Sweden's military and political power was great and a number of distinguished immigrants raised the intellectual level of the country. Foremost among these immigrants was probably the historian and natural law philosopher Samuel von Pufendorf, who was one of the learned Germans who were offered a Chair when a new university was founded at Lund in 1668; the province of Skåne, in which Lund is situated, had recently been won from Denmark by conquest. Pufendorf became one of Adam Smith's leading authorities on natural law, and he wrote on price formation and on taxes. Taxes should be just, which in Pufendorf's view implied a variant of the benefit principle which has since been advocated by Wicksell, Buchanan, and others.

An often analysed era in Swedish political economy is the eighteenth century, more specifically the period 1718–72, which has been called the Age of Freedom (i.e. freedom from royal absolutism). During this period 'the promotion of economic growth and modernization was the cornerstone of official policy' (Magnusson, 1987). It found expression in different kinds of measures. The first Chairs of political economy at Swedish universities were created during this period. The very first Chair was located in Uppsala, where Anders Berch took office in 1741; the Diet had resolved to establish the Chair in 1739.

This was the fourth Chair in Europe; the first was set up in Halle in Prussia in 1727, the second in Frankfurt an der Oder, also in 1727, and the third in Rinteln in 1730 (Liedman, 1986: 27). Both in Sweden and in Prussia the State had power over the universities; this Liedman regards as one of the reasons why those countries had Chairs in political economy before England and France.

The first Chair in Sweden, Berch's, like the German Chairs, was formally connected with cameralism and law. It was followed by three Chairs which all had a different determination, towards applied natural science: at Turku in 1747, at Lund in 1750, and a second at Uppsala in 1759.[2] Knowledge about nature is essential if one is to utilize nature economically, which was an object of the policy of the Age of Freedom.

Other measures to promote economic growth were a number of economic regulations. The 'Produktplakatet' of 1724 was a Swedish version of the English navigation laws. Subsidies were given to, especially, import-substituting manufactures. Domestic trade was regulated.

During the Age of Freedom there was lively internal discussion on economic matters, made possible by general freedom of the press. Supporters of the policy of regulation have, not unexpectedly, been called mercantilists, while the adherents of a greater degree of economic freedom have been labelled reform mercantilists (Magnusson, 1987). Some of the latter might rather be called physiocrats; a 'Swedish-style physiocracy' is discernible from the end of the 1760s. At the turn of the century Adam Smith was introduced to a Swedish audience by translations of extracts from *The Wealth of Nations* and by a book on his ideas translated from German. The ideas of the British classical economists were often disseminated in Sweden by German and French translations (Björkqvist, 1986: 47). This is, of course, just a reflection of the general cultural influences of the time.

The economic writing of the first eight decades of the nineteenth century in Sweden has received less attention in the literature than that of the eighteenth century; I think this is a correct judgement. There is no straightforward explanation, but we can make a few observations. First, at the end of the nineteenth century David Davidson and Knut Wicksell appeared on the scene, and compared with them their immediate Swedish predecessors may seem less significant. Second, during a large part of the century the historical school predominated, during another part it subsisted beside other movements. History is written by victors, i.e. by economists brought up in the classical/neoclassical tradition, who seldom regard the writings of the historical school, with its inductive method and organic conception of the State, interesting.[3] (One could argue that they should not regard the Age of Freedom as very interesting either, before the 1760s; and, not unexpectedly, more economic historians and specialists in the history of ideas than pure economists have studied the Swedish thought of this period.)

In the period 1815–30 the historical school defined official State ideology, and in political economy as a university discipline it dominated until the middle of the century. Subsequently, liberal ideas flourished; at the universities this meant an increased interest in the classical economists. Wicksell's predecessor in the Chair at Lund, G. K. Hamilton, was the most pronounced liberal – today we might say libertarian. Outside the universities liberalism had to compete for radical minds with the growing strength of socialism.

The transition to modern economics

Such was the atmosphere when David Davidson and Knut Wicksell arrived on the scene. Carl Uhr has a chapter on each of them in this volume. They were dominating Swedish economics around the turn of the century, although Gustav Cassel soon attained a respected position. We let them represent the era of transition to modern economics in Sweden.

Some scholars contend that modern economics began when the total economy was comprehended as a mathematical general equilibrium system by Walras in his *Eléments d'économie politique pure* in 1874 and 1877. It is, however, possible to find objections to any such dividing line. For instance, Lowry indicates that in a way Walras's approach did not begin with Walras but:

> has roots that reach back into Parmenedean and Pythagorean mathematical presumptions of a totally rational world order, perpetuated in Platonic thought and drawn upon in the Enlightenment with Copernicus' and Kepler's analyses of planetary motion, and the post-Newtonian image of astronomy and physics as the ideals of scientific precision. (1987: 3)

Others lay greater emphasis on marginalistic thought, and regard Jevons's *Principles* and Menger's *Grundsätze* from 1871 as the beginning of modern economics. We know, however, that marginalism can be found even earlier, for instance in von Thünen

4

(1826), Cournot (1838), Dupuit (1844), and Gossen (1854). A third party takes Marx as the turning point.

If we follow the convention of considering the 1870s, i.e. Jevons's, Menger's, and Walras's books, as the outset of modern economics, we can hardly find any fully modern economic literature in Sweden before Wicksell's writings in the 1890s. Davidson was younger – born in 1854, three years after Wicksell – but his books, written between 1878 and 1889, partly represent an older tradition. In Uhr's words, 'as a theorist Davidson denotes a transitional figure endeavoring to bridge the gap between classical, especially Ricardian, economics and neoclassical economics in the realms of value and distribution theories'. Wicksell was one of the earliest advocates of a marginal productivity theory of distribution, while it is questionable whether Davidson ever accepted it. Davidson had evidently no aspirations to an international reputation: he always wrote in Swedish. Wicksell published his first three books in German, and became a respected member of the international corps of economists. Davidson and Wicksell became close friends as time went on, often pondering the same economic problems, but often reaching different conclusions.

The theory of capital was one of the main subjects in economics at the time, and within this area of research both Davidson and Wicksell wrote their first book, in 1878 and 1893 respectively. For Davidson, with at least one foot in the pre-neoclassical tradition, capital formation is the main focus, while Wicksell confines himself to a stationary economy, which is easier to handle with the mathematical tools brought into vogue by Jevons and Walras. This shifting is a good illustration to Kuhn's (1970: 167) conclusion that 'there are losses as well as gains in scientific revolutions'.

Davidson and Wicksell both published books on taxation as well, Davidson in 1889 and Wicksell in 1896, besides contributions to government reports and numerous articles in *Ekonomisk Tidskrift*, which Davidson founded in 1899.

In personality Davidson and Wicksell were quite different. Davidson was polite and behaved as a well educated man could be expected to behave. Wicksell was a radical social reformer, and a stickler for principle who seemed to love provoking the public with his attitude on controversial issues. His two months in prison for blasphemy when he was a well known professor in his late fifties are a logical consequence of this posture. So are his strained relations with the presumptuous Gustav Cassel, whom Lars Magnusson scrutinizes in this book.

Consolidation and broadening

Gustav Cassel is sometimes considered one of the founders of modern economics in Sweden, together with Davidson and Wicksell. This is a questionable view, as the bulk of Cassel's output falls later than Davidson's and Wicksell's. When Wicksell had already published three books in the 1890s, Cassel was still a novice at economics. Therefore it is advisable to assign him to a later epoch.

Cassel had no great opinion of his precursors but considerable confidence in his own capacity. In his memoirs, *I förnuftets tjänst* (In the Service of Reason), he says that when he came to economic theory at the end of the nineteenth century he 'immediately found that it did not at all satisfy the demand for clarity and a firm quantitative foundation which [he] habitually took for granted, not only in pure mathematics but also in its applications in the natural sciences' (1940: 13). He thought that he could be the man to construct something better, and during a stay in Germany he decided to 'abolish the whole theory of value and to build up an economic theory directly on a study of price formation' (1940: 15).

Cassel's price theory reminds us of Walras's, and in his first serious study, 'Grundriss einer elementaren Preislehre' (1899), there are several references to Walras. It is an enigma that Cassel conceals this influence two decades later in his *Theoretische Sozialökonomie* (1918), and that he even denies it in his memoirs.[4]

Cassel was an economic guru in his day. His reputation was not restricted to academic circles; it was probably even higher among practical working economists and politicians, who appreciated a simple and resolute answer on a complicated question. As a consequence – if it was not a source of his fame – he had a lot of engagements in organizations working on solutions to international monetary problems.

Cassel's and Wicksell's reputations have developed differently, and to Wicksell's advantage, since their deaths. This is probably a just outcome. While Cassel often expressed his ideas in a telling way, the ideas themselves were not always very clear. Wicksell was almost the exact opposite. A first reading of one of his economics publications may result in a number of question marks in the margin. However, they may all be crossed out on the second or third reading, confirming Ragnar Frisch's (1951) words, 'the discovery of the fact that Wicksell is, after all, right will always be a matter only of patience and intelligence on the part of the reader'.

Wicksell left a larger and more cogent body of work on theoretical issues of permanent interest. Today few would deny his stature. Cassel has been subject to more divergent assessments. One scholar calls him 'the greatest scientific charlatan that Swedish economics has, so far, brought forth' (Södersten, 1970: 114). Another says, 'We must not treat Cassel the way he treated others. We must respect him as a pioneer. He was the first to dynamize general equilibrium into his "uniformly progressing state" . . .' (Brems, 1986: 158).

In 1904 Cassel acquired an (unpaid) assistant, Eli F. Heckscher. Heckscher was to become known to a wider audience for two things: the Heckscher–Ohlin theorem in international trade theory, and his contributions as an economic historian. To us he is interesting also because he has given rise to much of the traditional view of the early history of Swedish economic thought. Rolf Henriksson provides the chapter on Heckscher in this book.

Heckscher differed from Davidson, Wicksell, and Cassel in at least one respect. As late as in 1909, when he took up a Chair in economics and statistics at the Stockholm School of Economics, he had written hardly anything on economic theory, only on economic history. This was not, however, a serious drawback. At the time economic theory was considered merely one part of economics, not the whole discipline. His above-mentioned older colleagues, on the contrary, were predominantly theorists.

Heckscher was not, however, hostile to theory. His plea for theory in economic-historical research is well known. He proposed a combined approach, where methods used in history should be used to establish facts, and economic theory, i.e. neoclassical theory, should be used to interpret the facts. He would not plead for the traditional inductive method of the historical school.

In 1929 Heckscher's Chair was changed to a research Chair in economic history. A couple of years after that, in 1931, he published the work for which he is best known internationally, *Mercantilism.* This book was an outgrowth of his licentiate thesis of 1904. It illustrates how an originally limited purpose may beget new ideas which demand an enormous amount of labour to develop. Not surprisingly, people are often haunted by their dissertations for the rest of their life.

The Stockholm school

Both Cassel and Heckscher were adherents of traditional economic liberalism and sceptical about far-reaching public intervention. In their middle age in the 1920s and 1930s this position was challenged by a number of young economists, some of whom were their pupils. Erik Lindahl, Gunnar Myrdal, Bertil Ohlin, Alf Johansson, Dag Hammarskjöld, Erik Lundberg, and Ingvar Svennilson are usually assigned to this group, which Ohlin named the Stockholm school, and which is the subject of Björn Hansson's chapter.

The early 1920s and early 1930s were alike characterized by heavy unemployment in Sweden as in other countries. This

> gave inspiration to a new way of thinking within economics. During this decade [the 1930s] the foundation was laid for at least three macroeconomic schools: the Keynesian, where the central figure was, of course, Keynes; the Austrian, with Hayek as the leading name; and the Swedish or Stockholm school (Jonung, 1987).

When, in a paper in the *Economic Journal* in 1937, Ohlin coined the name 'Stockholm school' he argued that the theory of unemployment had been developed in Stockholm at the same time as Keynes was working on his *General Theory,* but that the Stockholm school, unlike Keynes, used a dynamic method. The Stockholm school was characterized by an analysis of aggregates, a distinction between *ex ante* and *ex post,* a period analysis throughout, a concern with the plans and expectations of individual households, and a casuistic approach. To the Stockholm school, moreover, could be attributed the ideas that a market economy has a large element of cyclical instability, that the government can and should control the business cycle by fiscal means, and that high employment should be the main concern, although price stability is also important (Siven, 1987). Björn Hansson focuses on 'the development of dynamic method, which is considered the differentia of the Stockholm school' compared with Keynes.

Did the Stockholm school disappear with the 1930s? In Hansson's opinion 'it was still influential in Sweden in the 1950s and there was even a sequel to the original development of dynamic methods'. Some traces are left in the international literature. Hicks was influenced by Lindahl in developing the theory of temporary equilibrium. But the Stockholm school did not live on in the same way as Keynes's thinking, and it was never much more than a national phenomenon.

There are several reasons. First, the Stockholm economists seldom addressed an international audience. They wrote mainly in Swedish, their work often taking the form of government reports. Second, their approach was in some respects difficult to reconcile with the then dominant or new techniques. They did not believe in constancy in economic relations. Consequently, econometric estimations of parameters in regression equations would be meaningless. They analysed special rather than general cases; interesting general statements were hardly considered possible to make. They emphasized the dynamics of the economy. Consequently, mathematization of their models was more complicated than mathematization of static models, and it was accomplished only to a small extent.

After the chapter on the Stockholm school there is only one complementary chapter, for two reasons. After the Stockholm school there is hardly any such thing as a unique Swedish economics. It has, with a few important exceptions, mentioned in the concluding chapter, been absorbed by, or, rather, has been eager to join, the Anglo-American mainstream tradition, which is, of course, not literally only Anglo-American. Second, as a general rule it may be wise to postpone a historical evaluation of the most recent contributions; their historical significance is not always apparent immediately.

Notes

1   That is not to say that the history of thought deals, or should deal, only with change. In a recent article Donald A. Walker (1988) epitomizes the proper scope of the study of the history of economic thought: 'An economist treats either present-day writings or older ones as the history of economic thought when he examines them in order to establish their characteristics, interpret them, and evaluate them in the ways shortly to be described. He may relate current doctrine to past doctrine, or examine past doctrine to see how it evolved into a subsequent state: or he may describe and interpret economic writings with no attempt to relate them to material either before or after them.'

2   In a historical perspective the leaning towards natural science should not surprise. Internationally, Swedish natural science and engineering seem to have been, and to be, more competitive than Swedish *belles lettres* and art. One opinion is that this has its roots in the fact that Sweden was 'civilized' comparatively late. It seems easier to reduce a technical lead than a *belles lettres* and scholarly lead.

3   A passage in Knut Wicksell's (1904) inaugural lecture may illustrate a neoclassicist's opinion of the historical school. Having declared that, as far as he knows, the positive good – consisting of certain empirical knowledge – achieved by the historical school has never been denied by its opponents, Wicksell states, 'But because of its one-sidedness and the purely negative, harshly deprecatory, even conceited and offensive attitude which it always adopts towards contemporary research of the theorizing and systematizing sort, this school has, in my opinion, hindered and harmed the development of economics, especially in Germany.'

4   Myrdal (1972) has suggested that Cassel had simply forgotten where he had got his idea from; he ceased intensive reading quite early and retained some constructive ideas which by and by he came to regard as his own. This evokes the question whether Cassel really could avoid recalling the original circumstances when he comments in his memoirs on those 'critics who, year after year, find it important to din that opinion into their readers, that my statement is entirely built upon Walras and devoid of originality' (1941: 434).

Chapter two

Before economics

Johan Lönnroth

The political economy of gods and lords

Before Christianity

The Roman author Tacitus (*c.* AD 100) wrote that the goddess Nertus (Earth) was worshipped by the people up north. When she came with her ox waggon, men had to lay down their weapons and do peaceful work. We do not know about her role for sure, but in most Old World religions fertility goddesses dominated as long as the human race lived at the edge of survival. So why not also in the Nordic countries?

With surplus production came private property, trade, slaves, and wars. The patriarchy took over on earth as in heaven. 'Allfather' Odin and Thor, who made thunder with his hammer, were made the highest gods, the so called 'Asarna'. And the goddess Nertus in some parts of Scandinavia was transformed into a man, Njord, who was the highest among 'Vanerna', the fertility gods. Also in this godly pattern there are similarities with other religions. (Eve was made of Adam's rib, etc.)

In one of the earliest poems in the Nordic tradition, probably with its origin in Norwegian language on the Orkney Islands, the son of Odin travels round the world and begets three sons of three different women. The first woman is dark-skinned, ugly, and twisted. Her son becomes the first father in the family of slaves, whose duty it is to dig in the mud, carry burdens, tend cattle, and fulfil other simple tasks of this kind. The second woman is of ordinary beauty and complexion. Her son becomes the first in the family of peasants, whose duty it is to make tools, build houses, and the like. The third woman is fair-complexioned and very beautiful. Her son becomes the first in the family of lords, whose duty is to govern and learn the art of writing.

In this way the division of labour and power on earth was given divine origin. (One can compare Plato's ideal State, with philosophers and military leaders, peasants and craftsmen, slaves and women.) Otherwise, we know little of how the Nordic peoples thought about political and economic matters before the Middle Ages and Christianity.

Husbandry literature

Sweden was gradually christianized and formed as a national state between the eleventh and fourteenth centuries. The Landskapslagarna (provincial laws) were written down from the beginning of the thirteenth century. They mirror a change in thinking about politics and economics. The old customary practices from the oldest laws from Västergötland and Uppland were gradually replaced by rules stemming from canon law and feudal Continental thinking.

Under the oldest laws, distant family relations had still a strong position in questions of heritage and maintenance burden. Under the later laws, nuclear family relations, the duty to pay taxes to God and king, and the right to give donations to the Church instead of inheritance against the will of relatives took over. If penalties are taken as a measure, labour opportunity cost was important in the system of law in fixing value and price. For example, if a free man made a female slave pregnant, he had to pay the owner goods or money corresponding to lost production until she was able to work full-time again. Luxurious living, interest, and profit from trade in excess of normal cost were banned (as everywhere in the Catholic world).

In the early sixteenth century humanistic and Renaissance literature from southern Europe reached Sweden, at first through the Church, later also through the nobility. Husbandry (*oeconomia* in Latin) literature with calendars, poems, and pictures about when and how to produce and to consume, began to circulate among educated landowners.

Probably the first original work written in Sweden in this spirit was the *Hushållskalendarium* (Household calendar) by Bishop Hans Brask in Linköping, written some time between 1503 and 1525. He calculated the requirements for inputs and outputs in agricultural production and described when to sow different crops, when to eat different foods, etc., over the year. It was a sort of *bondepraktika* (peasants' handbook) for the bishop's estate.[1]

The most productive and probably most advanced author in the husbandry tradition in the early sixteenth century was Peder Månsson. He was a monk from the Birgitta monastery at

Vadstena, then the leading intellectual centre in Sweden. In 1507 he was sent to investigate the shaky finances of the Birgitta house in Rome. As superintendent of the house he came into contact with the European husbandry tradition. In 1523 he was called home to Sweden and made bishop in Västerås.

Peder Månsson wrote a husbandry book in Rome and published it in Swedish in 1520. It was mainly a translation and partly an adaptation to Swedish conditions of *De re rustica* by Lucius Columella from the first century AD. There Månsson, as did Columella, spoke for rational agriculture run by engaged men and against absent landowners. He also wrote about handicraft and mining, where he tried to introduce new methods of production into Sweden.[2]

With Lutheranism and Gustav Vasa, intellectual contacts with German universities in Wittenberg, Rostock, and Greifswald became more important. Per Brahe (1520–90), a son of a sister of King Gustav Vasa, was one of the young noblemen sent to study at German universities. When he came back he was appointed supervisor of the royal castle in Stockholm and later he became a leading councillor behind the king. He was probably the leading brain behind the first State budgets under King Johan III (1568–92). He also became one of the biggest landowners in the country. In the last five years of his life Brahe wrote his *Oeconomia*.

The first part of Brahe's book is about the education best suited to young gentry, while in the second he wrote about the optimal housekeeping of the large landowner. He compared the system of direct rule by the owner of the estate with the system of tenant farming. If they use the first system, he advised his pupils to give their dependants just enough food in order to maximize the surplus. If they use the second, they should buy eventual surplus product from their tenants after deductions for subsistence consumption and rent.

Brahe's *Oeconomia* also contained a household calendar of the same type as Brask's and Månsson's. This calendar is very similar to a German *Oeconomia*, published by Caspar Jugel in 1617. This in its turn was founded upon Abraham von Thumbshirn's *Oeconomia* from 1569 or 1570, which makes it probable that Brahe had read and was influenced by von Thumbshirn. Brahe's own work was not published until 1677 and so it could probably have had very little influence outside a small circle of friends and relatives.

Gustav Vasa's homespun mercantilism

An interesting document of primitive mercantilist thinking in Sweden is a poem by a Bishop Henrik in Linköping from the

13

1490s (Lönnroth, 1940: 233). Here are some lines (some expressions in old Swedish are hard to translate):

> A king exporting silver and gold
> he is no good for the kingdom.
> Or if he buys estate and silver cups
> that is an evil couple.
> A good king makes a good coin.
> To wear expensive cloth and jewellery
> and to be without food – that is big shame.
> To wear rough homespun cloth is the custom.

Officially a State economic policy of this sort was implemented by King Gustav Vasa, the founder of Sweden as a national State (and, according to Gustav Cassel (1940: 11), one of its two greatest economists). But the demands for thriftiness and the criticism of luxuries were directed from the king to his subjects and especially to the Catholic Church. Luxury imports were forbidden, with the exception of the needs of the king himself and his court. The people were ordered to live simply and work hard. Land, silver, and gold were taken from the Church; Lutheranism was a suitable motive.

In a constant stream of letters the king gave economic instruction to his subjects. When he thought a town was inefficient for its purpose, he ordered its inhabitants to go to another. And when he thought that the peasants in a region were insufficiently productive, he gave their farms to friends he trusted and wrote to his constables that the State could make better use of this nice piece of land.

Johan Classon Risingh

During the seventeenth century, and especially under King Gustav II Adolf and his generals, the nation grew to an empire. But the economy was still too backward to support a national school of thinking in political economy. New ideas were mostly imported by foreign entrepreneurs like the Dutchmen Willem Usselinx and Johan Palmstruch or by imported intellectuals like Cartesius and Pufendorf.[3] A more developed commercial life was necessary to maintain the nation's greatness. So said Johan Classon Risingh, who, according to Eli Heckscher, was '... the first Swedish writer on economics'.[4]

Risingh was the last Governor of New Sweden (Delaware) and was made the scapegoat for the defeat in 1655. After failures in private trading projects, he was made customs official in Swedish Pomerania. He returned to Sweden impoverished in 1660. For private economic reasons he was never able to realize plans for the publication of a major tract on commerce. But in 1669 he managed to obtain subsidies to finance a short summary, or 'excerpt'.

As was common among contemporary mercantilist authors, Risingh started his 'excerpt' with the assertion that a thrifty, wealthy, and plentiful population was a major condition for the power and glory of regents. A wealthy nation also needs, in this order: godliness, defence, fisheries and agriculture, mining, handicrafts and trade, with a merchant navy. Trade should be based on contract, not on violence. It is a legal way of exchanging goods you have plenty of for scarce goods, and making a profit, and it helps the nation to keep the rate of exchange in balance with other countries, wrote Risingh (1669: 16).

Trade, he continued, consists of three parts: goods, money, and *wäxelen* (credit). As can be seen in other countries, you must have all three of them. Goods correspond to the human body, money to the soul, and credit to the spirit (*ande*). Those three parts must, in trade as in human beings, stand in the right proportion to each other.[5]

The theoretically most advanced part of Risingh's excerpt dealt with inflation and rates of exchange. If you have money you have power as well, he wrote. There are two sorts of value of money: 'intrinsic' value or *skrot och korn* (alloy and standard) and 'political' or 'face' value. 'High authority' must see to it that these two kinds of value correspond to each other in the right proportion.[6]

According to Risingh, debasement of the currency, that is, a lowering of the intrinsic value of the coinage, is not good for the national economy. For if the face value is too high compared with the intrinsic value, foreigners will use such 'bad' money to buy exports too cheap. But Risingh also warns (1669: 50) against putting too much gold, silver, or copper into the coinage. For if the face value is too low in relation to the intrinsic value, such money will be taken out of the country 'in secret' and 'bad' imports will be brought back in exchange. It is as difficult to set the right value on the coinage as to 'ride into the wind' (*rida mot strömmen*).

According to Risingh, the authorities ought to encourage the expansion of credit. A rate of interest between 3 and 10 per cent could be accepted. Companies too should be supported, since big trading enterprises need many persons to take part in *eventyret* (the venture). Investment opportunities and credit should be open to everybody, since closed guilds and excessive profit make people lazy (1669: chapter 14).

Risingh also spoke out for freedom of worship for Italians and

Jews, since with their knowledge and contacts they could develop trade. This could be seen in Holland. But, as if he had let slip a little too much freethinking, he ended the pamphlet with SOLI DEO GLORIA.

The spiritual climate of the 1670s in Sweden was not ready for trade policies and theoretical thinking of this kind. Moreover, Risingh died soon after the publication of the pamphlet, so he could not propagate its distribution. He was never mentioned by later mercantilist writers in Sweden. Not until the end of the nineteenth century was he rediscovered by the historian Ellen Fries.

The arithmeticians of utility

Hats and Caps

The level of population, production capacity, State income, and trade in Sweden was not enough to maintain the country's military position. Under the rule of Karl XII, at the beginning of the eighteenth century, the empire fell apart. Loans were accepted from Turkey, piracy was sanctioned by the State, and emergency coins were issued. But none of it helped. When Karl XII was shot dead in battle in 1718 the economy was in chaos. The public hanging of the Minister of Finance was poor consolation. There was an urgent need for political and economic reform.

The period between the death of Karl XII and the restoration of autocracy in 1772 by Gustav III is called the Age of Freedom. It was marked by a swing of power from the old rural nobility to merchant capitalists in the towns and from the king to the Diet of the Four Estates. The intellectual climate turned from glory to utility, from military and religious to materialist and scientific matters. England and France took over from Germany and Holland as the main sources of contacts and ideas in economic matters.

The general economic policy of the period consisted of protectionism and import substitution. The Produktplakatet (Commodity Ordinance) of 1724, the Swedish version of the English navigation laws, barred foreign ships from Swedish trade except when carrying cargoes of the ships' own nationality. Great importance was attached to the establishment of trading companies, of which the Swedish East India Company, with its base in Göteborg, first chartered in 1731, was the most successful example. Several 'decrees against superfluity' (*överflödsförordningar*) forbidding the use of imported luxuries, and subsidies to import-substituting manufactures were decided upon.

16

The new State-interventionist policy had a political party of its own. It consisted of men who were advocates of a strong policy of national self-sufficiency and of a militant policy of revenge towards the hereditary foe, Russia. They were called the 'Hats', the first clear-cut political party in Sweden. Their stronghold was the *nouveau riche* urban merchant and factory-owning nobility, often the profiteers of the policy of reduction in the 1680s. The Hats also dominated the upper levels of the military system, still bloated from the days of empire, and the State boards of commerce; some of them were leading figures in the Academy of Science.

The new policy, of course, met with opposition from those classes in society which had suffered a net loss as a result of the new policy: that is, people who had to pay more in the form of taxes or dead soldiers compared with what they won in the form of subsidies or market strength. This opposition came mainly from the old rural nobility, the Church, the peasants, and the lower classes in the towns. Their representatives in the Diet were called 'Nightcaps' by the Hats. So Hats and Caps formed a two-party system that lasted until the end of the Age of Freedom.

The number of publications on political economy during the Age of Freedom is so large that it is impossible to cover even the most important of them in this book. In a stream of pamphlets merchants, ironmasters, inventors, and State officials expressed their opinion on what to produce and how to make the nation richer. Most had a firm belief in the power of the State to further useful and sensible projects, and their proposals for State support usually happened to be consistent with their own private interests.

Nordencrantz

An incarnation of the new spirit and the great introducer of contemporary international mercantilist thinking was Anders Bachmansson, in 1743 ennobled to Nordencrantz. He was the most productive, and perhaps also the most politically important, economic thinker of the Age of Freedom. He studied in England, took over his father's merchant firm and became one of the burghers representing Sundsvall in 1727. In a stream of proposals, summarized in his *Arcana* (Secrets of Husbandry and Trade), published in 1730, he introduced the thinking of Thomas Mun, Charles Davenant, and other English mercantilist authors into Sweden.[7]

The *Arcana* was an act of homage to the importance of Nordencrantz's own kind in Sweden's underdeveloped peasant economy. He wrote that wealthy merchants were the 'heads of the civil being' and should consequently be given proportionate power.

17

And he wrote that envy, self-interest, and greed for power were the prime movers of human action. By means of wise laws and the influence of social conditioning these forces must be channelled into useful activity. This represented a very radical attitude, outside the boundaries of Christian values, in conservative Sweden (Lindroth, 1978: 103–4).

Nordencrantz also wrote in the *Arcana* that in a relatively infertile country with an unproductive peasant agriculture the produce of the land, the 'natural property' of the nation, can scarcely suffice for the nation's needs with regard to sustenance, clothing, and defence. The nation must therefore supplement its 'rural condition' with a 'bourgeois condition', in which the nation's raw materials are processed into man-made wealth; it must protect, support, and develop foreign trade, and by legislation prevent the wealth of merchants from leaving commerce.[8]

The *Arcana* also argued for the importance of the division of labour and for economies of scale, and drew a comparison with England: 'One main problem is the lack of sufficient division of labour ... time is wasted within our handicrafts as long as the bad old habit persists of one man doing all the tasks ... what one labourer does here is in England divided up between ten or twelve labourers.'[9]

Nordencrantz proposed that successful merchants should be ennobled and that children of factory owners and merchants who left their fathers' trade should be disinherited. In this way middle-class life should be made attractive to the nobility, so that their minds turned away from war and vainglory. He also said that monopolies and guilds were inimical to progress. But new industries must be protected against foreign competition (Arnberg, 1868: 66).

In the *Arcana* Nordencrantz argued for a stronger position for the study of economics and for a broader recruitment to the universities. He pointed out that the classical universities abroad – Oxford, Cambridge, and Leyden – had started from the study of simple economic problems, and in this way they had contributed to the economic strength of their nations. Once material needs were satisfied, those leading trading nations could afford to take up more spiritual subjects at their universities (1730: 146).

Berch, Linné, and the birth of academic political economy

Also in the Academy of Science and among the Hat party there was growing interest in economics. The new Hat government in the Diet of 1738–9 took concrete action in this direction. One move was to appoint Anders Berch, of the Board of Commerce, professor of 'jurisprudentiae, oeconomiae et comerciorum' at the Faculty of Law in Uppsala. Berch had been astute enough to defend a dissertation on the need for this kind of professorship in 1731 and he had cultivated the acquaintance of leading Hat politicians ever since. It was the fourth post of the kind in Europe; only three Chairs in the tradition of German 'cameralism' – two in Prussia and one in Hessen – can be seen as forerunners (Liedman, 1986: 27).

Berch was seen by the Caps as a mouthpiece of the Hat party and soon he became the target of political attacks. Perhaps this was the reason why his first major work on 'political arithmetic' was published anonymously in 1746. In it Berch tried to adapt the doctrines of John Graunt and William Petty to Sweden's language and society.

The main thesis in Berch's Swedish variant of political arithmetic was similar to that of its model: a large and industrious population, living near subsistence level, is the main condition for the welfare of the nation. To achieve this end, it was necessary to survey all aspects of economic life, and almost any kind of social experiment was permitted. Foreigners with special expertise should be attracted to Sweden. Colonization projects should be promoted. Berch referred approvingly to an example where ten prisoners of each sex were made to copulate and then sent away to Greenland as colonists (Johannisson, 1988: 98).

The author's name was soon discovered and Berch carried on his propaganda for political arithmetic in public. In a letter of 1749 to the new secretary of the Academy of Sciences, Pehr Wargentin, he tried to point out the consequences of the new method more concretely:

Every village could have its own principal occupation: one could concentrate on farming, another could breed cattle and produce butter, cheese, and hides, the third could breed sheep, a fourth develop a stud farm ... another do woodwork, etc. Then everyone could learn his trade thoroughly and be spared messing around with everything. Then the towns would know where to get their products in plenty and so they would not have to seek out and travel around to buy goods.... In conclusion, the country's housekeeping would be in good order, nothing too plentiful so that its price fell, nothing too scarce so that its price went up, and no task would be left undone, since each and every one would see to his own. And all this depends on the economic description of the country and how much a worker in every art and industry can achieve in a given period of time. (Translated from Heckscher, 1949a: 842).

Political arithmetic was probably an important source of inspiration for 'Tabellverket' – a system of collecting and publishing statistics on population – which under the direction of a special commission, led by Pehr Wargentin, was to develop the most advanced population statistics in the world. The collected data were then used for very advanced political arithmetic.[10]

In 1747 the new academic field got its first textbook, written by Berch. The main part of the book was something between a manual for producers and a catalogue of the political opinions of the Hat party. It was inspired by similar textbooks by German 'cameralists', but also by English seventeenth-century mercantilists and by Nordencrantz. The book was easy to read, compared with contemporary texts in the same genre. It was translated into German and used at several German universities. In Sweden it was to have an academic monopoly for eighty years to come.

The textbook starts with a humble dedication to King Fredrik I and the newly born Prince Gustaf. The intention of the author is only to write a textbook for beginners, not to compete with international literature for the highly educated. But if the Swedish youth read the the book, writes Berch, the prince will have 'good, industrious, and wealthy' subjects in the future.

Berch distinguishes between practical, private economics (*oeconomia privata*) and theoretical, political economics (*oeconomia publica*). The latter is important, but Berch does not share the German cameralists' inclination to subordinate the entire economy to the State and its financial ends. Individuals have a right to pursue their own interests and maximize utility and profit from private property. Private economics should give advice about this, but not about how to acquire the property, which according to Berch (1747: 9) is a subject for law, not for economics. The owner has the right to use private property freely, but only when it does not affect other people's lives.

The right to start new production and to choose a profession must be regulated by the State, wrote Berch. In this reckoning, the people should be divided into those who 'nourish' and those who 'consume'. The people employed in the State administration are among the latter. But they are necessary for production, since somebody must see to it that the division of labour in the nourishing part of the population is 'natural'. According to Berch (1747: 221) towns are especially useful for a State, not only because they make a certain division of crafts possible and the establishment of markets of considerable size, but also because they have fiscal functions in connection with the collection of taxes and dues on foreign as well as domestic trade.

20

Berch's textbook also included a more private and practical section, with a long catalogue of statements about the correct solution to various economic problems in everyday life. In 1754 he supplemented his textbook with a 'Theatrum Oeconomico-mechanicum' (an economic-mechanical theatre) – an exhibition in a house in Uppsala with objects illustrating his textbook and his lectures. In 1760 a German student described the contents of the theatre: there were a lot of different ploughs (Berch's speciality), different sorts of wood, furs from different animals, and a lot of other useful objects from nature and handicraft.

Another leading propagandist for a greater interest in practical economics was the famous botanist Carl von Linné (better known internationally as Linnaeus). His motivation was divine: in his *Oeconomia naturae* he wrote that it was the duty of human beings to extract natural resources, otherwise God would not have deposited them in the earth. To this he added the patriotic idea that the natural resources of Sweden were superior to those of any other country (Frängsmyr, 1971–2: 244).

If the economics of Berch was close to manufacturing and trade and so to physics and mechanics, the economics of Linné pointed in another direction. He argued for new professorships in *Oeconomia privata* with close links to botany and natural history. One of his pupils, Per Kalm, in 1747 obtained the first professorship of this kind in Åbo (in Finland). In 1750 a new professorship in economics, botany, and natural history was established in Lund. But the economic element in this symbiosis soon disappeared. It turned up again when Agardh got the job in the next century (see below). After that it was not until the twentieth century with the ecology movement that this was again to be seen as a natural combination.

Christiernin's monetarism

For a short period, from 1770 to 1771, Pehr Niclas Christiernin succeeded Berch as professor of law and economics. But the new university subject was then already in decline and Christiernin preferred to go over to a Chair in philosophy. But before that he produced a quantity theory of money, which according to a modern American writer 'in many respects constitutes a more sophisticated monetary study than that of Hume, Steuart, or Smith'.[11]

When Christiernin published this theory in 1761 the Swedish economy had been shaken for decades by monetary problems. After several decreases in the relative price of copper, the copper coins had become so big and clumsy that, by the 1720s, a horse

21

and cart were necessary for many payments. The national bank then introduced 'bank transport notes' in 1726. They were only a receipt for copper deposited in the bank but they were equal to the copper coin in value and acceptability. Bank credit was liberalized in the 1730s in order to promote industry and the cultivation of land as well as to aid factories (Myhrman, 1976: 174).

The war in Finland against Russia of 1741–3 and growing subsidies to manufactures created deficits in the State budget and in foreign trade. This situation unsettled the copper-standard monetary system, and in 1745 for lack of hard currency the national bank introduced a non-redeemable paper money in order to cover the State budget deficit. In 1747 the Hat government also set up *växelkontor* (exchange offices) to raise loans in foreign financial centres like Hamburg and Amsterdam and to use the money for a State-promoted economic growth programme. Entrepreneurs in manufacturing and commerce could use their partly finished commodities as collateral for loans. This policy was intended to increase domestic production and exports in order to cover the trade deficit and maintain the value of the currency.

The policy was quite successful as long as Swedish export prices for iron and copper were on the high side during the late 1740s and early 1750s. After that, however, the outbreak of the Pomeranian war (1757–64) in combination with worsening terms of trade led to a fall in the rate of exchange. The inflationary process in paper money that followed, reached its peak in the early 1760s, and led to an outburst of a political and economic debate of unparalleled intensity, with Christiernin's pamphlet of 1761 the leading contribution.[12]

Christiernin had studied Cantillon, Hume, Locke, Malynes, and other international writers, but the basis of his monetary theory was empirical observation of the inflationary process in Sweden. In contrast to most contemporary writers, Christiernin did not believe that the monetary unit had an intrinsic value, independent of supply and demand. He wrote:

> If metals could be obtained as easily as water, everyone would take as much as he needed and these metals would have almost no value.... When the quantity of goods increases a larger amount of money is needed.... The cost of all buying and selling is in proportion to the circulating money reserves and the speed of circulation.[13]

So in Christiernin's opinion the value of the Swedish daler had fallen because banknotes had been increased continuously above the quantity of goods and beyond public and private requirements. This increase in the issue of banknotes was a response to the lower rate of interest charged by the central bank and to the liberal credit policy. According to Christiernin (1761: 28) the right money supply was that required to support the current level of economic transactions at the current level of prices and output.

Christiernin argued that the general increase in money demand for domestic goods was accompanied by an increased demand for imports, which in turn caused a rise in the exchange rate. This increase in the price of foreign exchange in terms of dalers made Swedish exports less expensive in terms of foreign currency than before. At the same time, if Swedish imports in terms of dalers were more expensive than before, that would increase exports and decrease imports and so stop the rise in the exchange rate (1761: 32–3).

But Christiernin preferred not to rely on this automatic mechanism. An increase in exports could be brought about only by reducing the supply of goods delivered to the domestic market, so that the living standard of the home population was lowered. Also the rise in profits of the export industries would tend to lead to a greater concentration of wealth in the hands of a few. Christiernin therefore condemned the expansionary policy of the Hat government.

But he also warned against a strongly deflationary policy, since it could lead to a sudden decrease in production. It is easy for prices to adjust upward when the money supply increases, but getting prices to fall, he thought, was always more difficult. No one reduces the price of his commodities or his labour until the lack of sales forces him to. Any attempt to squeeze the money supply in order to reduce prices must necessarily result in unemployed resources and a reduction in national income. And if the price level fell, this would cause undue hardship among existing debtor groups and would make potential debtors reluctant to borrow, so the entrepreneurial class would be forced into bankruptcy (1761: 28).

The Diet resolved to approve the recommendation of Nordencrantz and others that the exchange rate should be reduced. The decision was meant to be kept secret, but it soon became obvious what the policy was. So violent speculation started against the Hamburg thaler, which fell in value far more steeply than had been intended. A serious unemployment crisis hit the export industry, just as Christiernin had said would happen as a consequence of a strongly deflationary policy. The Cap government had failed in its economic policy. The Hats returned in 1769, but the party system of the Age of Freedom had lost popular support.

Economic liberalism and its opponents

Anders Chydenius

The material basis for more liberal economic reforms promoting industrial capitalism did not yet exist. But in spite of this, Sweden – or perhaps we should confess that he was from Finland – can boast an outstanding example of a revolutionary liberal thinker from this period. Eleven years before the publication of *The Wealth of Nations* Anders Chydenius, a Finnish-born, Swedish-speaking clergyman, formulated a revolutionary economic liberalism in more uncompromising terms than did Adam Smith.

Chydenius probably knew no foreign languages. He studied under Peter Kalm, who was professor in Åbo. A decisive influence on him may have been such French social critics as Rousseau, with whom he became acquainted, mainly through Anders Nordencrantz.[14]

But Chydenius's economic liberalism also stemmed from his experience of life in his own home province of Österbotten (Ostrobothnia) in Finland. His deeper political involvement seems to have started in 1763, when he made a speech at a provincial council meeting in Gamla Karleby on the injustice of the existing system of trade, which excluded the small towns in the Gulf of Bothnia from foreign trade and shipping. His stance on this question contributed to his election as a representative for the lower Ostrobothnian clergy and the Caps in the dramatic Diet session of 1765–6. In 1765 he published several contributions to the debate. One of them in particular, *Källan till Rikets Vanmakt* (The Source of the Nation's Weakness), aroused strong feelings and several answers for and against (Uhr, 1963: 18).

Chydenius started his pamphlet with China, which he said was the richest country in the whole world. There they had no special trade privileges for towns, no difference between urban and rural industry, no fences, no customs, and no Productplakat (Navigation Act).

Chydenius's conclusion is worth a fuller quotation:

> My reader, put all your prejudices aside and you will see that free trade within and outside the country will promote even the smallest industry, stop the foreigner from skinning the country' and one citizen from exploiting another citizen. Security for the farmer to possess his land and freedom for him to produce what he likes will lead him ... to what is most profitable for him and the kingdom.... No political laws in the world could ever regulate this, that nature so easy and without strain carries out. (1765a: 42)

Another contribution from Chydenius to the debate in 1765, more modest in tone, but theoretically more advanced, was *The National Gain*. Here, through a sort of opportunity cost argument, he tried to show that State regulations and bounties lead to resources being driven away from activities more profitable to the nation. He was against any laws that hindered people from choosing their own trade and concluding their own contracts: 'When a stream is allowed to flow smoothly, every drop of water is in motion. When there are no hindrances, every workman strives for his daily bread and thereby increases the gain of the nation' (1765b: 56, 64).

But liberty for Chydenius had its limits when rich people exploited others:

> The more opportunities there are in a society for some persons to live upon the toil of others, and the less those others may enjoy the fruits of their work themselves, the more is diligence killed, the former become insolent, the latter despairing, and both negligent. (1765b: 70–1).

Equality, however, could not be achieved by State regulation. In a final plea Chydenius warned against too many laws, making it impossible for either judges or ordinary citizens to know them all. He wrote: 'I, for my part, cannot but sing with Lucidor, the Misanthrope:

> I hear many words, my thoughts are far astray
> I see so many lights that I mistake my way.
> Too much of arguing makes me confused, I fear,
> And though I Swedish know, I know not what I hear.'[15]

At the very end of 1765 Chydenius became acquainted with Christiernin's pamphlet of 1761. In a third essay for the Diet session published in 1766 about 'a natural system of finance' Chydenius changed his mind on the revaluation policy. The aristocratic leadership of the Caps saw this as a dangerous rebellion and he had to return home before the Diet broke up. His attack provoked an onslaught of counter-attacks and his opinions were therefore to be better known than Christiernin's earlier pamphlets.

When in 1772 royal autocracy was re-established under Gustaf III, the new king was seen at first as a liberal reformer. New pamphlets by Chydenius in 1777 and 1778, against restrictions on trade in the countryside and against the ill treatment of servants respectively, probably had a degree of influence on the king and his not very successful efforts to liberalize the trade and labour market laws. The king also recruited Chydenius as an adviser on his more successful proposals for freedom of worship. After that he was stigmatized by the clergy as the king's agent, so he was not re-elected to the Diet.[16]

Swedish-style physiocracy

Already by the late 1760s the tutor of Gustaf III during the king's minority, the ambassador in Paris and Lord Counsellor, Carl Fredrik Scheffer, in his 'Letters to the nation's council' had tried to introduce French physiocracy into Sweden in a translated, simplified, and revised form. In order to make the theory fit an economically more backward country and its current debate, Scheffer distorted the translations and turned them, in the words of Lars Herlitz, into a special 'Swedish-style physiocracy'.[17]

The translations modified the physiocratic doctrine above all on the following points. The physiocratic object of taxation, the net produce of landed properties, became in Scheffer's version 'the pure income of the land', depicted as a taxed surplus of agricultural production. The physiocratic precondition, that it was the leasing contract between the agricultural capitalist and the landowner that fixed what was available for taxation, was eliminated from the translation. Instead Scheffer presented general arguments for increased land taxation – in itself understandable against the background of relative decline in the land taxation income of the Crown during the Age of Freedom. The specifically physiocratic goal, however, is gone: to free agricultural capital and capital accumulation from all taxation.

The physiocrats' *classe productive*, the capitalistic tenant farmers, had no counterpart in the Swedish version and Scheffer also eradicated the physiocratic doctrine of the social and economic function of agricultural capital. There remained only a demand for money for agriculture, an observation about the profitability of draught animals, and a plea for private economic advice to the landowners.

Scheffer also tried to distort physiocratic doctrine in order to form an apology for monetary policy in Sweden up to the beginning of the 1760s, in the execution of which Scheffer himself had taken part. He also wanted to launch a polemic against the deflationary Cap policy of the year 1765. From this particular viewpoint, Scheffer was unable to share the views of the physiocrats as to the sterility of foreign trade. Nor could he support the physiocratic demand for the highest possible price on agricultural products and foodstuffs.

Thus transformed, physiocracy was able to occupy a central place in the context of ideas which characterized the Swedish debate. Scheffer was to become a leading counsellor of Gustav III. Hence the constitutional aspects of Scheffer's Swedish-style physiocracy also played a certain role, since its support for a strong Crown, private property, and civil liberties (within limits) was a very suitable ideology for his master.

Hans Järta

Almost every leading personality in Sweden who was of an intellectually impressionable age in the 1790s or early in the nineteenth century had romantic dreams about France and the revolution as long as France was victorious in war. Later they hailed the new constitution in Sweden in 1809 and welcomed the French marshal Bernadotte as the new king. When the tide of war turned against France in 1812–13 they, as did Bernadotte, switched sides. Now they mostly derived their impressions from the dynamism of English capitalism and economic liberalism. When they grew old, like the new king they became conservative defenders of the State, the Crown, the sword, and the Church.

One example of this pattern was the young nobleman Hans Hiertha, who as a student belonged to the radical 'Junta' in Uppsala. At the Diet session in Norrköping in 1800 he declared that he was giving up his noble title and changed his name to Järta. In 1809 he was one of the leading men responsible for the main part of the text of the new constitution. In the new government he was made secretary for financial affairs, where he defended liberal reforms and free trade. When he grew old he became a conservative politician.

Economic reorganization after the Napoleonic wars was of course one of the leading themes in the political debate after 1815. Big State loans had been raised in 1809 in order to finance the army and also in order to start building the Göta canal between Göteborg and Stockholm. Prices had trebled in the period 1800–15. Big profits had been made and big loans taken up in agriculture, and when the war was over depression loomed. In politics the same pattern of opinion as in the 1760s was revived: 'expansionists' gave priority to State support and protection of landowners in distress. They proposed *jordbruksdiskonter*, special banks for agriculture, a ban on corn imports, and support for purchases of domestic corn when the price fell below a certain level. 'Restrictionists' gave priority to a stable monetary system.[18]

Hans Järta was one of the restrictionists. He resigned from his post as Secretary of Finance in 1816, when the conservative reverend and minister Fredrik Bogislaus von Schwerin, with the aid of the new king, Karl XIV Johan (Bernadotte), managed to force protectionist measures through. In 1823 Järta published a pamphlet, where he collected his arguments on the economic debate after 1815. Its main themes were the price of corn and inflation, both important subjects in *national-ekonomin* (national economy), a term that now began to be used together with the traditional *stats-ekonomi* (State economy) or *politisk ekonomi* (political economy).[19]

Järta's pamphlet began with a rhetorical question: are landowners' profits more important than hungry workers? In order to get higher prices, speculators had bought land and hoarded corn during the war and taken out big loans to finance their business. In Järta's opinion it was wrong then to protect those profits by means of an expansionist economic policy.

Järta linked this expansionist policy with the overproduction of paper money and with credit expansion, created by new financial institutions:

> People often imagine the stock of money in a nation as a stationary weight placed on one side of the scales and the quantity of goods as a stationary weight on the other. But both are circulating in permanent interaction. The faster this circulation is, the less the quantity of money needed to further the turnover of goods.... Financial institutions, set up in order to aid business by augmenting a representative quantity of money, mostly fail to produce the desired effect. Instead they debase the value of money, destroy credit, and in this way restrain circulation.

Järta then gave a numerical example, to illustrate the detrimental effects of credit expansion (1823: 17).

Carl Adolph Agardh

One of Järta's expansionist and protectionist opponents in the Diet was Carl Adolph Agardh. He was a young student in Lund at the beginning of the century, who moved in the exalted circles around the poet Esaias Tegnér. He also was a botanist and a mathematician and in 1812, twenty-seven years old, he obtained a professorship in botany and economics at Lund, a post that was an offspring of the original Linné-inspired Chairs in private economics and natural history from the 1750s.[20]

In 1816 Agardh was ordained, he became the incumbent of a parsonage, and the next year he was elected to the Diet as a representative of the clergy. In 1821–2 he went to Paris and listened to a series of lectures by Say, of which *Traité d'économie politique* was translated into Swedish in 1823. But evidently Agardh did not believe in everything he heard, since at the Diet session of 1823 he definitely belonged to the expansionist and protectionist camp. He bitterly opposed the decision to sell State forests to private interests and he was against lower customs duties. He defended the Produktplakatet and called for an expansionary fiscal policy with among other things bigger loans to farmers.

In 1829 Agardh collected a series of dissertations, defended by pupils, but written by him. According to the author, they were written early in the 1820s and were inspired by Say, whom Agardh considered the most brilliant follower of Adam Smith and his 'liberal system'. In the first dissertation Agardh started with a short history of the world, where his main conclusion was that in the long run the poor nations conquer the rich ones. In an equally short history of economic ideas, he considered the 'mercantile system' and also Quesnay to have been replaced by the 'liberal system'. But this system too had been rejected by the 'experience of practical men' and by 'an instinct, which makes statesmen reluctant to carry it out' (1829: 7–11).

According to Agardh, there are two different theories of society. In one of them it is supposed that the State is a product of human reason. This theory is supported by Hobbes, Locke, Rousseau, and modern liberal thinkers. For them State economy is reduced to a simple theoretical reflection on the origin and distribution of wealth. In the second theory of society, men can reach reason only through the State. This theory is supported by Hume, Burke, Montesquieu, and others. Only with this second theory does State economy become an important science for political practice, wrote Agardh (1829: 27–8).

He continued to criticize the teaching of Smith and Say, who he thought had overestimated the role of labour and underestimated the role of natural resources in the creation of national wealth. Among the different schools of economic thought, Agardh thought that the physiocrats, despite their 'mistakes in practice', best understood the nature of value and wealth. Wealth is a means to reach power, but it is not the same as power itself. 'The glitter of wealth has deceived statesmen and State economists of all ages. Only the physiocrats had a feeling that there is a higher goal for State economy than quantities of surplus value' (1829: 80).

What, then, was this higher goal of State economy? Apart from the divine aspects of the question, Agardh argued for public works in order to create jobs and lighten the burden of poverty. Reclaiming land for agriculture, the Göta canal between Göteborg and Stockholm, and later the railway network were among his favourite projects. The projects could be financed through domestic State loans. Since future generations would inherit the wealth created today, it was only fair that the burden of debt was laid on them.

In 1835 Agardh was made bishop in Karlstad. As we shall see, he was influenced by liberalism. But as a whole, in public speeches, as a member of the Diet for the clergy and in a giant work, written in co-operation with C.E. Ljungberg and published in four parts in 1852–7, he continued to defend his old opinions. He insisted that the basic subject matter of economics was not the wealth of the nation but its power to defend its independence. And he continued to argue for State intervention to stimulate and protect domestic industry.[21]

Erik Gustaf Geijer and Anders Stenkula

In the first half of the nineteenth century, capitalism gradually grew within the shell of the old agrarian and conservative society. A new class of industrial employers and progressive landowners with economic liberalism as their ideology came into power and a new pattern of thought also gradually penetrated the State bureaucracy and the academic world. The institutions of law and economics mostly remained, to the last, bastions of conservatism. But even here new voices were heard.

The famous 'defection' in 1838 by the historian Erik Gustaf Geijer was to become an important symbol of change from conservative to liberal dominance. Before that, as a professor of history and a member of the Diet, he had been a leading member of the conservative 'historical school'. In a letter to Hans Järta he wrote, 'I am leaving the historical school, since I have been more and more convinced that history cannot give – only modify – the principle of action and that this principle on the contrary must be a contribution from each epoch.'[22]

In 1847, the year of his death, Geijer published a newspaper article entitled 'An economic dream'. In it he described an economic system of liberty and harmony. 'So at last all the industries and trades flowed into each other ... and the working hours danced around the rising sun in deliberate heavenly and harmonic paths. That was the heavenly performance at the sight of which I woke up.'[23]

The teacher of finance and law at Lund, Anders Stenkula, was a devoted follower of Geijer. In a textbook of 1839 he introduced classical English liberalism. 'Swedish agriculture could be compared with a mole: it digs and digs, but not much is accomplished. But in industrial production, new methods and new thinking are produced. And in *The Wealth of Nations* we have a new theory of "State economics", where we can find the explanation of this.' In this way he introduced his subject in an ambitious book published in 1839.

Mercantilism fostered war. To oppose free trade or to bind wealth to certain families is to go against the laws of nature, wrote Stenkula (1839: 40). The State must foster all the talents of the people, but it must accept that differences in ability are distributed by nature. The idea of absolute equality might be defended with the eloquence of a Condorcet or a Godwin: it can 'caress imagination', but it disappears like 'smoke' in confrontation with reality.

Stenkula continued with Ricardo, who in *Proposals for an Economical and Secure Currency* (1819) saw the bank crisis of 1797 as a result of panic. Ricardo thought the banks should have continued to pay out money. He also explained the relation between the price level and the quantity of money. Stenkula tried to put the theory in a mathematical form: if v is the total quantity of goods, y is the average number of transactions in goods, p is the total sum of money values, and x is the average number of transactions for a sum of money, then (1839: 104) $vy = px$.

Stenkula then turned to Malthus and undertook a mathematical and Swedish interpretation of his theory of population. He also thought that immediate action must be taken to prevent the realization of a gloomy Malthusian future. Moral abstinence must be upheld. It was also necessary to stop the splitting up of farms into smaller units, to make the incidence of land taxes more even, and to establish freedom of trade and industry.

The Bastiat fan club

By the end of the 1840s the ideas of the English and French movements in support of free trade were spread throughout the growing Swedish liberal press. Johan August Gripenstedt, from 1856 to 1866 the Minister of Finance and a leading promoter of liberal reforms, was particularly influenced by the leader of the French movement, Frederic Bastiat, whose *Sophismes économiques*, Part I, had been translated into Swedish in 1846 (Gasslander, 1949: 119; Heckscher, 1954: 237).

Compared to Gripenstedt an even more ardent defender of Bastiat's 'natural order' was Gustaf Knut Hamilton, who in 1859

31

got Bergfalk's Chair at Uppsala, now renamed 'Administrativ rätt [law] och nationalekonomi'. In 1862 Hamilton moved to Lund, where he stayed for the rest of his life. He was to be famous for two reasons: he tried to prevent Knut Wicksell from getting his professorship (but had to agree in the end) and he bestowed upon his son the christian name of Bastiat.

In a textbook of 1858 Hamilton described his idol as having '... with a sharper intellect than anybody else defended the importance of the Economic World Order' (p. 82). For Hamilton, neither Ricardo, nor Malthus, nor Say was defending this 'natural order' with enough consistency. Say believed that nature – and not only labour – can generate value, and this was wrong, according to Hamilton: '... and it places a weapon in the hands of those socialists and communists who in later times have raged against freedom and private property' (p. 68).

As one would suppose from this, Hamilton was a firm believer in labour as the only source of value. In a series of lectures for a 'workers' association' in Stockholm in 1864, published – according to the author – after '... demands from members of the working class', he argued for profit-sharing schemes and workers' associations as incentives to work. Referring to John Stuart Mill, Hamilton said that this kind of economic organization would 'ennoble simple workers to make noble experiments' in production. It would also 'stir the general conscience of society' (1865: 145).

Another series of lectures given the same year as Hamilton's were by the *docent* (senior lecturer) in *statskunskap* (literally 'state-knowledge', akin to the English concept 'political science'), Wolter Arnberg, at Uppsala. In the first lecture Arnberg outlined a short history of economic thought. Political economy he described as a 'young science', striving after universality and born in the spirit of the French revolution, 'when people at last understood that society is formed not of estates or of classes, but of individuals' (1864: 2).

Arnberg too evidently belonged to the 'Bastiat fan club'. It is the French economist, he wrote, who has given the best account of 'the natural organization of society', which is characterized by the fight for survival, competition for development, and consumption as the ultimate goal of human activity (1864: 36).

In his second lecture Arnberg developed his own theory of capital and value. Capital investment has its roots in the noblest human qualities, namely forethought and consideration. 'Capital is the son of labour,' that is, the result of past labour, which has not been immediately consumed but made useful to facilitate future work and production. Therefore capital has a right to profit and interest, and this incentive is also needed for future saving. With a growing supply of capital, however, the rate of profit and interest must fall. This can be seen by comparing England, with its lower rates of interest, with Sweden (1864: 37).

Arnberg continued: social welfare grows in proportion to a growing division of labour and growing markets. Market value is determined by supply and demand. A surplus of supply over demand leads to falling value, and a shortage leads to increasing value. With freedom to enter or cease production, value will settle at the level of production cost, since, if value is higher, capital will flow into that kind of production, and if value is lower, capital will flow out. But, with reduced capital mobility, production will go on even at a loss (p. 44).

In the third lecture Arnberg compared the systems of free trade and of protectionism. The latter leads to high costs and inefficient use of resources. Arnberg wrote: 'When the Protection system points at a new industry and says, "This is my doing," then it forgets that it has taken labour and capital from other more natural industries, which would have yielded far greater benefits from the amount of toil and cost invested' (1864: 60).

As can be seen, Arnberg was a pioneer, coming close to some of the ideas of professional economics, established fifty years later. He was also a pioneer in another respect – in the history of economic thought. In 1868 he published a comprehensive survey of the thinking of Nordencrantz, Berch, and their contemporaries. Arnberg condemned their ignorance of 'the laws of production and exchange'. Such ignorance he said had contributed to the failure of the factories and of the monetary system towards the end of the Age of Freedom. But he did not adjudge the thinking of the period to have been vain, since out of its failures and ideas grew the new true science (1868: 248).

Arnberg was later to become managing director of the Upplands Enskilda Bank, secretary of the parliamentary budget commission, and head of the central bank. His opinions then established themselves as the new official State ideology, manifested in the foundation in 1877 of the Nationalekonomiska Före-ningen (Association of National Economists). Of this association leading employers, members of the royal family, and almost everyone with economic or political power was soon to become a member.

Socialist economics and its opponents

Marx mitigated by God

Every ideology in Sweden has tried to incorporate Geijer as part of its heritage. In some of Geijer's lectures from the 1840s people have even looked for expressions which might conceivably bear a socialist interpretation:

> capital, as such and in its impersonal meaning, is in reality only labour performed.... Money representing capital's power would therefore oppress labour. This is in accordance with the common view today, that the power of plutocracy, that is, of wealth and money, has succeeded the power of nobility, clergy, and royalty.[24]

Geijer met and was influenced by Hegel, and Marx read his Swedish *History* in a German translation. Marx quoted several excerpts, mostly about the medieval law system and the making of the Swedish State, since at the time he was working on the *Kritik des Hegelschen Staatsrechts*. And in *Das Kapital* there is a passage about the Swedish 'Reduction' (the reversion of alienated lands to the Crown) under Karl IX, probably a respite from the study of Geijer's *History*. Geijer's famous expression, 'En händelse som ser ut som en tanke' ('An event looking like a thought') sounds like Hegel, and Marx may have liked its dialectic flavour (Meurling, 1983: 84).

As early as in 1847 Swedish communists had organized the publication of an early draft of the Communist Manifesto. But, in order to adapt the pamphlet to Swedish conditions, some alterations were made. On the front page 'Workers of the world, unite' was replaced by 'The voice of the people is the voice of God', 'revolution' was toned down to 'radical transformation' and a passage in the manifesto about feudalism as a past stage of history was deleted. The editor may have thought either that feudalism still existed or that it had never existed in Sweden.[25]

Davidson's and Wicksell's error

During the high tide of economic liberalism in the 1850s and 1860s, socialist movements and ideas were practically non-existent in Sweden. It took the combined effect of the publication of the first volume of *Das Kapital* in 1867 and growing German influence after the war of 1870–1 for Marx to come back to Sweden. The first professional economist in Sweden to investigate deeper into the political economy of Marxism was David Davidson (see chapter 3), who in his dissertation of 1878 had a four-page footnote about the labour theory of value in the first volume of *Das Kapital.*

Davidson blamed Adam Smith, and his idea of labour as the only source of wealth, for having inspired the socialist theory of surplus labour as the source of capitalist income. Either Smith's theory of value is wrong, or you must admit that the socialist theory is right, wrote Davidson. But nowadays we have come to understand also that goods from nature which have had no labour expended on them can have value.[26]

Knut Wicksell (see chapter 4) was known in the early 1880s as a neo-Malthusian left-winger and a radical opponent of the king, the Church, and the sword. In a lecture in November 1886 to a liberal workers' association in Stockholm he attacked Marxism. Hjalmar Branting – party leader after August Palm and later Prime Minister of Sweden – wrote in *Socialdemokraten* that it was a pity to have to count someone like Wicksell with his materialist conception of life as an opponent of social democracy. But as a national economist he regrettably belonged to the school of Mill and Spencer, 'which has got stuck in empirical analysis and has not been able to achieve a synthesis'.[27]

Later the same month Wicksell gave another lecture. According to a new article by Branting, he was now criticizing the Swedish socialists for underestimating the threat of overpopulation and was also attacking the Marxist labour theory of value for neglecting nature as a source of wealth. Reading between the lines, it is clear that Branting considered Wicksell a formidable opponent.[28]

Wicksell v. Wermelin

Probably the only party ideologist who attempted an independent interpretation of Marxist political economics during the pioneering years of the 1880s was the journalist, poet, and bohemian Atterdag Wermelin. He was offended by Wicksell's attack on Marx, and challenged him in public in an advertisement in *Socialdemokraten.* So a debate between the two was organized at the workers' association in Stockholm. Branting was the secretary of the meeting and he gave a detailed account in the party journal.[29]

According to Branting, Wermelin opened the debate by saying that Wicksell had attacked the 'popular form' of Marx's 'fundamental statement' about labour as a source of wealth instead of its 'scientific form', which was that 'labour was the source of all wealth *in its social form* – *its value*' (Branting's emphasis). Wermelin also said that Marx was fully aware that nature too was needed to produce 'use-values'.

Wicksell replied that this 'scientific' form of the statement was also wrong and that, if nature is the mother of production, labour is at best 'the small boy clinging to his mother's apron strings'. He continued by asserting that Marx was wrong when he claimed that 'use value and exchange value were not strictly comparable' and that utility and scarcity, and not only labour, had an influence on exchange value. Wicksell also denied that capitalists necessarily always exploit workers. To prove the point he took an example where a capitalist invests in virgin forest in the north of Sweden and thereby creates new jobs and new income for the population.[30]

Wicksell also claimed that use value and exchange value were not at all 'non-comparable quantities', as Marx had said. As a matter of fact there was no doubt at all that utility played a role in the determination of exchange value. You could understand that labour alone did not decide exchange value when you considered the rising price of cotton after a bad harvest. In that case the amount of labour performed could very well be greater, compared with a good harvest.

Wermelin answered that, if satisfaction really was part of the determination of value, it could only give 'relative', but not 'absolute', value. He also said that he had difficulties with the example, since he was no expert on cotton, but in the case of rye he knew that a bad harvest would consume practically the same amount of labour as a good one. And concerning Wicksell's instance of the capitalist up north, he just wanted to note that the people themselves could have started production themselves equally well without him.

An angry worker said that Wicksell's Malthusianism meant 'a society after the example of bees and ants, where a small minority could have children but the rest were infertile and a working bunch of slaves'. Another opponent said that Wicksell had forgotten to ask himself how the capitalist got his capital. August Palm, also present at the meeting, said that 'it was clear as daylight' that labour alone is the source of wealth. And Axel Danielsson, later to become a leading ideologist and the main author of the 1897 party programme, said that Wicksell's Malthusian ideas could be put to good use by the bourgeoisie to prevent the revolution.

The discussion ended at half past twelve after the chairman had pointed out that Wicksell had not answered the question whether he wanted nature to be publicly owned or not. But Wermelin probably had the feeling that he had lost the debate, at least in the eyes of Branting and the thinking section of the public. In 1887 he wrote a pamphlet on the value theory of Marx, where he tried to give a better answer to Wicksell. The phrase 'Labour is the source of all wealth' was only 'a popular expression intended to make the hearts of the millions beat faster' (p. 8).

Wermelin's new pamphlet was reviewed by Branting, who was evidently not impressed. He wrote that the 'truth of socialism' was not necessarily coupled to the theory of value. The socialist conception of life, in his view, was based more on the 'inevitable development of history' than on 'abstract economics' and I, for my part, wrote Branting, 'think that it is safer that way'.[31]

Gustaf Steffen

It is a remarkable fact that the three new professors of national economics at the beginning of the twentieth century – Wicksell at Lund, Gustaf Steffen at Göteborg, and Gustav Cassel at Stockholm – were all in their youth looked upon as different types of socialist, or at least as close to the labour movement.

As a young man Gustaf Steffen was immortalized as the dogmatic socialist in a novel by August Strindberg, with whom he had travelled in France and whom he had tried to win over to socialism. Steffen studied under Wagner and Schmoller in Berlin, moved to London in 1887, and became closely involved with Philip Wicksteed and the Fabian Society. His political opinions were influenced by them all.[32]

Steffen soon became the leading exponent in the Swedish press of neoclassical and Fabian criticism of the labour theory of value. In 1890 he wrote a pamphlet on 'Jevonsism', where he exhorted the Marxists to heed the new signals. In 1892 he also gave lectures at London University about labour economics and the labour movement, where he argued for social reform in the spirit of the German historical school type of State socialism. The lectures were reported back to Sweden in the form of a stream of articles in the social democratic and liberal press.

Steffen brought together his lectures and articles from his German and English periods in a substantial work published in 1900. There he wrote that Marxism was a doctrine for a 'narrow workers' socialism' during its 'primitive stage', when its leaders were agitators and 'bitter enemies of the upper classes'. In its more 'mature form' socialism gets leaders who are 'social scientists or politicians' (p. 192).

In Steffen's opinion, this mature form of socialism must reject the labour theory of value. Marx drove Ricardo's theory *in absurdum* when he made labour the source of all wealth and when he drew 'the false conclusion that the capitalist was unnecessary'. Marxism also grossly underestimated the spiritual resources of the working class and the importance of moral qualities in modern society (1900: 240–2).

37

In 1914 Steffen summarized his views on Marxism. Marx was right in that 'capitalist private property must yield to economic citizenship for the proletariat'. But it is a construction in the spirit of Hegel that the world order will collapse, and Marx is wrong if he believes that the proletariat is capable of power and leadership. The reform of private ownership is a 'means' and not an 'end' for socialists. Therefore they must prepare for socialism within the bounds of capitalism (1914: 87, 138).

The defeat of Marxist economics in Sweden

Cassel, in an article of 1899, suggested that it was not easy to attack Marx, who had said very little about what he meant by socialism. Instead Cassel analysed what he took to be the more interesting type of socialism in its 'modern German sense', by which he meant the State socialist system of Rodbertus. Cassel's main point of criticism was that Rodbertus thought that wages could follow labour content in his socialist system, and that to this extent he had not understood the nature of 'scarcity rent'.

Cassel returned to the problem of distribution under socialism in 1901. Now he referred to Bernstein, 'who wanted to raise the proletariat to the level of the bourgeoisie and not the other way round, as Marxists normally do'. Even Engels had said that it should be possible to get rid of class differences without a decline in total production. But, according to Cassel, statistics from Prussia showed that it was impossible to increase the standard of living of the working class by taking money from the rich, since that would hinder capital accumulation. When the worker himself learned to form capital 'emancipation in real-economic terms' could come (1901: 130).

In an article in a conservative newspaper in 1908 Cassel summarized his ideas about Marx and socialism. 'The Marxian theory is dead, but socialism lives on.' But socialism can survive only as a political struggle for a better life for the workers. When it is turned into a class struggle and seeks to get rid of capitalism, it must be attacked.[33]

Wicksell, in a paper of 1899, wanted to 'iron out the contradictions between the socialists and the new theory'. He conceded Marx to be right on the point that capital has its origin in labour and not in the thrift of capitalists. But this was a problem of only 'ethical and social interest'; from 'economic aspects' it was of no interest.

Three years later Wicksell sharpened his position. Marx had led the social democrats on 'the wrong track'. Why should workers and employers not agree on the price of labour as buyers and sellers do for other goods? Marxism makes the social democrats indifferent to economic reforms. And this is dangerous for the working class at a time when the number of monopolies and cartels is growing, a fact which according to Wicksell showed that 'socialist planning' was gradually spreading within the limits of capitalism (1902, 1905).

In 1892 Branting tried to blend Marxism and marginalism in an ambitious pamphlet. He referred to Steffen, Wicksell, Jevons, and Böhm-Bawerk and the 'new theory of value', which was 'embraced by the majority in the scientific world'. Marx's 'law of value' still 'almost' held true, but prices would also follow the rules set up by this new theory. Branting did not want to go into the question of how the Marxists had answered the Jevonsists, but the issue was not very important, since Engels once said that Marx had not founded his demand for socialism on the labour theory of value.[34]

From the turn of the century the political economy of the labour movement was shaped more by academic professionals than by amateurs. Branting and the other leaders of the Social-Democratic Party were practical politicians without the time or the inclination to produce an effective defence of Marxist political economy against the attacks of academic authorities like Wicksell, Cassel, and Steffen. Probably this was one of the reasons why Marxism, or at least its political economy, failed to penetrate the labour movement in Sweden.[35]

Summary

In his speech at the golden jubilee of the Nationalekonomiska Föreningen on 29 January 1927, Eli Heckscher claimed that in former days economists – mercantilists as well as liberals – had also been spokesmen for different political interests. But now he thought they no longer spoke for anything other than their own science.[36]

The latter part of this statement is wrong, in the present writer's opinion. It led Heckscher to look back at the old thinkers before Davidson and Wicksell through falsely unpolitical neoclassical spectacles. And, given Heckscher's importance as the leading historian among the founders of modern *nationalekonomi*, his judgements had a big impact on the autobiography of Swedish economics.

The first part of the statement is probably less controversial. Economic thinking before the neoclassical school was closely connected with law and practical politics. Kings and priests spoke for their right to collect surplus production. Mercantilists spoke for

39

the merchants and physiocrats for the landowners. The historical school spoke for the *status quo*, classical liberals for profits and capitalism, and the followers of Marx for wages and socialism.

Until the twentieth century Sweden lagged far behind the other countries in its economic development. Because of language and differences in political and economic conditions, the most advanced international thinking in political economy could not be fully understood in Sweden at the time it was written. Published economic texts were often translations or home-cooked versions of texts in other languages in order to make them fit less advanced economic and social conditions.

In medieval times, influences came mostly from Christian and humanistic thinking in southern Europe, transformed via German Hanseatic towns and Denmark to suit a peasant economy with a weak feudal system. In the sixteenth century German technology and mercantilist thinking were imported to suit the war economy of autocratic Vasa kings. In the seventeenth century the Dutch took over from the Germans as chief ideologists when the small super-power tried to develop its trade. In the first half of the eighteenth century English mercantilist thinking was imported to suit merchants and factory owners. In the second half of the century a distorted version of the teachings of the French physio- crats reached Sweden.

During the first part of the nineteenth century English and French influences (Smith, Say, Bastiat) competed for dominance when economic liberalism penetrated a country that lagged about half a century behind their own in its capitalist development. In the 1870s the German language regained a leading position through schools of thought on both wings of the political spectrum, from left to right. Moreover those schools were interpreted in a way that suited relatively more rural, peaceful, democratic, and pragmatic traditions.

But foreign influences should not be overrated. Swedish politi- cal economists also made original contributions of their own. Men like Nordencrantz, Christiernin, Chydenius, Järta, and Arnberg not only used international texts but also evolved their thinking from practical experience of Swedish society. Because of the smallness of their language area, and underdeveloped systems of communication, they never got a chance to reach an international public. Had they written in another language, some of their works could have become classics in the international history of ideas. Seen in their historical environment, most of them, in the present writer's opinion, were quite as brilliant as any leading modern figures among the authorities on what is now called *nationalekon- omi* in Sweden and economics in the English-speaking world.

Notes

Erik Lönnroth, Bo Sandelin and Carl G. Uhr have given valuable advice in the preparation of this chapter.

1 See the term *hushållsbok* ('husbandry') in *Kulturhistoriskt lexikon för nordisk medeltid* 7 (1962).
2 *Bondakonst*, ed. Granlund (1983), and Lindroth (1975: 181). The second part of Granlund's 1983 edition, *Barnabok*, is a translation of *Institutio Principis Christiani* by Erasmus of Rotterdam.
3 Usselinx tried to start the first large Swedish trading company: see Franklin Jameson in *Papers of the American Historical Association* II, 3 (1987). Palmstruch started a private bank in 1656, the first European producer of paper money. It went bankrupt in 1668 and Palmstruch was executed. But Palmstruch's bank was succeeded by Riksens Ständers Bank (the Bank of the Diet of the Four Estates), which was established as a national bank and which has been called by a modern writer 'Next to John Law's Banque Royale, the most important mercantilist monetary experiment attempted in Western Europe during the pre-Adam Smith era' (Eagly's introduction, in Christiernin, 1971: 3). Cartesius was invited to Stockholm by Queen Kristina. Pufendorf wrote his major books at the University of Lund; see Bo Sandelin in *Ekonomisk Debatt* 7 (1987).
4 Heckscher on Risingh (1954: 114). For more about Risingh see Lönnroth (1987).
5 Risingh (1669: ch. 3). This idea was probably inspired by Gerard Malynes in his *Lex mercatoria* (1622); see Heckscher (1935–6: 697).
6 Risingh (1669: 34). The expression 'skrot och korn' comes from the German 'Schrott und Korn', which is translated as 'alloy and standard' in *Langenscheidts Taschenwörterbuch* I, *Englisch–Deutsch* (1851).
7 Lindroth (1978: 105). The main works by Mun and Davenant were translated into Swedish in 1732 and 1734.
8 The last part of this section is taken almost word for word from Herlitz (1964: 118).
9 Nordencrantz (1730: 135), cited by Magnusson (1987: 422).
10 At the request of the commission an author even succeeded in calculating that the average farm worker in Sweden had the exact 'political value' of 5,758 daler $10^{2/3}$ öre copper coins! See Johannisson (1988: 150).

11 Christiernin (1761: 23). For the following passage on Christiernin see also Persson and Siven (1988).

12 Heckscher (1949a: 817). The average annual number of publications in political economy exceeded thirty during the period 1761–72, more than ten times the average for the rest of the century. Most of them dealt with monetary problems and policies.

13 Christiernin (1761: 142), partly cited after Ohlin (1959: 8).

14 According to Virrankoski (1988: 108) the impulse came primarily from Nordencrantz's *En vördsam föreställning uti et Omständeligit svar* (Stockholm, 1759).

15 Chydenius (1765b: 90). Lucidor was the pseudonym of the Swedish poet Lars Johansson (1638–74). The translation was by 'Englishmen in Stockholm' (Schauman's preface, ibid.: 5).

16 The pamphlets were *Landthandel* (1777) and *Tankar om husbönders och tienstehions naturliga rätt* (1778). See Virrankoski (1988: 117).

17 The Swedish title of Scheffer's letters was *Bref till herrar riksens rad.* See Herlitz (1976: 113–14; English summary). The following description is mainly a quotation from this summary.

18 See Andréen (1958) on the debate between expansionists and restrictionists.

19 Järta (1823: 1). Modern 'economics' is called *nationalekonomi* in Sweden.

20 The section on Agardh's life is based mainly on Wadensjö (1987) and Wallerius's biography (1975).

21 *Försök till en statsekonomisk statistik öfver Sverige* (Statistical Essay on the State Economy of Sweden).

22 The concept of a historical 'school' was used by Geijer long before the German counterpart was known in Sweden. See also Björkqvist (1986: ch. IX) for an analysis of the historical school and its representatives in Finland. (Sweden lost Finland in 1809, and the Swedish-speaking thinkers in Finland after that year are not treated here. Instead they may be found in Björkqvist, 1986.) The letter from Geijer to Järta is reproduced in Geijer (1980).

23 The article is reproduced in Geijer (1980).

24 The whole lecture is reproduced in Geijer (1980).

25 Bäckström (1972: 81), who writes that Per Götrek was the editor. According to Olausson the text in the Swedish version was by Carl Rudolph Löwstedt.

26 Davidson (1878: 22–7). In *Capital* I Marx cites Petty, who once said that nature is the mother and labour the father of material wealth; see Marx (1970: 38). In his critique of the Gotha programme in 1875 Marx also wrote, 'Labour is *not the source* of all wealth. *Nature* is just as much the source of use values (and it is surely of such that material wealth consists!) as labour ...' (Marx, 1971: 11; emphasis in original). Evidently Davidson was not aware of this, and we shall see that he was not alone in his error.

27 *Socialdemokraten,* 5 November 1886, unsigned article that must have been by Branting.

28 'Knut Wicksell och socialismen', *Socialdemokraten,* 26 November 1886. The article is reproduced in Branting (1926, I).
29 *Socialdemokraten,* 17 December 1886. (From a microfilm version at the university library in Göteborg.)
30 Marx was well aware that the capitalist plays a role as entrepreneur in capitalist production. He often stressed too that profits are an important incentive in choice of technology and capitalist growth. See, for example, the first pages of Marx's commentary to Adolph Wagner's textbook of political economy.
31 *Socialdemokraten,* 6 August 1887, cited after Olson (1983: 38).
32 See Lönnroth (1989) for a fuller biography of Steffen as political economist.
33 'Socialismen', *Svenska Dagbladet,* 12 February 1908.
34 Branting (1906: 68). Marx knew that short-run market prices are determined by the joint forces of supply and demand. The 'law of value' stated that labour values are 'centres of gravity' for market prices under three conditions: if exchange 'ceases to be purely accidental or merely occasional', if commodities are produced 'in relative quantities that approximately correspond to the mutual need', and if 'no natural or artificial monopolies enable one of the contracting parties to sell above value, or force them to sell cheap, below value' (Marx, 1981: 278–9). The law is wrong on any reasonable interpretation.
35 A paper, 'The defeat of Marxism as Economics: The Swedish Example', is forthcoming in 1990 in *Perspectives on the History of Economic Thought,* Vol V ed. William J. Barber. A short history of the political economy of Marxism in Sweden in the present century can be found in the Swedish version; see J. Lönnroth, 'Den marxistiska ekonomilärans nederlag i Sverige', in J. Bohlin, B. Fridén, U. Herlitz, A. Kihlström, A. Molander, and M. Rantanen (eds.) *Samhällsvetenskap, ekonomi och historia: festskrift till Lars Herlitz,* Göteborg: Daidalos, 1989.
36 *Nationalekonomiska Föreningens Förhandlingar* (1927).

Chapter three

David Davidson: the transition to neoclassical economics

Carl G. Uhr

Life and career

David Davidson was born in 1854, the eldest son among nine children of the German Jewish merchant family of Isaac and Rebecca Davidson, who had settled in Stockholm in the later 1840s.[1] As a teenager David must have been a gifted student, for already in 1871, at the age of seventeen – a year or two younger than most of his classmates – he matriculated at the University of Uppsala to study economics and law. There he made rapid progress, completing an undergraduate degree in 1872, and an advanced pre-doctoral degree in 1877. In 1878 he earned his doctorate with a dissertation, the title of which may be translated as 'A Contribution to the Theory of the Economic Laws of Capital Formation'. That same year he was appointed a *docent* in economics at Uppsala University, in which capacity he served until 1880. Then he was advanced to the rank of professor *extraodinarius* (a professorship without tenure) pending the anticipated resignation of an older colleague who was called to a Cabinet post. However, the colleague decided to continue both his professorship and his Cabinet duties for nearly a decade, until his retirement in 1889. Then Davidson was appointed to replace him as professor *ordinarius*. For thirty years Davidson served the University of Uppsala as a professor of economics and a member of a succession of parliamentary committees on problems of monetary and trade policies, on taxation and public finance, until his retirement (mandatory at the age of sixty-five in Sweden's universities) in 1919.

During the 1880s Davidson wrote four more works in monograph form, as distinct from the greater part of his writing, which, from 1899 to 1939, was in article form in *Ekonomisk Tidskrift*. The titles of his monographs translate as *A Contribution to the*

History of the Theory of Rent (1880), *Central Banks of Europe* (1886), *Commentary on the Finance Acts* (1889a), and *Taxation Norms for the Income Tax* (1889b). Only two of these, *History of the Theory of Rent* and *Taxation Norms*, are of doctrinal and economic policy interest and will be considered below.

Soon after being appointed a *docent*, Davidson was given a grant and leave by the Uppsala Faculty of Law for research and studies abroad. In 1879 he left to attend some courses by K. Knies at the University of Heidelberg. In 1886 he received another grant to study income tax legislation in the former Hanseatic cities of Bremen, Hamburg, and Lübeck, and the Swiss canton of Basel.

In 1899 two events occurred which had a lasting bearing on Davidson's life, the first of which made it more complete, and the second of which enhanced his communication with the then existing handful of Swedish economists and, more particularly, extended his influence over the coming generation of economists. First, at the age of forty-five he married. Second, at his own risk and expense he started Sweden's first economic journal, *Ekonomisk Tidskrift*. Davidson remained owner and editor of (and for most of its first decades also a main contributor to) *Ekonomisk Tidskrift*, for forty years, until 1939. Then, at eighty-five, he turned it over to younger colleagues, Ingvar Svennilson and Erik Lundberg. Several years later they changed both the title and the language of this prestigious journal from Swedish to English. From 1965 they issued it as the *Swedish Journal of Economics* and in 1975 changed its name once more to the *Scandinavian Journal of Economics*.

After retirement in 1919 Davidson devoted his energies entirely to editing and writing occasional articles for *Ekonomisk Tidskrift*, and to service on parliamentary committees called to study and advise on monetary and fiscal policy problems. In recognition of his long teaching career, his successful launching of *Ekonomisk Tidskrift* and his service on government committees, in 1920 he was elected a member of the Royal Swedish Academy of Sciences. In his various activities he was in frequent contact and collaboration with his colleague Wicksell, and also a frequent and constructive critic of both Wicksell and Cassel. However, neither they nor he endeavoured to establish a distinctive following or 'school' of disciples. In fact, while their teaching, writings, and public services reached and influenced a fairly large public of students, academics, business people, civil servants, and politicians, they had surprisingly few 'disciples' who, later on, became outstanding economists and as such could carry forward some of the ideas and analyses of their mentors.

In terms of their orientation and allegiance as mature economists, one can say that Wicksell's's primary disciples were Erik Lindahl and Bertil Ohlin; Cassel's were Gunnar Myrdal and Erik Lundberg, while Davidson in the main had only one disciple, the noted economic historian Eli Heckscher.[2] It was these 'disciples' who, in their turn, founded and became the leaders of the 'Stockholm school of economics'. However, in this circle it seems, at first glance, that Davidson's role as mentor and inspirer was much less than that of either Wicksell or Cassel. These matters are difficult to evaluate. But there can be scarcely any doubt that Davidson's influence over the 'school' was considerably less, especially in matters of economic theory, than that of Wicksell.[3] Still, how it measures up to that of Cassel, whose role was also less than that of Wicksell, is more problematic and will be left in abeyance here.

In monetary policy during World War I and its aftermath, and from the turn of the century in taxation and fiscal policy, Davidson's influence was quite direct and probably greater than Wicksell's. But as an economic theorist his influence on younger economists and students was apparently small and indirect, exerted in the main by what he and others published in *Ekonomisk Tidskrift*.

As a theorist Davidson appears a transitional figure endeavouring to bridge the gap between classical, especially Ricardian, economics and neoclassical economics in the realms of value and distribution theories. From an intellectual history standpoint, his transitional position is of considerable interest, for others of his generation, notably Alfred Marshall and Philip Wicksteed, had to make a more or less similar transition. Davidson crossed this bridge in a controversy about these subjects carried on by correspondence with Wicksell.

As for Davidson's recognition internationally, relative to the great attention Wicksell's work has attracted (especially posthumously) it was practically non-existent until the later 1930s, when such scholars as Brinley Thomas (1935, 1936) and years later Ralph Turvey incorporated synopses of some of Davidson's analysis in their own treatises. This lack of recognition outside Scandinavia was due to two circumstances, the language barrier and the fact that he never consolidated his work in treatise form. Unlike Wicksell and Cassel, who published their major works in German between the 1890s and the early 1920s, works which were translated into English in the 1930s, all Davidson's writings were published in Swedish; none was translated. Moreover, they were scattered between his five early monographs, 250 signed articles in

Ekonomisk Tidskrift plus a number of unsigned ones recording his reactions to current problems and to the writings of others, plus chapters contributed to government reports.[4]

David Davidson died in Uppsala in March 1942, where he had spent almost all his adult life. He was then in his eighty-eighth year. Posthumously, in 1951, the Swedish Academy of Science struck a gold medal in his honour. Its text seems most appropriate and serves well as an epitaph to Davidson's unassuming and scholarly career:

> Scientiam sagaciter penetravit
> Nova voce ditavit.[5]

Capital theory

In 'Capital Formation' Davidson opened with a concise doctrinal review of capital and related concepts, beginning with Turgot, then Adam Smith and J.S. Mill, with brief comments on Dunoyer, J.B. Say, and Rau. From F. Hermann's *Staatswirtschaftliche Untersuchungen* (1832) he adopted an emphasis on gross investment in the creation of capital and on the indefinite durability in service of fixed capital goods under proper maintenance and eventual replacement. Then he turned to C. Menger's *Grundsätze der Volkswirtschaftslehre* (1871), from which he adopted Menger's hierarchical classification of commodities into goods of the first, or lowest, order (consumer goods) and goods of a higher order (capital goods). The relative order of a good was higher the further back it was used in the production stages from raw materials to finished consumer goods. Davidson also illustrated the essential complementary relationships which prevail and are necessary in production processes between higher- and lower-order goods used in combination in production-stage sequences. Then he linked Knies's treatment in *Geld und Kredit* (1873–6) of credit and credit institutions with Menger's analysis to show how credit mediates and enhances the transformation of real savings, his 'goods reserved for the satisfaction of future wants', into real investment in goods of a higher order.

He criticized Menger on only one point, in interpreting Menger as holding that real capital was identical with the totality of produced means of production. In contrast to this, Davidson (1878: 43) stated his own view that 'Capital and its formation are activities by which present goods are reserved for the satisfaction of future wants, whether or not those goods are used as means of production, as by far the majority of them are.' In a much later context (1913, 1917) he corrected this by saying, 'Savings do not necessarily lead to the formation of new capital, not if they are lent to consumers, only if they are lent to producers who use them for producing capital goods' (1913, 5: 28 ff.). The circumstances in which savings might not be fully transformed into real investment came to play an important role in his (and also in Wicksell's) analysis about the turn of the century and subsequently; but more of that anon.

He went on to consider the motives for saving, i.e. for 'reserving goods for future wants', and attributed them to people's concern about the future of their families, especially the future of their children and the parents' economic security in old age. He noted how large a role an unequal distribution of income and wealth plays in capital formation. On high incomes the wealthy can satisfy many more wants, and wants of declining to negligible importance, than can persons of middling to small means. To the wealthy sooner or later – often sooner – there comes a point at which the importance of their future wants outweighs that of the least and the lesser of their present wants. This induces them to save. In this manner Davidson made it clear that income, like most things, is subject to diminishing present marginal utility, but not necessarily to a simultaneous and equally fast declining future marginal utility.

One notes in this connection that, unlike Böhm-Bawerk, Davidson did not dwell at length on the allegedly widespread obstacles to saving, overestimation (especially by the young) of future provision and underestimation (except by the aged, who in extreme old age may no longer have any savings) of future needs.

Davidson then went on to point out that 'goods reserved for future wants' could be traded with others for use by them in current production. Such trades or exchanges would be made in return for a commitment by the users to the erstwhile owners of disposal of future goods of greater value than the goods surrendered, a value that would increase with the duration or length of time in the future over which the commitment was to run. In this way, Davidson brought clearly into focus the close relationship that exists between credit and credit institutions and capital formation. He also implicitly explained the basis of interest, which Böhm-Bawerk (1889) was to call the 'agio', namely the *quid pro quo* (here disposal of future goods of greater value than goods surrendered), for which owners of 'reserved goods' would make them available mostly to entrepreneurs (but also to consumer borrowers) in a credit exchange for use as real capital in production.

All along Davidson had stressed that goods 'reserved for future wants' also could and to a great extent would be transformed in current production into goods of greater and more valuable future uses, whether they were so transformed by their owners or by entrepreneurs after a credit exchange. Here Davidson anticipated what Böhm-Bawerk a decade later was to refer to as the 'technical superiority of present over future goods of like kinds', and what we now refer to as the productivity of real capital or of 'waiting'.

It is surprising that Davidson, restricting himself in 1878 to an 'explanation of the laws of capital formation', did not bring these three strands of his analysis to a common focus as an explanation of interest, as Böhm-Bawerk was to do with his trinitarian explanation, known as the 'three grounds of interest', in his *magnum opus, The Positive Theory of Capital* (1889).[6] Whether or not, as he read Böhm-Bawerk's works, Davidson himself regretted that he had not consolidated his reasoning of 1878 more closely we do not know. In any case, at this stage Davidson had considered capital chiefly from its supply side, paying scant attention to its highly variable demand side.

In his early work one notes that Davidson paid almost no attention to the variable time dimension with which the use of capital endows production processes. But by the 1890s he seems to have adopted the substance of Böhm-Bawerk's capital theory and along with it Wicksell's more sophisticated reconstruction in *Value, Capital and Rent* (1893) and also in *Lectures on Political Economy* I (1901). This can be seen from the following statements in Per Jacobsson's shorthand notes of Davidson's lectures in the autumn term of 1913 and 1917 respectively:[7]

Capital is directly proportional to the investment period.
   Capital has two dimensions, a certain breadth, the result of a certain input of labour and land services, and a certain time span. (1913, 26: 127)
   Increasing the investment period increases the productivity of capital but at a progressively decreasing rate, unless diminishing returns on lengthening this period are offset by labour-saving inventions. (1917, 24: 173–4)
   The relation between lengthening and the period of production and distribution is that lengthening increases the return on capital and reduces the real wage, and at the same time an increase in the share of labour in the total product, correspondingly a reduction in the share of capital provides an inducement for lengthening the period of production. (1917, 26: 191)

The last statement, which shows a direct relationship between capital formation and changes in distributive shares, led Davidson to link his earlier observation that savings invested in consumer loans create no new capital with the concept of a real wages fund. The latter is also an object of the investment of savings, which, as such, likewise creates no real capital unless and to the extent that the workers are directed to produce capital goods. Then he defined a concept of 'enterprise capital funds' which are used both for paying real wages and for acquiring or producing capital goods. Under certain circumstances, he pointed out, the greater proportion – in the end, all – of these funds might be used for paying real wages and little or none for capital goods. Alternatively, when the conditions are reversed, the greater proportion of these funds are used for producing capital goods. Out of these relations he developed a model of capital formation for a hypothetical society and then applied relevant features of the model to a monetary economy, and on that basis generated a hypothesis for explaining business cycles which we sketch as follows.[8]

We have a community where land is initially a free good and the people are self-employed nomads living by hunting, fishing, and gathering berries. They have no real capital other than simple tools. Yet some of these nomads realize a surplus over their consumption needs and use or save and invest it in clearing fields and building huts in order to settle in agriculture. To cut a long story short, as this succeeds, the initial settlers expand their farms by hiring nomads at slightly better real wages than are available from hunting and the like. They set these nomad labourers chiefly to producing capital goods and facilities for the improvement and expansion of agriculture, and these activities are referred to as 'lengthening the period of production'. From their steadier and better wages some of the nomad labourers save a portion in order eventually to settle themselves as farmers in the outlying areas. Within a generation practically all the former nomads are either settled in farming or are labourers for the settlers. At that stage a labour shortage develops, as there are almost no nomads left to transform into new farm labourers, and real wages have risen and are rising. The larger of the settlers are still saving and trying to expand and improve their farms further. But by now almost all their saving goes in real wages to workers who now produce mainly consumer goods.

This bucolic situation is disrupted as labour-saving technological innovations are introduced, to lift reduced profit prospects and induce renewed lengthening of the production period. Some workers are now laid off. Real wages decline, and laid-off workers compete with others still employed at lower wages. Returns on capital improve. Eventually the unemployed find work again at lower wages as innovations motivate further expansion.

However, this transition is not likely to be smooth. Often it involves a crisis. As laid-off workers reduce their consumption, unintended commodity stocks accumulate at falling prices. The real wages of those remaining at work increase for a time as commodity prices fall and money wages fall too but more slowly, with a lag behind commodity prices, and fall less than the latter. Meanwhile interest rates have been reduced and are still falling while returns on capital are beginning to rise. Once the recession reaches a turning point as innovations still brighten profit prospects, this may lay the basis of an upward cumulative Wicksellian process, at interest rates lower than returns on capital, a cumulative process which, in its turn, may end in another crisis a few years hence.

The foregoing sequence shows similarities with the problem Ricardo encountered in his famous chapter 'On machinery'. It motivated Wicksell to state, 'The capitalist saver is thus fundamentally the friend of labour, though the technical inventor is not infrequently its enemy' (1934a: 104).

One can paraphrase Davidson as saying of business cycles in the aftermath of World War I that continuous capital formation at a trend or rate generally higher than the growth trend of the labour force, in conditions of intermittent impact of technological change, generates economic fluctuations. The distributive shares effect of this is that in the absence of labour-saving innovations the increase in real capital occurs not to any significant extent through a reduction in real wages but rather through real savings.

Davidson's attitude towards business cycles was very matter-of-fact, to a degree one of indifference. Cycles come and go. They involve structural adjustments for some economic sectors more than others. To be sure, they give rise to unemployment, but they are generally of short duration, with fairly rapid recovery, like the crises of 1907–9 and the post-World War I depression of 1920–2. Not much can be done about them apart from pursuing a stabilizing monetary policy and avoiding disturbances and retaliatory trade policies.

However, in the course of the Great Depression, which was deeper and longer-lasting than earlier ones, his position changed. At first, as the government trotted out a series of large public works programmes to contain and reverse the rise in unemployment, he was apprehensive that such 'authoritarian interventions', as he called them, might lead to a permanent expansion of the public at the expense of the private sector of the economy. But as these and related recovery measures proved successful, so that the country's recovery was in substance achieved in the course of 1936, he became almost enthusiastic, saying:

> I have limited my task to indicating the measures needed for reducing the *effects* of unemployment to the minimum, something I consider Sweden has solved tolerably well recently. The means are to provide unemployed workers with *real* work for the duration of the crisis, and *only* for that duration. The result is that the country's labour force does not deteriorate in periods of general unemployment, and this is a decided gain. (*E.T.* 1937: 57)

He indicated that the best way to go about preventing the effects of future crises would be for the government to pre-plan public works to contain unemployment and to have such projects in readiness, to be quickly put into action when the need arose and to be equally quickly tapered off when the crisis had passed. As compared with this, he rejected most of Keynes's recovery proposals as he found them in the *General Theory*, about which he said:

> This [the Swedish] mode of meeting the unemployment problem is characterized by the fact that the structure of our economic life is by and large not altered by the measures taken against unemployment. Keynes's proposals are quite the opposite of this ... [they] assume important changes in the economic structure of society which would greatly restrict economic freedom and private initiative. ... To a certain extent measures of a Keynesian type have been introduced in Hitler's Germany and Mussolini's Italy. (ibid.)

This may suffice to reveal Davidson's concern with economic instability. His originality in this sphere was limited to an application of the Wicksell effect to the relations between a variable wages fund and the flow of savings intended for capital formation. As for his concession to government action by countercyclical variation of the budget between expenditure and revenue in order to cope with unemployment, this signifies that despite his advanced age in the later 1930s he was not intellectually inflexible but able to adjust to the exigencies of the time.

One more facet of Davidson's capital theory remains to be considered, his answer to a query which had once occupied both

Ricardo and J.S. Mill, namely the ancient query whether the rate of interest would fall to zero in an economy where continuous capital formation went on at a rate greater than the growth rate of labour. Wicksell (1893, 1901) had answered this in the negative both for a stationary and for a progressive economy. Davidson shared his position, with one very hypothetical reservation. Under the Wicksell effect a part of savings intended for capital formation is absorbed in rising real wages, with the result that the social marginal productivity rate of capital is smaller than the interest rate. Under continuous capital formation the social marginal productivity rate of capital may fall to zero while the interest rate, though very low, would still be greater than zero, according to Wicksell. Davidson's only reservation about this was that the interest rate could conceivably also go to zero if the workers were to save the increases in their real wages which capitalists' savings brought them under the Wicksell effect, a most unlikely eventuality.

Cassel had argued that the interest would always be positive (1) because all capital formation would cease before it fell to zero, and (2) even if it got to zero momentarily, it would soon rise because the demand for fixed capital would become limitless at a zero rate. Davidson's reasoning on this was that the first point is doubtful unless one assumes a zero growth rate of labour and no labour-saving technological change; then there would be no further use or demand for additional capital. The second reason, he said, was plainly wrong. Fixed capital is subject to two charges, interest and maintenance/depreciation. If the interest charge is eliminated there is still the maintenance to be met. As an example, even if workers had luxurious houses built at zero interest to live in, their demand for this form of fixed capital would not be limitless once they realized they would have to meet the maintenance costs (Wicksell, 1954: 127–39; 1934a: 177–80, 209; Cassel, 1918: 191; Davidson, *E.T.* 1914: 91–105; 1919: 241–2, 251, 254–6). From the foregoing one can conclude that Davidson, like Ricardo, liked to argue from 'strong cases'.

The history of rent and Davidson's neo-Ricardian theory of value

Davidson's *History of the Theory of Rent* is an excellent historiographical survey, beginning with Boisguillebert in the seventeenth century, proceeding to the physiocrats and Adam Smith in the eighteenth, and through most of the nineteenth century, ending with Rodbertus and Knies. One wonders why he omitted Marx;

probably because on rent Marx was less explicit than Rodbertus, and in terms of orientation the two were related. About two-thirds of this concise work (118 pp.) is taken up with the theories of Ricardo, Malthus, Jones, von Thünen, Rodbertus, and Knies. Davidson's survey showed clearly that by the 1880s the concept of rent had changed very little from its traditional association with land, as a demand-determined, unearned return to owners of land. The generalization of this concept as a return on any factor temporarily or permanently in inelastic supply had not yet achieved general acceptance (as it did after 1890, largely owing to Marshall), although both Schäffle and Mangoldt and, via them, Davidson were aware of the need to extend the concept.

Davidson undertook the survey to clear up his own position on value theory in view of the challenge to the classical theory coming by 1880 from what was later to be called neoclassical theory. He did this by a thorough exegesis of Ricardo's value theory, begun in *History of the Theory of Rent* and carried on in his lectures of 1917 and in two long articles he wrote for *Ekonomisk Tidskrift* (1919: 231–59; 1923: 191–254). 'Possessing utility, commodities derive their exchange value from scarcity and from the quantity of labour required to obtain them' (Ricardo, 1817: 12).

Concerning this and some later statements from Ricardo's work, which Davidson selected and approved of as revealing his own position, Davidson emphasized that it showed, notwithstanding widespread misinterpretation of Ricardo to the contrary, that Ricardo did not claim that commodity values are determined solely by and are strictly proportionate to the amount of labour required for their production. He went on to say that Ricardo had explicitly recognized that:

1. When two goods embody an equal amount of labour, but one commodity has a longer period of production than the other, the exchange value of the former will be greater relative to that of the latter than would follow from the respective amounts of labour embodied in them.

2. When fixed capital is used in production, the rule that the values of goods are proportionate to the amount of labour used in producing them is valid only if (*a*) the fixed capitals have the same durability, their values being proportionate to labour embodied in them, or (*b*) if the capitals have the same value their durability must be in proportion to the labour quantities in question.

3. In all other cases of the use of fixed capital, the yield or profit on capital affects the exchange values of commodities.

4. Accordingly, Ricardo concluded, the value of a commodity must be identical with its cost of production, inclusive of profit on

capital. In fact there is an explicit statement on this, which Davidson quoted (Ricardo, 1817: 47).

Moreover, Davidson emphasized that Ricardo's treatment (*a*) applied only to reproducible commodities, and (*b*) concerned only their relative or exchange value, not their absolute value. 'Absolute' commodity value was a problem Ricardo found intractable after struggling with it in section VI, 'An invariable measure of value', in chapter I of his *Principles*.

Like Ricardo, Davidson took the position that the real, absolute value of a commodity depends on the quantities of scarce primary factors of production which must be used in producing it. Absolute value might also be expressed as a ratio, not that of the exchange ratio between a pair of commodities, but a ratio determined by the degree of scarcity of the primary factors of production. When the production function of a commodity, produced on marginal (no rent) land, changes so as to require less labour and more capital input, the commodity's absolute value also changes, but we cannot tell by how much for lack of a common unit of measurement by which to translate units of labour input into equivalent units of capital input, or vice versa. The three primary factors are incommensurable with respect to each other. It is true that this problem is not insoluble, as both Ricardo and Davidson thought. It has been solved in an ingenious fashion by Sraffa (1960). But that was long past Davidson's time and had nothing to do with his doctrines, and for that reason we need not discuss it here.

As Davidson was aware, in the marginal utility theory of value, the 'absolute value' problem does not emerge in the form it did for Ricardo, and in that connection he referred to a point that had arisen between Ricardo and J.B. Say. Say had claimed that the degree of utility determines the value of commodities. Ricardo denied this, saying that, if two communities had the same quantities of commodities, they would be equally rich, but the value (in Ricardo's sense) of their respective riches would depend on the comparative difficulties with which they were produced.

Davidson took exception to this and regarded Ricardo's position of denying any role of utility in the determination of value as extreme. For himself, Davidson regarded the marginal utility theory of value and his own neo-Ricardian 'theory of objective economic value' as complementary to one another rather than competitive. He felt certain that relative scarcity affects and serves as a basis also for the marginal utility valuations which guide individual decisions as to spending and the allocation of income, and hence acts on demand:

> The development of the magnitude of value is very different in the two theories [Ricardian versus marginal utility theory].... When productivity increases (ratio of labour input to output declines) then the [Ricardian] value of this output would decline in the same proportion as productivity increased. But this principle does not hold under marginal utility theory. Marginal utility of a unit of output does *not* decline *pari passu* with the increase in the quantity of output ... it may decline more or less than in proportion to the increase in output.... The difficulty is that subjective value also depends on objective circumstances. It depends on the supply or availability of goods, and this is an objective condition which the individual can influence only slightly, if at all. So when one tries to explain the objective via the individual value, we see that behind the individual valuation there are objective conditions at work. (1917, 22: 152–3)

Cassel (1918) rejected all value theories, especially the marginal utility theory, as useless metaphysics and urged that prices and price relationships should be taken as the fundamental data of economics. Wicksell responded with a long review in *Ekonomisk Tidskrift* (1919), since translated as 'Professor Cassel's system of economics' and appended to Wicksell (1934: 219–57). In it Wicksell defended marginal utility theory with a scathing review of the first half of Cassel's tome and praising him for its second half and his work on business cycles. Since both Cassel and Wicksell had spoken, Davidson felt it incumbent on himself to bring out his own view on value theory, and so in a long article in *Ekonimisk Tidskrift* (1919), the title of which translates as 'Some problems in economic theory', we get a full statement of his 'theory of objective economic value'. It is most concisely presented in Davidson's own words:

> Marginal utility theory asserts that individual economic values are expressed by marginal utility.... Still, it is certain that a person's individual economic valuation and the marginal utility of his supply are parallel expressions of the same cause, *scarcity*.... Scarcity also gives rise to another valuation, different from the individual valuation, as it concerns different kinds of resources or goods as such without regard to the circumstance that they are included as component parts of individual persons' supplies. The existence of goods of different kinds necessitates such a further valuation, the purpose of which is to determine objectively how much of a certain good or resource corresponds to a given quantity of another good.... This

valuation is needed to determine what changes in the composition of a person's supply are called for because of scarcity.... *The result of this kind of economic valuation is appropriately called objective economic value....* Objective value is the same for rich and poor alike, which is *not* the case with individual valuation. (*E.T.* 1923: 211–12; emphasis in original)

... A commodity quantity ... which is always the output of the same quantity of productive power [Davidson's expression for factor inputs] represents *as a rule* an objective value of constant magnitude. This is to presuppose ... that production and the flow of output of commodities equal the demand for them and the variation to which the demand for them is subject. Otherwise it is possible for the magnitude of objective value of a commodity to change even though it continues to require the same quantity of productive power for its production as before. (*E.T.* 1923: 228; emphasis in original)

Thus objective values are invariant only in dynamic equilibrium between aggregate demand and output, when no changes in productivity occur and factors are used in optimal combinations so that the output/input ratio of each commodity is constant. But if production fails to anticipate and adjust to variations in demand, as often happens, then objective values will change even if given commodities require 'the same productive power' for their production as before. This seems a very brittle resolution of the objective or absolute value problem, although it represents a substantial clarification of the nature of that problem over the manner in which Ricardo had to leave it.

As Davidson became aware, his objective value theory did not gain any wide acceptance, nor, so far as I know, any followers among the Stockholm economists. Still, for all that, Davidson's emphasis on resource and commodity scarcity served him and Sweden well in managing some monetary problems during World War I.

Having seen the reservations and qualifications with which Davidson accepted the marginal utility approach to economic value, we now turn to his reaction to a closely related concept, the marginal productivity theory of distribution.

The marginal productivity theory of distribution

Davidson's discussion of the marginal productivity of distribution was fragmentary, moving from rejection to reluctant acceptance.

The determinacy of marginal productivity distribution had first been proved by Wicksell in 1893 (in *Value, Capital, and Rent*, 1954: 148–53) and then by Wicksteed in *The Co-ordination of the Laws of Distribution* (1894). But because this theory was demonstrated for production at constant returns to scale, it was criticized on the basis that few, if any, industries operate with linear and homogeneous production functions, and because the indivisibility of many factor inputs would block the freedom of factor substitution which was assumed. Aware of these issues, Wicksell published two articles in *Ekonomisk Tidskrift* (1900, 1902; since translated in Lindahl, 1958: 93–120, 121–30). There he proved that marginal productivity distribution is determinate regardless of whether production goes on at constant returns to scale or at diminishing returns, but not at continuously increasing returns to scale, so that production functions can reach their maxima under maintenance of free competition. At those maxima, firms have corresponding cost curves that reach their minima, or points of minimum unit cost. Competition would force firms to produce at minimum cost, and then production runs as if at constant returns to scale, and marginal productivity distribution is determinate.

In correspondence with Wicksell in 1902 Davidson objected to this with an example purporting to show that this distribution left a significant residual. Let land be a free good, in $Q = f(K, L)$ we increase the factors equiproportionally by one thousandth, but do it first *seriatim*, with $b = K/1{,}000$ and $a = L/1{,}000$. Using $(b + K)$ while keeping L constant, we get a marginal product, r. Then, increasing L to $(a + L)$ while keeping $(b + K)$ constant, we get another marginal product, w. Next we increase both factors simultaneously by one thousandth and get a joint marginal product $f[(b + K), (a + L)] - f(K,L) = \Delta Q$. Now, said Davidson, $(Q + \Delta Q) - [r(b + K) + w(a + L)] > 0$ so $\Delta Q - (r + w) > 0$ and we have an undistributed residual. The reason is that when any one of several factors is increased singly, with the others constant, its output is subject to diminishing returns, compared with what its contribution to output would be when all factors are increased equally and simultaneously.

Wicksell's reply was that the *seriatim* marginal products of the separate factors are approximately equal to the respective partial differentials of the production function,

$$r = \frac{\delta f}{\delta K}\ dK, \qquad w = \frac{\delta f}{\delta L}\ dL$$

and the joint marginal product from increasing them simultaneously and equally equals the total derivative of the production function,

$$\Delta Q \simeq dQ = d[f(K, L)] = \frac{\delta f}{\delta K} \, dK + \frac{\delta f}{\delta L} \, dL$$

and so $\Delta Q \simeq (r + w)$, with no significant residual.

To make this crystal clear, Wicksell set up a three-factor production function with the firm's output $Q = \sqrt[3]{K \cdot L \, d \cdot L}$. Then *seriatim* he increased each factor equiproportionally by a thousandth, and the marginal product from each of the factors was $0 \cdot 0003332Q$, and the sum of their three separate marginal products was $0 \cdot 0009996Q$. The result from increasing them simultaneously was a joint marginal product of $0 \cdot 001000Q$. Thus the difference between ΔQ and dQ was $(0 \cdot 0010000Q - 0 \cdot 0009996Q) = 0 \cdot 0000004Q$ or $4Q/10,000,000$, a second order magnitude that can be ignored. This probably convinced Davidson that marginal productivity distribution is determinate, but we cannot be sure, for in a lecture in 1913 he said, 'The attempt to determine distribution according to marginal productivity has failed, but the attempt has by no means been given up' (1913, 4: 22).

In this lecture, much of which was repeated in 1917, Davidson dwelt on the several restrictive assumptions on which the marginal productivity theory of distribution rests, such as (1) free competition in all markets (no unions, cartels, or monopolies), (2) great resource and factor mobility between industries, (3) in the long run firms adjust the scale of operations and factor proportions so as to produce the minimum-cost output, (4) no technological change occurs to shift production functions, but at the same time capital formation (usually at a rate greater than the growth of the labour force) is an on-going process.

Given these assumptions, Davidson apparently conceded the determinacy of marginal productivity distribution. But in return for the concession he was anxious to show that this distribution principle was applicable only over a limited range. He set up some numerical models to reveal these limits. A summary of what he intended his models to show is all we can allow space for at this point.[9]

An upper limit is reached when production is at full capacity and a labour shortage is developing while capital formation is attempted at a rising rate. This brings the Wicksell effect – as originally interpreted in the 1920s – into play. Savings are progressively absorbed in rising wages and in the end are fully absorbed. Then capital formation stops and the social marginal productivity rate of capital may be close to or at zero, while the interest rate, though very low, is greater and positive. A lower limit can also be reached under excess productive capacity and unemployment. Net capital formation (as distinct from maintenance of the existing capital stock) stops for a time and real wages decline until they reach the subsistence level. At that point, if the marginal productivity of labour is less than the subsistence real wage, the marginal productivity principle of distribution can no longer be applied. The deficiency between the marginal productivity wage and the subsistence wage must then be made up by social or private transfer payments of one kind or another.

In this connection Davidson had the unique perspicacity to point out – something which no economist before and exceedingly few after him have noticed – that, when we consider factor distributive shares, we define and measure the shares of capital and land in net terms, but not those of labour. Labour's real wage has to defray what are the equivalent of repairs, maintenance, and depreciation on capital before any net return is derived, in addition to its net livelihood, so to speak. The reason labour's share is taken gross is, of course, that it is very difficult to distinguish the maintenance costs from the real net return in the gross real wages received by different grades of labour (*E.T.* 1919: 241).

The economic impact of technological change, omitted above when the basis of marginal productivity distribution was defined under restrictive assumptions, was by no means neglected by Davidson. Like Ricardo, he considered labour and machinery to be in constant competition with each other. While he recognized that widespread adoption of automation gave rise to technological unemployment, he emphasized that, with a lag behind the layoffs, it also generated a 'new scarcity', with employment-creating effects as improved and new products from the new technology were brought to market to replace older products, and it also rendered many kinds of existing capital equipment obsolete.

He observed that technological change led to more and more concentration of industry, and economic power, in a few large firms that replaced smaller ones and restricted price competition in formerly highly competitive markets. As a response to this concentration of employer-power, and, to Davidson's mind, as an appropriate countervailing power, a trade union movement develops, becoming federated and national in scope. It was mainly the skilled workers who became organized and gave the labour movement its strength. Unlike most conservatives of his time, Davidson was not tempted to seek the solution to strikes and disturbed industrial relations in breaking unions up and severely restricting their freedom to bargain collectively.

He also visualized that in the political arena the labour movement would succeed in obtaining minimum wage and other forms of protective legislation. But this, he observed, would benefit primarily an 'aristocracy' of relatively skilled labour. It would leave a majority of the labour force as an underclass of semi- and unskilled workers, deplorably under-educated, and exposed more than others to economic insecurity and poverty. As an alternative to such a development, he suggested, it would be better both for labour and for the nation as a whole to press for reduced hours of work as an alternative to constantly pushing for higher and higher money wages. With labour having more free time, it would be feasible for the government to greatly expand vocational as well as general educational facilities, especially for younger workers, in order, as he put it, 'to prevent an increasing inflow of the unskilled into the labour force'.

In looking back on Sweden's economic development over the last six decades it is clear that Davidson's vision has been fulfilled, even over-fulfilled. However, to Davidson's mind, as a cause of cyclical economic instability in particular, disturbed industrial relations take decidedly second place to the consequences of inept monetary policies.

Monetary theory and norms of monetary policy

Davidson approached monetary theory via his concept of objective economic value – defined as constant for goods which are the output of given quantities of 'productive power'. One wonders why he chose this approach in view of the fact that, as we have shown, the concept is vague to indeterminate except in a general equilibrium, and in view of the further fact, which he himself admitted, that:

> It is of the utmost importance that the values of commodities should be expressed correctly. However, *the magnitude of the objective value of commodities cannot be observed directly,* but only through the medium of the prices of commodities ... [which latter] depend on two factors, their own objective values and the value of money. (*E.T.* 1932: 106; emphasis added)

In one of Davidson's longest articles (*E.T* 1923: 191–254) he set out the conditions under which the supply of money would have a constant objective value. As his statement was rather long

(193 ff.) we summarize it in paraphrase:

In a given state of technology, if the supply of money (*MV*) *is kept in a constant ratio to the output capacity* of the growing resources of the economy, then the supply of money would have approximately a constant objective value relative to the variable objective values of the commodities which make up the real national product and are exchanged by this money.

This is entirely a supply-side definition of the objective value of money, without any attention to the demand side, or to the rate of interest which affects that demand. Davidson also intimated that it was a task of monetary policy to see to it that the money supply was kept at a constant ratio to the growth rate of the economy. In this he anticipated one of Milton Friedman's monetary policy aims.

A key concept in Davidson's monetary analysis was the following:

With respect to a supply of money, the following proposition holds true: its value is the same as or identical to the objective value of the volume of commodities which are turned over per unit of time by means of this money supply. (*E.T.* 1923: 219)

This then defines the purchasing power of money in terms of the not directly observable objective values of the commodities traded. To keep that purchasing power constant, the money supply has to be kept, as in the paraphrase above, in constant proportion to the economy's growth rate.

To make his meaning clearer, Davidson drew a categorical distinction between the value of a supply and that of one of its units respectively for any commodity and for money. The value of a commodity supply is the product of the value of the commodity unit multiplied by the units in the supply. In the case of money the exact opposite holds. It is the value of the money supply which determines that of the money unit, for the values of its money units are only quotients of the value of the money supply. Having said this, Davidson supplemented his distinction by a model, the purpose of which was to show that the objective value of a supply of money cannot be increased (or decreased) by increasing (or decreasing) the number of money units in that supply.

His model cannot be included here.[10] It featured a gold coin currency with fixed quantities of gold coins and of five commodities. The exchange ratios between these six items were shown and were kept fixed throughout. One defect of the model was that the exchange ratios were said to represent the objective values of the commodities and gold, yet nowhere was it shown how these exchange ratios, crucial to the model, were derived from the objective values of respective commodities. Davidson took this model through sequences of uniformly increased, then uniformly decreased, output, and he applied it also to a gold certificate currency with fractional reserve banking and finally to an inconvertible currency.

Having spent so much effort on the quantitative dimension of the supply of money, Davidson gave its other dimension, its circuit velocity, V, a much shorter treatment. Like Wicksell, Davidson regarded V as a function mainly of variations of demand deposit credit issued by banks in a system of fractional reserve banking, and this form of credit, more than other forms, as increasing the virtual circuit velocity of money. Deposit credit, viewed as nearly synonymous with V, imparts a significant elasticity to the supply of money. Within broad and rather vague limits, however, deposit credit could be 'managed' by applying the tools of monetary policy, changes in discount rates, in open-market operations, in reserve requirements, used selectively, alternately, and/or in combination.

Davidson regarded an increase in V as the equivalent, in its effect, of 'increasing the number of quotients into which the money supply is divided' in the proportion $[M(V + \Delta V)]/MV$. Accordingly, only if V were constant, with a given quantity of money units, M, in circulation, would the price level be determined by the objective value of the volume of goods transacted per unit of time. And in his models Davidson assumed V to be constant.

In his review (*E.T.* 1913: 87–107) of Irving Fisher's 'compensated dollar' proposal, in *The Purchasing Power of Money* (1911, 1922: 337 ff.) to stabilize the purchasing power of gold certificate dollars within a narrow range of fluctuations in a price-level index, say between 97 and 103, by increasing or decreasing the bullion weight per gold certificate in proportion to the rise of the index above or decline below the level of 100, Davidson worked through a sequence of Fisher's proposal. Davidson found that, in a succession of repeated applications of Fisher's schema for reversing an inflationary sequence, the proportions of unregulated demand deposits created under fractional reserve banking to the total monetary circulation would increase progressively. This would erode and diminish the stabilization efficacy of Fisher's proposal.

This confirmed Davidson's insight that constraints placed on M would be only partly effective, because they could be offset by a rise in V, by expansion of demand deposit credit. However, Davidson reasoned about this in terms of the 'needs of the circulation' without relating the elasticity of the monetary system to the 'price' of expanding the volume of deposit credit, i.e. without relating it to the interest rate. Davidson had no concept of a 'real balance demand' for money. Consequently his treatment of V could not play a role in the controversy of the mid-1930s between Pigou and Keynes, carried on since then between the Keynesians and the Chicago school about the nature and role of (1) liquidity preferences, (2) real balances, and (3) other forms of assets in the portfolios of firms and individuals in the sensitive nexus between interest rates, investment, and employment.

With the foregoing aspects of monetary theory as background, we turn at this point to Davidson's norm for monetary policy. His aim was to keep the monetary mechanism neutral with respect to objective commodity values. To that end, he said, 'The monetary mechanism should be so regulated that the prices of commodities are in an invariant proportion to the magnitude of the objective and variable values of commodities' (*E.T.* 1923: 225–6). He published this 'norm' in 1923, but before that, during World War I and its aftermath, he had criticized Wicksell's aim of price level stabilization by an active discount rate policy as inappropriate in periods of changing productivity, and he had also criticized Cassel, who considered Sweden's inflation in 1915–20 as due to the overissue of inconvertible banknotes and too liberal reserve credit provided to banks by the Bank of Sweden. Davidson emphasized that owing to wartime blockades 'commodity scarcity' had increased. Increased commodity scarcity leads to a rise in the price level which has to be put up with until the scarcity is relieved, for monetary policy can do little or nothing about it. He also worked up an index of commodity scarcity which he subtracted from the official price index. He found that about a third of Sweden's inflation was due to increased commodity scarcity, and the rest to ineffectiveness and/or miscarriages of monetary policy.

Assuming that productivity was not changing, in 1922 Davidson said:

> In order that neither inflation nor deflation shall occur, it is necessary that the quantity of money be permitted to increase in the same proportion as population and real capital. (*E.T.* 1922: 102)

But when productivity is changing:

> If the quantity of money is adjusted to changes in population and real capital, then, when productivity changes, the price level

should decline in proportion to the increase in productivity, and when productivity declines, it should rise in proportion to that decline. The price of the composite commodity unit which represents the price level index should vary in the same proportion and direction as that quantity of productive powers (i.e. factor inputs) which is requisite for the production of the composite commodity unit. (*E.T.* 1922: 103–4)

Before we consider how Davidson thought these adjustments might be carried out, let us pause for a moment to try and find an approximation in real life to what Davidson called 'objective values of commodities'.

Since objective commodity values cannot be observed directly but must be inferred from commodity prices, there are two variables to consider. Commodity prices depend on (1) the objective values of the commodities themselves, and (2) the value of money. To make the money supply achieve and maintain a constant objective value of its own, it must be kept, as Davidson said earlier, in a constant ratio to the output capacity of the growing resources of the economy. Assuming that this can be done by appropriate monetary and other economic measures, using a money supply kept at that ratio would give commodity prices which are free from distortion on the part of the monetary mechanism. To go from such distortion-free prices to objective commodity values, one would have to consider the inputs per unit of output needed for the production of any commodity, for it was observed above that 'commodities which are regularly the output of given quantities of productive power (of factor inputs) have as a rule an objective value of constant magnitude'. So it would be necessary to determine the input quantities needed per unit of output for any given commodity and then multiply those inputs by their distortion-free market prices as a statement of the resource cost per unit of output of the commodity (and in that cost an allowance must be included for the industry's average profit rate). The result of such a calculation would be the commodity's 'objective value'. In real life seasonally and inflation-adjusted annual rates or possibly moving average rates of unit cost prices (inclusive of a profit allowance) of commodities might be a fairly close approximation to Davidson's 'objective commodity values'. It was also Davidson's view that objective values would serve as a guide in allocating income to consumption, investment, etc., for longer-term decisions by individuals and firms, and by government policy organs, rather than for day-to-day household decisions about how to spend the weekly grocery allowance.

Now how should the adjustments be done so as to (1) keep the money supply, MV, in a constant ratio to the economy's output capacity on growing economic resources, and (2) induce or force a movement of the price level that will be inversely proportional to any change in factor productivity? This was a compound problem, which Davidson, surprisingly enough, did not investigate in any depth, and on which neither Wicksell nor Cassel made much headway, either. The three of them thought the required adjustments could be achieved to a tolerable degree by flexible and variegated changes of interest rates within the structure of interest rates.

The problem was not simple, and required more specification than Davidson had given it. Within the framework of his norm the adjustments worked best for capital. With no change in productivity, let real capital alone increase. Its rate of return declines, and the banks reduce interest rates to suit, so MV increases, hopefully only to the extent that real capital has increased.

Next let the labour force alone increase, again without change in productivity. Labour's marginal value product declines, and with it real wages, but at the same time the return on capital rises. If banks do not raise interest rates to match, they may lay the basis of a Wicksellian upward cumulative process. As they raise interest rates this will not increase the money quantity to match the increase in labour. If MV stays constant, the difference between the increased rate of return on capital and the lower interest rate may so stimulate capital formation that it exceeds voluntary savings and a part of it becomes financed by 'forced savings' via absorption of some of the wages fund as real wages decline. The distribution of income shifts in favour of capital and the national product increases but with a larger proportion of capital goods in its commodity composition.

Now let population or the labour force and real capital remain constant, but productivity of capital alone increases. Since real capital has not increased quantitatively, there is no need to adjust the money quantity, which we assume was in the proper ratio of the economy's output capacity. Now the objective values of goods decline in relation to the increase in capital productivity, and real wages increase. The price level tilts downward, with more of a dip for goods produced with greater than average capital-intensity. Demand may be assumed to adjust to the increase in size and the change in the composition of the national product, and some workers who became unemployed as capital productivity rose rapidly in some industries are re-employed. Davidson did not proceed to investigate the more complicated case of labour alone increasing quantitatively, real capital staying nearly constant, but the productivity of capital alone increasing; this would have called for some amendments of the rules stated in his monetary policy norm.

Meanwhile Davidson became well aware of the difficulties which arise under monetary policy executed mainly by changes in interest rates. Raising such rates can readily halt or even reverse an inflationary sequence. But if rates are already low in a period of stagnation, say at 2 per cent, there is very little stimulus to be got from reducing them further to 1·5 or 1·0 per cent. He was also aware that monetary policy can do very little about changes in market structure, which proceed from many relatively small firms in intense competition to the development of a few large-scale enterprises which restrict competition and raise prices sharing the market as oligopolies.

For the longer-term future Davidson visualized an indefinite number of years of gently declining price levels as the response under a properly adjusted monetary mechanism of prices or price levels to a continuous decline in objective values of commodities and a continuous rise in real incomes that technological progress held in prospect. How very unlike that vision is the development which has taken place since the mid-1920s in Western Europe, North America, Japan, and some other parts of Asia! Technological progress has been rapid and real incomes have risen, but price levels certainly have not been on a gentle secular decline. That part of Davidson's norm seems like a randomly straying counsel of perfection for the world's developed economies in the last decades of the twentieth century.

For all the sustained effort Davidson put into his writings on money and monetary problems, they did not have as much influence at the level of economic policy as his less voluminous monographs and essays on taxation and public finance.

Taxation and public finance

In *Taxation Norms* (1889b), taking income as the best measure of his ability to pay, Davidson said the principle for levying an income tax ought to be one of so designing the tax that the marginal utility of income given up for the tax should be no greater than the marginal utility the citizen receives in public services for the tax he pays. Since income is subject to diminishing marginal utility, this implies that the rate of taxation should rise progressively with the relative magnitude of income. From his studies of income taxes in Germany and Switzerland he concluded that the authorities had never succeeded in designing and consistently applying a schedule of tax rates according to either of two criteria, the 'equal proportionate sacrifice' or the 'equal marginal sacrifice' schedules.

The progressive rates that have been proposed ... have neither imposed an equally great sacrifice on the wealthy as on the poor, nor have the authorities made as much use of the tax-paying ability of the wealthy as they have of the poor. (1889b: 129)

As a tentative proposal aimed at parliament, Davidson worked out (1) an income tax rate schedule, (2) an estimate of its tax base and (3) of the revenue it would bring in, and, along with that, (4) a schedule allocating the estimated revenues to government functions classified and arrayed (5) in descending order of social indispensability. He did this for a hypothetical community of 100,000 families with an aggregate annual income of US $100 million (Uhr, 1975: 104–8). With some excise taxes continuing even after a general income tax had been introduced (as it was in Sweden in 1902, thirteen years after *Taxation Norms* was written) it was both equitable and practical to exempt all families (in the 1890s) with incomes less than $1,000 a year (slightly more than subsistence level). Accordingly his income tax would start at 5·9 per cent on first-bracket incomes of $1,000–$1,999. Then it would rise over a succession of five brackets to a peak of $100,000 and over, on which the tax rate would be 42·3 per cent.

On his estimate of the prevailing income distribution, of the 100,000 families, only 30,000 would have to pay income tax, and the aggregate tax base would be $85 million. He estimated the tax would come to an average of 16·9 per cent of this base, and would yield a revenue of $14·35 million. That revenue might be allocated as follows to government functions labelled as: (1) *indispensable*: law enforcement, defence, public education, 50 per cent; (2) *facilitating*: transport and communication networks, etc., 30 per cent; (3) *convenience*: public parks, public libraries, extension of postal services to savings banking, etc., 12 per cent; (4) '*luxury*': buildings and equipment for government departments, and impressive embassies and consulates abroad, 8 per cent of revenues. For the 1890s this schema of Davidson's must have surprised and shocked members of Sweden's parliament, for in the few countries in Europe which already had progressive income taxes the top rates were about 5–6 per cent of incomes.

Davidson was well aware that matters of tax rates and income brackets would be decided by political compromise in parliament. Given, then, a parliamentary schedule of tax rates, for the purpose of making the income tax the dominant component – a role it would merit because it was more equitable than other taxes and, under self-declaration, easier to administer and enforce – of the country's revenue system, the vital matter was to make its base as broad as possible. To that end the tax should apply not only to income in the form of wages, salaries, interest, rent, and profits, but also to any net increments to the taxpayer's net worth which had accrued between the end and the beginning of the tax year.

Why? Because, along with ordinary income, net gains or accruals of one sort or another confer potential consumption power or power of utilization and disposal over economic resources to owners of net value-accruing assets. It is in proportion to the citizen's relative command over economic resources that he should be taxed, both for the protection of his rights to them and for the several other kinds of public services which are extended to him and them by government.

While Davidson had at first argued that net worth gains should be taxed on an accrual basis, he soon retreated from that position and conceded that they could not be taxed except on a realized basis, after sale or bequest of the assets involved. Among other concessions he allowed that inheritances among gains should be taxed at lower rates because their former owners had in most cases already been taxed on those gains. Also people with widely fluctuating incomes – farmers, commission agents, and so on – should be allowed to average their income over a term of years and be taxed on the average.

In principle business firms would not be taxed at all under his proposal, for their net returns are owned by stockholder-taxpayers who are taxed on such returns. But he was aware that companies do not usually distribute all the profit earned, and, since they keep a large proportion for internally financed investment, they ought to be taxed on that. Consequently he approved of an Act that was passed taxing companies on their profits after allowing them a deduction from their net profits of 6 per cent of the value of the invested capital as an allowance for dividends. When he was further urged to make a distinction in tax rates, lower for 'earned' than for 'unearned' incomes, he rejected the idea on the ground that on the same income a wage worker and a *rentier* have the same consumption power. While the *rentier* has much more leisure than the wage worker, he should not be taxed extra for it, since relative leisure time is not a part of the tax base. Still, he recognized that most wage-earners can save very little towards economic security in old age. Because of this he indicated that the level of income exempt from the tax might be raised by lifting the first bracket beyond $1,000. But he doubted whether it would do much good, because the tax relief would be minimal, and that little might very well not be saved for the rainy day. That problem had to be solved by social security legislation, of which Sweden had almost none until 1913, when a tax-supported national old age pension law was passed, for pension levels which were entirely inadequate. It was later enactments in the 1930s and after World War II that provided 'cradle to grave' economic security for the Swedish people.

The breakthrough for Davidson's desire to tax net worth gains applied in principle (though not in the form he had suggested) with the income tax of 1910. A new, steeper income tax was passed, in which taxpayers were required to declare their net worth along with income. A fraction, one sixtieth, of the taxpayer's net worth was computed as a 'wealth element' implicit in and added to his regular income, and the sum of both was then taxed according to the rate schedule. With many changes since then, this 'wealth' title remains a feature of Sweden's income-and-wealth tax, but the wealth element is taxed at much lower and very mildly progressive rates relative to the regular income. But the fact that this 'wealth tax' has survived is doubtless attributable to Davidson's work and influence after the turn of the century.

Taxes are, of course, a major part but not all of public finance. There is also the matter of the public debt, concerning which questions were raised in the 1920s whether a public debt necessarily has to be amortized. Elsewhere in Europe the resoundingly emphatic answer would have been 'yes', but in Sweden the question made sense, and Davidson's resolution of it merits attention even from the perspective of the contemporary scene in the United States.

During the nineteenth century Sweden had borrowed heavily both abroad and domestically to get its railways, canals, and power projects built. A tradition had developed that if a government project could not be financed even partly by user fees, it would have to be financed entirely by taxes. But if user fees could meet a significant part of its cost, then it might be financed by a combination of public borrowing and taxes, provided that the user fees would be sufficient at least to pay the debt service charges, including amortization. By the 1920s Sweden was practically free of any foreign debt and had become a creditor country. Also much of its domestic public debt had been paid up. The value of government enterprises and projects substantially exceeded that of its public debt. Hence the question, why amortize? Why not keep on refinancing?

Davidson's answer was that amortization would still be necessary, since the government's projects were subject to obsolescence. At the same time the annually budgeted amortization could be used to reduce the need for borrowing for new projects. As an example, he said, suppose a project has been approved which will cost $480 million, and which will have an annual net return from user fees of $20 million. At 5 per cent interest those returns suffice for a loan of $400 million. But budgeted amortization allowances come to $150 million. Since $80 million of the cost would, in any case, have to be tax-financed, as the capitalized user fees come to only $400 million, then, instead of borrowing that amount, borrow only $250 million and use the amortization amount of $150 million plus $80 million from taxes for the rest. By this method the ratio of public debt to public or government assets will have declined, for a Δ public debt of $250 million is offset by a Δ public assets worth at least $400 million (*E.T.* 1927: 26–7).

Before bringing this chapter to a close, we refer once more to Wicksell, not only because he served on several of the finance and tax committees to which Davidson was called, but also because his approach to taxation and public finance provides such a distinct contrast – not necessarily a contradiction – to that of Davidson. Davidson was a cautious and hesitant social reformer while Wicksell was a bold one (Uhr, 1951: 834–8; 1960, 164–90, 328–37).

Wicksell (1896) took the position that taxes must ultimately become voluntary contributions made on the basis of the 'benefit principle' rather than on that of the 'ability to pay principle' by the citizens to the government for its services. But, for that to be possible, the existing distribution of income and wealth must be so changed by redistributive taxation and by other means that the reformed distribution will be approved as acceptable by a nearly unanimous social consensus. Along with this change would also have to come universal adult suffrage (adopted in 1918), proportional representation, simultaneous decisions on government expenditure for various purposes and on the revenue and/or borrowing needed to finance them, with the decisions requiring approval by a 'qualified majority' (two-thirds or better) in parliament. In an economy restructured along these lines progressive income taxes sustained on the benefit principle would be used for much the same purposes, at similar rates and tax bases as Davidson wanted. Consequently Wicksell collaborated with him on several finance committees during World War I and the 1920s.

As it has turned out, the political reforms Wicksell wanted have been adopted. While simultaneous approval of expenditure and revenue decisions has not been formally made, under Sweden's 'double budget' there is much better co-ordination between expenditure and revenue than there used to be, but decisions are still by simple majority. The former great inequalities in distribution of income have been reduced significantly, and, while the current distribution does not rest on a nearly unanimous social consensus, it seems probable that it may have the support of some two-thirds of the public.

Moreover Sweden's Welfare State has become greatly developed, most of it with Davidson's implicit blessing, and along with it the public sector has expanded considerably, to some extent at the expense of the private sector of the economy. Meanwhile Davidson's progressive income tax, after much expansion and steepening, no longer plays the dominant role in Sweden's revenue picture. In 1931, on the eve of the Social Democratic Party coming to power (from 1932 for forty-four years to 1976, and then again from 1982), Davidson had the perspicacity to foresee in broad outline some of these developments which have occurred since his time. On the basis of the trends he was discerning he visualized that Sweden would be transformed into a quasi-socialist economy, which he referred to as 'a socialist economy which retains the form of capitalism'. Concerning such an economy he had the following to say:

> In a socialist economy which retains the form of capitalism the scope for choice in providing services to the citizens at uniform prices or taxes regardless of the citizen's income and wealth is greatly narrowed. In such a society taxes on citizens in payment for public sector services *must* be so designed that despite great inequalities in income and wealth between individuals, the needs of *all* citizens for public services are *equally* satisfied, and this requires payments by citizens to the government – i.e. taxes – to be *proportional to their income and wealth.* Consequently, it is certain that the scope for application of progressive taxes is *reduced* to the extent that the proportion of society's public sector expands and increases. (*E.T.* 1931: 176)

In this respect Davidson's prophecy of nearly six decades ago has been fulfilled. In the later 1940s direct progressive taxes accounted for about three-quarters of total revenue, while now they account for about one quarter, with proportional social security taxes and rather heavy regressive value-added taxes providing almost all the remainder (except for a few per cent of revenue coming from the traditional excises on alcohol and tobacco, etc.).

Notes

1 The first section of this chapter is based on Heckscher (1952), 111 ff., and on the biographical piece by B. Ohlin on Davidson in *Svenskt Biografiskt Lexikon* (Swedish Dictionary of Biography) X (1931), Stockholm: Bonniers.

2 Neither Lindahl nor Ohlin completed his doctorate under Wicksell's supervision. Lindahl attended Wicksell's courses until 1916, when Wicksell retired; he finished his doctorate in 1919 under Wicksell's successor, E. Sommarin. Ohlin was probably too young, barely seventeen, by 1916 to have done course work with Wicksell. He finished his doctorate under Heckscher. As a mature economist he was more a follower of Wicksell, and in foreign trade theory of Heckscher, than of Davidson or Cassel. For that matter it may be said that all the economists of the Stockholm school were influenced by Wicksell because they studied his writings in depth during their professional training.

3 Heckscher (1952: 116) puts Davidson ahead of Wicksell: 'Davidson was the founder of economic science in Sweden. Wicksell, who began as a mathematician, did not follow his example until fifteen years later (1893, when Wicksell published *Value, Capital and Rent*) and it was a work in German, and Cassel only began writing at the turn of the century. Davidson was thus strikingly ahead of the others in time, especially since Wicksell was three years his senior.'

4 Most of Davidson's writings are articles in his journal *Ekonomisk Tidskrift* (1899–1939). They are referred to here simply by year and page reference, e.g. *E.T.* (1919: 241 ff.), and no further details are given in the bibliography. Anyone looking up such an item in a library would in any case have to read Swedish, or have it translated, so neither the title of the article nor a translation of it is needed to locate it. Then there are Davidson's course lectures of 1913 and 1917. The late Dr Per Jacobsson had made shorthand notes of them; his daughter, Dr Erin Jucker-Fleetwood, kindly lent me her copies. I assume she will give them, if she has not already, to the Davidson archive of correspondence and published writings at the University of Uppsala, where they may be located, or information about their location obtained. These lectures are simply cited here by the year and

the page numbers in the typed binders. The five early monographs are Davidson (1878, 1880, 1886, 1889a, b).

5 Heckscher (1952: 135). Freely translated, this Latin epitaph reads, 'With great acumen he penetrated his science and gave it a new voice.'

6 Böhm-Bawerk would not have been aware of Davidson (1878) because of the language barrier. He may have heard of Davidson via Wicksell, who was in correspondence with Böhm-Bawerk from the 1890s onwards.

7 A brief description of the lectures (see note 4 above) is to be found in Uhr (1975: 122–7).

8 For a fuller but still concise account of Davidson's model of capital formation and his business cycle hypothesis see Uhr (1975: 32–40).

9 For a fuller discussion of these relationships see Uhr (1975: 122–34).

10 Davidson's model is developed in Uhr (1975: 81–8).

Chapter four

Knut Wicksell, neoclassicist and iconoclast

Carl G. Uhr

Life and career

Johan Gustav Knut Wicksell was born in Stockholm on 20 December 1851, the youngest of Johan and Christina Wicksell's five children.[1] His father was a produce merchant who became fairly prosperous in his later years. Knut's mother died when he was not quite seven, an event that greatly affected him. His father, who subsequently remarried, died in 1866, when Knut was about fifteen. The stepmother, whom the children did not like, and an aunt, of whom they were fond, took care of them for a time, but soon they were old enough to be on their own. Knut's father left an estate of sufficient size to provide for secondary and some university education for the boys (Knut had a brother one year older, Axel) and for secondary and vocational education for the three girls. One of Knut's sisters married a prosperous farmer landowner, another sister worked her way up through the corporate structure of Sweden's telegraph and telephone system, and the third sister became a physical therapist, practising in Stockholm.

In 1869 both Knut and Axel enrolled at Uppsala University, Knut to study mathematics, for which he had shown unusual aptitude at high school. He made rapid progress in his studies and within two years had earned his first degree, a B.Sc. in mathematics and physics, in 1871. His brother Axel left the university after three terms without a degree: eventually he emigrated to the United States in the 1880s, where he remained until his death in 1930.

One reason for Knut's early progress at the university was that he lived, practically speaking, the life of a virtual ascetic. At the time of his father's death he had come under the influence of a very pietistic Lutheran minister in Stockholm and had become a decidedly devout Christian. This phase of his youth lasted until 1874, when he went through a spiritual crisis in which he lost his faith and emerged, and for the rest of his life remained, a strictly rationalistic agnostic.

Until 1873 Wicksell maintained himself on a very modest income from his share of his father's estate, on a small inheritance from a grandmother, and on small grants from private foundations. In 1873-4 he filled a vacancy teaching at a grammar school in Uppsala, and the year after that he worked as a private tutor to the son of an ironmaster. From time to time he also found it necessary to borrow small sums from his sisters. Actually, Wicksell's financial position remained precarious (except during his years of study abroad, 1885-9, on grants from a private foundation) most of his adult life, until 1900, when, at the age of forty-nine, and supporting his wife and two school-age sons, he was appointed to the law and economic faculty at Lund University.

In 1875 he passed two of three required examinations for the pre-doctoral degree, *Philosophiae licenciatus* in mathematics (after which the doctorate is completed by working up a dissertation and defending it). For various reasons he delayed his third examination for the *Phil. lic.* degree for a decade until 1885. His doctorate, which was to be in economics rather than mathematics, was not completed until another decade had passed, in 1895. On the face of it this seems and was a strange record for someone who, as it turned out, was to be among the world's four or five leading economists in the era 1890-1930.

During the intervening twenty – actually twenty-four – years (for after the doctorate in economics in 1895 he was also obliged to earn an LL.B. degree in law in order to qualify for an appointment in economics which, at the time, was offered only by the Faculty of Law), he engaged in a variety of pursuits in addition to studies and research.

In the mid-1870s he began to doubt whether he would be able to make any contribution to mathematics, and his interest shifted more and more towards the humanities and social sciences. In this transitional phase of his career he became active in student organizations, and in literary and theatrical sessions and productions, to which he contributed. He even wrote several poems and a play (in the spirit of Ibsen) which was performed in Uppsala and some adjacent towns. As he became known for his ready wit, and his talent as an orator and debater, he was elected a curator of the students' union in 1877-9. At this juncture he moved from his one-room lodging to share a flat with two congenial fellow graduate students, H. Öhrvall in medicine and T. Frölander in law. This inconspicuous event was to have an abiding effect on his life. The three men became fast and lifelong friends. On several occasions in later years when Wicksell's career was seriously threatened, these two friends proved to be very supportive and effectively helpful to him. One circumstance which bonded their friendship was their common reaction to and interest in a book Wicksell bought, a work translated into Swedish in 1878, *The Elements of Social Science*, by Dr G. Drysdale, originally published in London in 1854, with the challenging subtitle *Physical, Sexual, and Natural Religion, An Explanation of the True Causes of the Three Primary Evils of Society – Poverty, Prostitution, and Celibacy*. This thoroughly neo-Malthusian treatise openly discussed matters unmentionable in 'polite society' of the 1870s and 1880s, such as sex, methods of birth control, prostitution for the poor among the young as the only alternative to psychologically harmful celibacy, the need for family planning, and for limiting population growth in order to raise the standard of living of the working classes above bare subsistence. This tome, which was read and discussed jointly by the three friends, firmly converted them to its standpoint. It was this work, supplemented by a study of some of J. S. Mill's essays, which induced Wicksell to take the fatal step of accepting an invitation from a temperance society in Uppsala to give a fee-paid lecture on 'The most common causes of habitual drunkenness and how to remove them'.

His lecture, in February 1880, met with a mixed reception, but a summary of it was reported in the press, and that led to demands that he repeat the lecture a week later in a much larger hall, which filled to overflowing. There he attributed alcoholism, widespread among factory workers, to the poverty and monotony of their lives, crowded into cheap, insanitary housing. For young workers earning too little to afford marriage this led to their using the services of prostitutes. Among the remedies he suggested, he urged that the medical profession be assigned the task of disseminating information to the public about sound and safe birth control techniques, and for the public health authorities to set and enforce acceptable standards of sanitation and of room-space per occupant in housing in the factory districts of cities and towns.

The reaction to his address was strong. The press organs of the Young Socialists and of some of the student organizations praised him. Medical and temperance bodies ridiculed or reviled him, while the non-socialist press questioned his competence to give advice on the sensitive issues he had covered.

From now on he was marked as newsworthy. His future public appearances – and there were to be many – would be attended by reporters who would briefly state the gist of his talk and then devote more space to the audience's reaction, particularly to negative and critical comments, and to how he responded. Most of the reportage characterized him as an eloquent, non-revolutionary radical social reformer.

Later in 1880 he published his lecture as a tract, and along with it a pamphlet, 'Answers to my critics', both of which sold several thousand copies, and yielded him a modest income. In fact this became something of a pattern. Between 1880 and 1885, and again in 1886–7, after his return from his first year of studies abroad, Wicksell turned into a radical public lecturer and journalist. He earned his subsistence by paid public lectures, in a few cases followed by publishing tracts based on them, and by paid articles on various 'social questions' written for local newspapers, including some as far away as Finland. He lectured both in Uppsala and in Stockholm, and occasionally in some other towns, and wrote in a neo-Malthusian spirit on marriage, population control, socialism, prostitution, spiritualism, and so on.

As mentioned earlier, in 1885 he set aside these public activities for a time in order to complete the third and last requirement for a *Phil. lic.* degree in mathematics by a research paper. But by now he definitely wanted to switch to the social sciences rather than take a doctorate in mathematics. To do this beyond elementary or undergraduate level he would have to go abroad; the social science disciplines had not yet become separate fields in Swedish universities but were secondary subjects sandwiched among the faculties of law, philosophy, literature and humanities, and the like.

At this time his sisters received a favourable offer for the rented properties of Johan Wicksell's estate, and after obtaining the brothers' assent, accepted the offer. Knut's share of the proceeds was sufficient for him to pay off old debts and to maintain him for a year of study abroad. So in autumn 1885 he took off for London. There, apart from contacting Charles Drysdale (son of G. Drysdale, who was continuing his father's neo-Malthusian organization and publicity), he spent his time at the British Museum and elsewhere studying the classical economists and the more recent works of Cairnes, Jevons, Walras, and Sidgwick.

Having spent his patrimony, he was forced to return to Sweden in summer 1886, and to resume public lecturing and writing for newspapers. Meanwhile 'fortune had smiled on him', sort of, subject to a delay. In 1885 a wealthy young man, Victor Lorén, died, leaving his estate to a foundation bearing his name, for the purposes of promoting study and research in the social sciences. While still in London Wicksell had been informed that the Lorén Foundation was preparing to award him a grant to study economics at the universities of Austria, Germany, and elsewhere for three years. Relatives of Victor Lorén contested his will in the courts, and lost, but by then distributions from the foundation had been held up for over a year.

If the Lorén Foundation had not given Wicksell that large grant, and subsequently smaller ones for each of the five works he published between 1893 and 1906, he could hardly have become an economist, much less a major figure in that discipline. In spring 1888 he was in Vienna attending lectures by Carl Menger. Then he went to Berlin to follow the courses by Adolph Wagner on public finance. In spring 1889 he returned to Sweden to seek a lectureship in economics at the University of Stockholm, where he was turned down as being 'too notorious' a person. He decided to spend the remainder of his grant period, nearly two years, in Paris. Heading in that direction, he took a detour via Oslo to contact a young lady, eleven years his junior, Anna Bugge, a high-school teacher, whom he had met and liked at a conference in Copenhagen. In Oslo he proposed a common-law marriage to Anna, who, out of consideration for the feelings of her parents, rejected his proposal in favour of a legal marriage, whereupon he left in a huff for Paris.

It seems necessary to mention that, in spite of his many public appearances, his past activities as a leader of the student body, and the like, on a one-to-one as distinct from a group basis, Knut Wicksell was very shy, nervous, and sensitive in the company of young women. Actually he had had very little female company apart from that of his sisters. Also, on three occasions some years earlier, when he had become infatuated, nothing came of it. In one case it was because he never met the young lady, whom he had only seen and pined for at a distance. In the other two cases it was because the ladies married suitors with better prospects.

None the less, not long after he had found somewhere inexpensive to live, Anna Bugge, with whom he had remained in correspondence, joined him on her own initiative. They declared themselves informally 'married' at a little private celebration to which they had invited a few close friends, among them Öhrwall and his wife.

In Paris Wicksell attended lectures by Leroy-Beaulieu on public finance and by Desmoulin on population. At this point he also began to publish in economics. His first article, which translates as 'Empty stomachs – full warehouses', appeared in a Norwegian journal (1890a), soon followed later that year by a second (1890b). It was fluctuations in the rate of capital formation, he inferred, that generated the cycle of prosperity and depression. He concluded that the high rate of capital formation in the recovery phase failed to be sustained because consumption demand, though rising, lagged behind the rate at which production capacity expanded on a growing capital base.

In summer 1890 he and Anna returned to Stockholm, anticipating the birth of their first child, a boy, Sven, born in October. Their second and last child, also a boy, Finn, was born in 1893.

Since he could not qualify for a faculty appointment in economics without a law degree, Wicksell had no alternative but to return to earning a precarious livelihood as a freelance journalist and public lecturer. This brought him into further difficulty.

In 1892 the government was considering an increase in compulsory military service to strengthen the country's defences. Wicksell gave a lecture in Stockholm on the question 'Can Sweden protect its independence?' He argued that, no matter how long conscription might be extended, it would never be adequate for defending the country against an invasion by a major military power – a point with which most of his listeners probably agreed. But they disagreed vehemently as he went on to say that in such circumstances the best thing would be to disarm and release the manpower and other resources committed to defence for other domestic purposes, and then to enter into an alliance with the Russian empire, with its far greater military resources. In return for the protection thus provided, the Swedes with their long tradition of democracy might then play a civilizing role in gradually preparing the Russian masses for democracy.

This performance had a further negative impact on his public image. To the majority of the Swedish public he was already viewed pejoratively as an irreligious freethinker, an advocate of birth control and of trial or common-law marriages, and now, in addition to being called a 'moral nihilist' in many quarters he was also labelled a 'defence nihilist'.

At this stage he intensified his efforts, begun in 1890, to publish professional-level articles and books, as distinct from popular tracts, in economics. His essay 'Kapitalzins und Arbeitslohn' (1892) formed the basis for his marginal productivity theory of distribution – one of Wicksell's main contributions to economic theory – which he developed further in his first treatise, *Über Wert, Kapital, und Rente* (1893), translated as *Value, Capital, and Rent* in 1954. That remarkable work attracted almost no attention in Sweden until years later, but it was reviewed favourably by Böhm-Bawerk and Walras.

Next he turned to a scrutiny of the system of taxation in Sweden, first in a tract 'Our taxes: who pays and who ought to pay them?' (1894), issued under the pseudonym Sven Trygg.

There he made it clear how very regressive the country's taxes were. This, he concluded, was due to the fact that only the upper and middle classes could vote, as income and property qualifications excluded almost all the workers and most of the small farmers from the franchise. His analysis in that tract was refined and extended in his second treatise, *Finanztheoretische Untersuchungen* (1896), where he urged that the major part of the revenue burden should be shifted from indirect to direct and progressive taxes on income and wealth. There he also developed his proposal for an 'equitable' system of taxation. It involved an application of the marginal utility principle to the functions of the public sector with the benefit principle as the basis of progressive taxes. It featured a new methodology (essentially one of marginal cost pricing) for pricing pure and less-than-pure public goods, the services of public utilities, and the products of market-sharing oligopolies and cartels.

In 1894 Wicksell applied to the faculty at Uppsala University to have *Value, Capital, and Rent* accepted as a doctoral dissertation. His request was turned down with the suggestion that it might be used as the basis of a *viva voce* examination to supplement his *Phil. lic.* degree.[2] David Davidson, whom he had come to know from the time of his 1880 lecture to the Uppsala temperance society, was appointed chief examiner, and Wicksell passed with very high marks in May 1895. Still aiming for the doctorate, on 29 May 1895 he defended the first part, 'Theory of the Incidence of Taxation', of his *Finanztheoretische Untersuchungen* as a dissertation, which was accepted, again with Davidson as chief examiner, and Wicksell was awarded his degree *magna cum laude*. That out of the way, he began research on monetary theory and policy, which he completed in 1898 with his third treatise, *Geldzins und Güterpreise* (translated as *Interest and Prices*, 1936). That work was the home of his famous 'cumulative price level fluctuations or processes', allegedly generated by a divergence between the rate of return on newly created real capital and the bank-dominated market rate of interest.

Now he applied to both Stockholm and Uppsala Universities for an appointment as a *docent*, but he was rebuffed, so it was said, because he lacked a degree in law.

From 1890 he had maintained his family slightly above subsistence level by earnings from newspaper articles, occasional but less frequent lectures, and some royalties on his tracts and from a succession of Lorén grants. Now, in autumn 1897, in real hardship with no more money coming in from the Lorén Foundation, he decided to move from Stockholm back to Uppsala to devote all his energies to cramming his way through law courses as fast as possible to a *Juris candidatus* or LL.B. degree. To do so he had to borrow for the maintenance of his family from his friends, Öhrvall, a physician, and Frölander, a banker-lawyer, both of whom were doing very well. In less than two years (undergraduates usually take four), in 1899, he had earned the requisite law degree. And where did all this get him? Not far. He was appointed a *docent* at Uppsala University but without fixed salary, so his income would depend on how many law students, at a given fee per head, attended his tutorials – hence back also to more journalism.

At Lund University Faculty of Law a new professorship was being created because an older professor's post was regarded as overloaded, and his courses in economics and law as related to taxation and some other economic matters were to be transferred to the new position. Wicksell and three others, among them Gustav Cassel, applied for the post. As the other candidates (Cassel for lack of a law degree) were eliminated as insufficiently qualified, the appointment was offered to Wicksell in November 1901. But parliament, in approving the position, had not voted enough money for a full professor's salary, so Wicksell had to accept it as professor *extraordinarius*, with the promise that the position would soon be upgraded. For reasons we need not go into, the upgrading was delayed until January 1904. Thus Wicksell had had to tread a tortuous path over thirty-five years, from 1869, when he enrolled at Uppsala University, until now, at the age of fifty-three, when he was finally established as a full professor.

At Lund University his courses in the law relating to economics, mainly to the tax code and the regulation of foreign trade, were well attended, but his courses in economics, an optional subject, attracted few students. He soon found out that the latter lacked the background to get much out of one semester spent on his *Value, Capital, and Rent* and a second on *Interest and Prices*. So he changed his presentation from pure to applied economics, to subjects such as agriculture and industry, commerce and consumption, social insurance, social movements, crises, and inflation. He had good relations with his students, who admired him for having the courage of his convictions and were amused by his idiosyncracies – his fisherman's peaked cap rather than a bowler or a stovepipe hat, his nondescript, mostly unpressed clothing while most of his colleagues lectured in formal dress – swallowtail coat, boiled shirt, black tie, pinstripe trousers, well polished shoes, and all – his bringing a shopping bag to the lectern as he collected his groceries shopping on the way, and, in winter time, his walking along with the family goat, pulling a pram which had seen better days to carry the many books he had borrowed from the university library.

In 1901 he published his fourth treatise, *Lectures on Political Economy* I (translated in 1934), which represented an expansion and improvement, especially in capital theory, over what he had presented eight years earlier in *Value, Capital, and Rent.*

In 1905 he issued one of his last and best tracts, *Socialiststaten och nutidssamhället* (The Socialist State and Contemporary Society). There he made it clear that he visualized a mixed, not a completely socialist economy (i.e. one which retained a significant but no longer dominant private sector) as inevitable in the future. Under universal adult suffrage, which he anticipated, the workers would be the political majority. As such they would not indefinitely tolerate the great inequalities in income and wealth and the economic instability (of employment and economic insecurity or dependence in old age) of *laissez-faire* capitalism without seeking and taking remedial measures.

He warned against drastic measures of income redistribution by a workers' government suddenly come to power. Such action would effectively stop all private capital formation before the workers' regime had developed the means to replace it by public or collective accumulation. A socialist economy is best built gradually by peaceful means and under democratic governance. Nationalization initially of banking, insurance, natural monopolies, and cartels might suffice if followed by substantial expansion of tax-supported services by the public sector in education, health, and social security. For the sake of efficiency, he held it best to leave farming and most varieties of genuinely competitive enterprise in private and/or co-operative ownership.

Consequently he argued for a form of market socialism with a well developed Welfare State. It is surprising to recognize the great extent to which his social vision has become a reality in Scandinavia as a whole after slightly more than fifty years of social democratic rule since the 1930s.

In 1906 Wicksell published his fifth and last treatise, *Lectures on Political Economy* II, on money and credit, in part an expansion and revision of what he had put forward in *Interest and Prices.* Yet it was more than that. The lectures were epoch-making less for their particular findings than for the broad framework and methodology they provided for the analysis of money and credit. They were first translated into German (1922), where, in the midst of Germany's hyper-inflation, they were read with greater than usual interest, and then rendered into English in 1935.

Wicksell's work at Lund proceeded tranquilly until 1908, when, against the advice of his wife and friends, he decided to make a test case of himself. Under an ancient statute, in three or four recent cases young so-called 'anarchist agitators' had been sentenced to a brief prison term for 'disturbing religious peace by public blasphemy'. Wicksell considered this an infringement by the courts of the freedom of speech and of the press guaranteed by Sweden's constitution. He decided to fight it by his lecture in Stockholm on 'The Throne, the Altar, the Sword and the Bag of Money', in which he satirized the story of the immaculate conception.

Wicksell was tried and convicted of public blasphemy and, over the protests of probably a plurality of liberal opinion, was sentenced to two months in prison. In 1909, after a higher court had upheld the decision, he was allowed to choose his jail, and he selected one, reputed to be among the best, in a small town in southern Sweden. He suffered no hardship other than that the university withheld his salary during the two months that he was a 'guest of the government'. During that time he wrote his last tract, *Läran om befolkningen, dess sammansättning och föränderlighet* (The Theory of Population: its Composition and Modes of Change, 1910). Apart from the clear demographic analysis he presented in it, he reiterated the conclusion he had reached in the 1880s, that, with partial depletion and increasing scarcity of natural resources, Sweden's optimum population should be 3 million instead of (the then) 5 million inhabitants. Likewise, for Europe, he urged a reduction of its population to three-quarters of its 1910 size.

Like Malthus and several other writers on population, while he acknowledged that technological change increases the productivity of given resources, he failed to see that new technology also, in many cases and in the long run, virtually increases existing resources. This happens when former waste products are turned to productive use (corn cobs become plastics) and when the number of uses to which existing resources can be turned increases (there are now several new uses for silicone and some other minerals). This is not to say that overpopulation cannot occur but that forecasts about it on given resources and given technology are subject to high error margins.

The law under which Wicksell was convicted was repealed some time after 1910, so his personal test case met belatedly with success. But the real aim of his challenge to the established national Lutheran Church – to break its monopoly of religious instruction in schools – was not achieved, although that 'monopoly' has been eased in the course of educational reforms.

His years at Lund University were very productive. He wrote

85

some fifty articles, most of them for Davidson's journal, *Ekonomisk Tidskrift*. He took an active part in the tax reforms of 1910, in the national pension legislation of 1913, and, after the outbreak of World War I, along with Davidson, played an important role in legislation relating to banking, currency and exchange controls.

As his retirement approached he and Anna faced new hardships. They insisted on moving back to Stockholm, where wartime inflation was more in evidence than elsewhere, especially in housing. After only sixteen years of university service Wicksell's pension would be considerably smaller than that of most of his colleagues who had served twenty-five or more years before being pensioned. Fortunately, help was 'just around the corner'.

Two friends of his in parliament succeeded on a motion to have his pension raised. Then these parliamentarians and several other friends, including Davidson and Heckscher, got together as a group and by their personal contributions raised enough money to buy a plot for a house and garden and begin construction to Anna's specifications in Mörby, a suburb of Stockholm. To complete the building Wicksell had to negotiate a small mortgage. Thus by Christmas 1916 he and Anna had moved into the new house, the first they could call their own.

The years 1917–26 were probably the happiest in their lives. Freed from financial worries and the burden of law courses related to taxation, Wicksell could devote all his time to economic research and consultation. From Mörby he wrote twenty-nine articles on wartime inflation and how to roll it back. He became a consultant to the Governor of the Bank of Sweden and, along with Davidson, a member of the parliamentary Committee on Banking and Credit, and then of the Committee on Taxation of Income and Property, 1918–22.

He also remained very active in the Stockholm Political Economy Club, which had been organized by Heckscher, and was made its president in 1917–22. It was a source of satisfaction for him to be sought out by the club's younger members, several of whom were graduate students, to advise and share in their research problems. Thus his teaching did not stop with retirement, for Emil Sommarin, the brothers Gustav and Johan Åkerman, Erik Lindahl, Bertil Ohlin, and probably others not listed in his literary remains, such as Tord Palander, Erik Lundberg, Ingvar Svennilson, and Dag Hammarskjöld consulted him about their dissertations in addition to benefiting from studying his treatises.

His wife Anna, who had taken a law degree at Lund in 1911, now became a leading figure in the women's suffrage movement and later in the peace movement connected with the League of Nations. Stockholm gave her more opportunity to be effective than Lund.

In spring 1926 Wicksell was working on an article 'Zur Zinstheorie' for a festschrift in honour of Friedrich von Wieser when he fell ill with a stomach disorder which was complicated by pneumonia. He died on 3 May 1926, aged seventy-four.

His widow, then a Swedish delegate to the League of Nations, survived him until 1928. Their elder son, Sven, became a professor of statistics at Lund University; he died in 1939. The younger son, Finn, died from an accident in 1913 at the age of nineteen as a medical student at the university.

Knut Wicksell would doubtless have objected to the elaborate funeral that was arranged for him, evidently with Anna's consent. Throughout his life he had steadfastly rejected as meaningless and offensive to his sense of rationality all pomp and circumstance, academic formalities along with marriage ceremonies, baptism, and confirmation for his children.

Wicksell's contribution to economics

Wicksell's works attracted much less notice and discussion during his lifetime than they have received since. They became familiar first to economists in Scandinavia, and then to a small and scattered number of scholars and writers in Austria, Germany, and France. A very few English-speaking economists first became aware of Wicksell's writings in the late 1920s and early 1930s. It was when J. M. Keynes was completing work on the first volume of his *A Treatise on Money* (1930) that R. F. Kahn told him of the Swedish economist who had expressed similar ideas some thirty years earlier in *Geldzins und Güterpreise*. At Keynes's request Kahn translated that work as *Interest and Prices* (1936), and he and Keynes also arranged to have *Vorlesungen* or *Lectures on Political Economy* translated.

These volumes, which showed a degree of kinship with some of the ideas of the 'Keynesian revolution', received considerable attention from Anglo-American economists after Keynes's *General Theory* had come out and by 1939 when Lindahl's and Myrdal's works, respectively *Studies in the Theory of Money and Capital, Monetary Equilibrium*, and then *Selected Papers on Economic Theory by Knut Wicksell*, edited by Lindahl (1958), became available. Thus it was Wicksell's monetary analysis that first received widespread international recognition.

His work on capital theory received attention much later. *Über Wert, Kapital, und Rente* was not translated until 1954 and, together with cognate chapters in *Lectures on Political Economy* I, did not receive much intensive analysis and exegesis until the capital theory controversy broke out in 1966 between 'the two Cambridges' and simmered on into the 1970s. Least widely discussed has been *Finanztheoretische Untersuchungen*, on public finance and taxation. Only one part of that treatise, 'A new principle of just taxation', has been translated (1958a).

Monetary theory

In his work *Interest and Prices* (1898) and in its later extension and refinement in *Lectures on Political Economy* II (1906) Wicksell made a significant contribution to economics, effectuating two essential linkages, succinctly indicated in the words both of Ohlin (1934: xiv), that 'Wicksell bridged the gap between price theory and monetary theory', and of Brems (1986: 205): 'in his *Interest and Prices* capital theory met monetary theory and the barrier between them was broken for good'.

Wicksell was moved to do research on general price movements in nineteenth-century Britain by the statements and findings of Thomas Tooke (1846) and in Tooke and Newmarch's monumental study (1838–56). Their findings contradicted the general interpretation of the relations between price-level movements and levels of interest rates, based on the quantity theory of money. According to that interpretation, an increase in the quantity of money, *ceteris paribus*, would not only raise prices generally approximately in proportion to the increase in money but would also reduce interest rates, since the supply of loanable funds would have increased without an equivalent rise in demand.

Tooke and Newmarch's data showed that periods of rising prices and high investment are periods of high and rising interest rates. Their studies also showed that rising prices, i.e. a rise in the price level, generally precede any significant increase in the quantity of money, so it is the latter that adjusts to the former rather than the other way round, and that rise is accompanied by rising, not by falling, interest rates (Wicksell, 1936: 44 ff., 81 ff.; 1935: 164, 173, 182, 206–7).

As he set himself the task of explaining this phenomenon, it did not mean that Wicksell rejected the so-called 'simple quantity theory of money'. In the long-run or at the secular level and for economies without a well developed credit and banking system, for what he called 'pure cash economies', he regarded that quantity theory as valid at the secular level. The gold and silver inflow to Europe from the Americas in the sixteenth and seventeenth centuries greatly increased the quantity of money, brought on the 'price revolution', and reduced long-term interest rates from the levels they had maintained before Columbus sailed.

However, Wicksell's research centred not on very short-run nor on secular-run price movements but on intermediate ones associated with business cycles of irregular ten-to-twelve-year periodicity. Moreover the 'money' he reasoned about was an elastic money supply, *MV*, characteristic of economies with a well developed system of credit and fractional reserve banking. As Ohlin (1936: xiv) put it, 'by his brilliant assumption of a pure credit system he [Wicksell] successfully escaped from the tyranny which the concept "quantity of money" has until recently exercised in monetary theory'.

In *Lectures on Political Economy* II, Wicksell made it clearer than he had done in *Interest and Prices* that he had chosen a macroeconomic approach to his task when he said:

> Every rise or fall in the price of a particular commodity presupposes a disturbance of the equilibrium between demand and supply for that commodity.... What is true in this respect of each commodity separately must be true for all commodities collectively. A general rise in prices is therefore only conceivable on the supposition that the general demand has for some reason become, or is expected to become, greater than supply.... Any theory of money worthy of the name must be able to show how and why monetary or pecuniary demand for goods exceeds or falls short of the supply of goods in given conditions. (1935: 159–60)

Since aggregate demand could differ from aggregate supply, he imposed a division of these two aggregates into two categories: aggregate demand into demand for consumer goods and saving, and aggregate supply into output of consumer goods finished and ready for immediate consumption and of real capital goods such as raw materials, equipment, and structures to be used in future periods of production for the enhancement of output of both categories of goods.

> The sum of money income will then usually exceed the value of consumer goods, but the excess ... is annually saved and invested in production – [it] will not produce any demand for present goods but only for labour and land for future production.... The accumulation of capital consists in the resolve of those who save to abstain from consumption of a part of their

89

income in the immediate future. Owing to their diminished demand... for consumption goods, the labour and land which would otherwise have been required in this production is set free for the creation of fixed capital for future production and consumption and is employed by entrepreneurs for that purpose with the help of the money placed at their disposal by savings. (1935: 192–3)

Wicksell presented his theory about the influence of interest rates on general prices (price levels) as a 'working hypothesis' for which he found some historical and empirical support (1936: 165–77). His hypothesis focused on a shifting relationship between explicit loan or money rates of interest and implicit 'natural' – or 'real' – rates of interest. But these changeable rate relations are played out within a general framework, as follows:

... in the last analysis the money rate of interest depends on the supply and demand for *real capital* ... the rate of interest is regulated by the profits from the employment of capital itself and *not* by the number or quality of the pieces of metal [i.e. currency, whether of metal or paper, and whether convertible or not] which facilitate the turnover of its products. (1935: 190; emphasis in original)

Consequently rates of interest on lending could not for long exceed the rate of return or profit earned by the employment of real capital in production. But for appreciable periods the lending rate could be lower than the rate of return on real capital, especially in economies with developed banking and credit systems.

That the 'natural' or 'real' rate of interest, which is crucial in Wicksell's analysis, corresponds to the marginal value productivity of real capital is obliquely explained or defined in *Lectures* II as the marginal productivity of waiting:

If ... present goods and services *for which payment need only be made in the future* fetch on average a higher price [higher than the unit cost price under pure competition] corresponding to the level of loan interest ... this is due to the fact that labour and land, if their fruits are not to be consumed immediately, may assume such forms as to give them a greater marginal productivity ... than in their present form. If banks or lenders in general demand exactly the higher price corresponding to the difference [the marginal productivity of waiting] the equilibrium will be attained [i.e. the lending rate here included in the higher price will correspond to the natural or real rate of interest]. (1935: 185; emphasis in original)

This was not a very clear and precise definition, and a more ambiguous one in real or barter terms was given in *Interest and Prices*:

There is a certain rate of interest on loans which is neutral ... to commodity prices and tends neither to raise nor lower them. This is necessarily the same as the rate of interest which would be determined by demand and supply *if no money were made use of* and all lending were in the form of real capital goods. It comes to the same, then, to describe it as the current value of the *natural rate of interest.* (1936: 102; emphasis added)

In *Lectures* II the natural or real rate of interest was stated more clearly as follows:

The rate of interest *at which demand for loan capital and the supply of savings exactly agree,* and which more or less corresponds to the expected yield on newly created real capital, will then be the normal or natural real rate. It is essentially variable.... And at the same time equilibrium must *ipso facto* obtain – if not disturbed by other causes – in the market for goods and services, so that wages and prices will remain unchanged. (1935: 193; emphasis added)

Now banks, within fairly wide limits set by reserve requirements, can create additional money by way of deposit credit and can offer this credit at lending rates which are lower than the natural or real rate of interest. Usually this happens not by the banks deliberately setting a lower lending rate, but by the banks maintaining a given lending rate which, in the initial equilibrium, was equal to the natural rate, but from which level the natural rate has gradually risen subsequently. As long as this condition continues entrepreneurs earn extra profits above the break-even returns they had in the initial equilibrium under pure competition. These extra profits motivate expansion. In competition with one another entrepreneurs now offer higher wages in an attempt to pirate fully employed labour from one another. At the same time the increased return on real capital has increased investment demand and the supply of savings from increased incomes, and the proportion of consumer goods in the gradually increasing national product diminishes. As workers and others spend increased money incomes the prices of consumer goods rise, the prices of capital goods having already risen by capitalization of anticipated greater profits. Thus the price level rises, and round by round in a price–wage spiral it keeps on rising as long as the lending rate remains lower than the natural rate.

In *Interest and Prices* (1936: 139–54) Wicksell presented a detailed model of how the cumulative price level movement or cumulative process operates, and a related, more up to date model is provided by Uhr (1960: 236–46).

In an upward cumulative process the banks are ultimately forced by an internal or external cash drain to raise the lending rate approximately to equality with the natural or real rate. At least momentarily that may generate an equilibrium. But, especially if the rate adjustment had to be rapid and took the form of one or two relatively large changes rather than a succession of small, fractional percentage-point increases, that equilibrium will prove unstable and likely to be followed by a downward cumulative process, with or without an intervening crisis. As Wicksell put it:

> The two rates of interest still reach ultimate equality *but only after and as a result of a previous movement of prices.* Prices constitute, so to speak, a spiral spring which transmits the power between the natural and money rates of interest. But the spring must first be sufficiently stretched or compressed. In a pure cash economy the spring is short and rigid; it becomes longer and more elastic in accordance with the stage of development of the system of credit and banking. (1936: 135–6; emphasis added)

Similarly in *Lectures* II:

> If ... a change occurs in the natural rate ... the money rate should undergo a corresponding change, but there exists ... no other connection between the two than *variations in commodity prices,* caused by the difference between them. And that link is elastic, like a spiral spring. (1935: 206; emphasis in original)

However:

> A complete correspondence [between the two rates] is not to be expected [because] profit on capital varies greatly in different

undertakings. In addition there is the difference between interest on short and on long-dated loans, of which only the latter corresponds to the real rate. (1935: 208)

This last statement must be an inadvertent error. Suppose the lending rate remains lower than the natural rate for a little over two years, while an upward cumulative process is gathering steam. During such a period several thirty-year bond issues may be floated at first at 6 per cent and later at 7 per cent rates, while the real rate as gauged by corporate profit rates is higher still. Consequently long-term interest rates may serve as a proxy for the real rate only in times of price-level stability, and that may have been what Wicksell meant.

His working hypothesis is aptly summarized in his statement that:

Fluctuations in commodity prices [price levels] which are *not* directly caused by changes in gold production [or by other major external causes, such as blocking the Persian Gulf and shutting off half or more of the world's supply of oil] must therefore have another cause ... namely changes in the real rate of interest, [to which changes] the lending rate *does not adapt itself quickly enough* ... so that the influence of the banks on commodity prices ... is a consequence of their passivity, and not of their activity, in the loan market. (1935: 205)

Before we proceed to consider some criticisms Wicksell's theory encountered and to which he responded, let us pause for a moment and consider the innovations in methodology and analysis he brought in with his working hypothesis.

We have already observed that his approach was macroeconomic but structured so that aggregate product is divided into consumer goods and capital or investment goods, and aggregate income or GNP is divided into consumption spending and saving, the former clearing the consumer goods market and the latter clearing the market for capital goods, *provided* that lending rates and real rates of interest are in an appropriate adjustment of approximate equality.

With his cumulative processes he launched a dynamic form of analysis with the moving price level as the equilibrating variable. Little or nothing was said explicitly about aggregate product, but he must have implied that that product increased along a growth trend in the upward cumulative movement and decreased in the downward process. But since he assumed full employment all along, and prices equally flexible upwards and downwards for commodities and production factors, his downward cumulative movement took no cognizance of mass involuntary unemployment. Nor in his discussion of the demand for money and 'the needs of the circulation' did he arrive at the concepts of 'real balances', 'real balance effects', and 'liquidity preferences'.

Finally, his method of treatment was to analyse a sequence of disequilibria, a disequilibrium analysis, in contrast with the prevailing comparative static equilibrium method.

Wicksell's solution or recommendation was that the monetary authority (and the central bank and the commercial banks subject to its policy directives) in order to achieve and maintain price-level stability should adjust its discount or lending-rate policy to the movement of a weighted general price index. As that index rises above its base-year level of 100, lending rates should be raised, and when it falls below it they should be reduced. The hoped-for result under such a policy might be that price-level and money-value variations would be reduced to approximate stability, to a narrow range of variation from about 97 below to 103 above the base-year level.

This was an aim with which most might agree, provided it were attainable, as Wicksell's analysis indicated, and attainable without significantly adverse side effects. Over the period 1899–1925 a number of issues were raised against the proposal, first and last by Davidson, and, among others, by von Mises, Cassel, von Hayek, Lindahl, Ohlin, and Myrdal. As often happens, in several cases the issues were not properly joined (reminiscent of the protracted controversy between Ricardo and Malthus) and Wicksell's answers were not always apt. However, eventually and at various times during this quarter-century he had to concede some points to his critics and especially in 1925, when he wrote a major article, 'The monetary problems of the Scandinavian countries' (*E.T.* 1925: 205–22).

We shall comment briefly only on a couple of points raised against Wicksell's theory before citing the concessions he made of exceptions to his price stabilization norm in that article of 1925, and at the same time we refer interested readers to Uhr (1960: 255–307), where the several (six or seven) issues that were raised are discussed and fully documented.

It was Davidson who reviewed *Interest and Prices* quite favourably in the first volume of his journal, *Ekonomisk Tidskrift* (1899), but he also pointed out that if lending rates are properly adjusted to real rates, and then productivity increases, the proper policy is to let the price level decline or vary inversely to the productivity increase. This would both avoid having to alter lending rates and it would also be more equitable, letting people on fixed incomes share in the benefits of increased productivity. But, apart from that, and of greater importance for Wicksell's theory, was the circumstance that if the decline in prices was to be prevented by reducing the lending rate, this would lay the basis for an upward cumulative process, as that lending rate would then be lower than the real rate. Wicksell did not respond directly to Davidson on this, and in substance repeated his recommendation in *Lectures* II 1906, upon which Davidson reiterated his criticism.

Ludwig von Mises (1912) raised a fundamental point, and a little later he was independently joined in it by Cassel and Davidson, namely that real interest rates and lending rates are interdependent. Thus if the lending rate is lower for a time than the real rate and an upward process gets started, it will before long force the real rate down to the level of the lending rate. Why? Because as prices rise in the upward wage–price spiral, while voluntary savings decline, forced savings and capital formation based on them will greatly surpass the decline in voluntary saving. Then real capital will increase more and faster than other factors, and the real rate will decline with its declining marginal value productivity towards the level of the lending rate, and the cumulative process will subside, perhaps without a crisis.

In the preface to the second edition of *Lectures* II in 1915 Wicksell half-heartedly conceded that this was possible, if very unlikely. After a round or two of the upward wage–price spiral, entrepreneurs begin to anticipate further price increases, and then the upward process accelerates, while the additional real capital formed from forced savings takes time to be produced and is added in production only with a lag behind the price spiral.

During World War I, when the belligerents and soon the neutrals too jettisoned the gold standard and began to finance the war and neutrals the defence of their neutrality by *fiat* money issues and/or by public borrowing for large budget deficits at artificially low bond rates, Wicksell became fully aware that central banks, and commercial banks following their policy, were powerless to control, let alone roll back, the inflationary consequences of governmental wartime deficit financing.

These monetary upheavals were accompanied by the increasing scarcity of many commodities, some of which were no longer produced as plant and facilities were converted to producing munitions and war *matériel* while others could not reach their customary markets in the usual volume because of blockades, submarine warfare, and so on. In Sweden's case it was chiefly coal and oil for the country's manufacturing industries that were becoming increasingly scarce. Davidson paid particular attention to increasing commodity scarcities and even computed an index number for them which he subtracted from the official index of wholesale prices to show that between a third and a half of Sweden's inflation since 1914 had been caused by increasing commodity scarcities. The rise in prices due to such scarcities would have to be put up with until the scarcities were relieved, for monetary policy action on them would be useless.

Implicitly Wicksell agreed with this and then proposed to alleviate the scarcity and rise in prices by urging the government to impose a steep export duty on Swedish timber and wood pulp, then in great demand, and use the proceeds to subsidize imports of oil, coal, etc., and deliver them below world market prices for industrial uses where the scarcity was felt the most.

However, it was after the war and the first short, sharp post-war depression of 1920–2, and after Sweden had returned to the gold standard in 1924, that he felt there might be sufficient monetary tranquillity to take a look towards the longer future, when he wrote the article of 1925 with concessions or exceptions from his price stabilization norm. The exceptions were for (1) *fiat* issues of money and/or (2) large-scale budget deficits by governments, (3) 'gold invasions' and (4) autonomous decline in productivity or 'increase in commodity scarcity'. For these conditions he would let the price level rise, since monetary policy could not reverse them. 'Gold invasion' was the term applied to the burgeoning Swedish balance of payments surplus during the war years, when the country's exports were snapped up at any price while imports were impeded, and the surplus was paid in gold shipments. The result was an accumulation of excess gold reserves which served only to keep lending rates lower than they would otherwise have been. So in 1916 this 'gold invasion' was to be blocked by relieving the Bank of Sweden from having to accept gold at the fixed pre-war mint price instead of the lower world exchange price. This policy was urged by Wicksell, Davidson, and Cassel, and when enacted in 1916–18 it may have staunched the inflow somewhat, but it was sabotaged by the Danes and Norwegians as members of the Scandinavian Monetary Union, since they had not passed any similar legislation.

In any case, it should be noted that Wicksell was willing to let prices rise for increased commodity scarcity, which can be equated to a decline in productivity, but he was not willing, as Davidson repeatedly urged, to let the price level vary inversely to or decline in proportion to increases in productivity. His reason was that he regarded increases in productivity as slow-acting forces. At points of impact in any given industry the increase in productivity of new technology can be dramatic, but soon the new techniques are modified and adapted in several other industries so that their effect is disseminated gradually over the economy. In view of this, and the fact that in the industrial economies markets for most manufactured products are subject to various and increasing degrees of imperfect competition, he said that with increasing productivity it was a matter of either accepting his price stabilization norm or no norm at all. He felt certain, for industrial relations reasons among others, that it was better to let increases in productivity be reflected in rising money incomes at stable prices than in rising real incomes at falling prices.

This completes our account of the main features of Wicksell's monetary theory. The heritage he left behind was extended and restructured by his followers in the 'Stockholm school' of economics which flourished from the closing years of the 1920s into the 1940s. We cannot go into the transformation his heritage underwent at the hands of the leading Stockholm economists – Lindahl, with his intertemporal equilibrium analysis, and Myrdal (especially if blended with Lundberg, as was not the case), with his dynamic disequilibrium analysis, employing an expectations perspective and methodology, the *ex ante ex post* analysis. The most extensive restructuring of Wicksell's monetary analysis was undertaken by Myrdal, and we shall give only a glimpse of it here. Myrdal summarized Wicksell's conditions for monetary equilibrium in the triad:

1. The real or natural rate of interest must reflect the marginal value productivity of real capital used in production.
2. Lending or money rates of interest which equal the real or natural rates generate an equilibrium and clear the capital market, with investment demand for capital being equal to the supply of savings.
3. A stable general price level results if, and only if, the crucial conditions (2), which make (1) determinate, are given.

Myrdal restated the Wicksellian variables in *ex ante* and *ex post* terms, and indicated how, by analysis of *ex post* results and comparing them with the *ex ante* calculations which preceded them, one arrives at an insight into which side and in what direction of monetary equilibrium the economy is drifting. On the basis of such an analysis Myrdal also set up three conditions for monetary equilibrium, the first two of which are similar to

97

Wicksell's conditions (1) and (2) but are stated in *ex ante ex post* difference terms. But the third condition is entirely different. Given conditions (1) and (2), they do not guarantee a stable price level, whether of both consumer and capital goods or of consumer goods only, but tend instead to secure something different, called 'business stabilization'. Business stabilization involves using monetary and, when necessary, other policies as well to adapt flexible prices to the absolute levels of inflexible prices. Capital values and prices of many finished commodities are flexible, whereas wage rates, and the products of natural and regulated monopolies, and of industries with oligopolistic sharing of markets, are inflexible (Myrdal, 1939: 35–8, 73, 90–1, 98–9, 133–6, 176–9, 191; Uhr, 1960: 313–27).

In contrast to Wicksell, who assumed pure competition on all markets, Myrdal relaxed that assumption to take cognizance of the fact that most industries in modern economies function in markets of varying degrees and severity of imperfect competition. This reconstruction by Myrdal of Wicksell's equilibrium conditions sounds realistic and plausible, until we ask how the adaptation of flexible prices to the levels of inflexible ones is to be achieved. For that he did not supply any answer.

Along with the Stockholm school reconstruction of Wicksell's monetary theory came the recognition, reinforced by the slightly later 'Keynesian revolution', that monetary policy *per se* is a brittle staff on which to lean for economic stabilization purposes, unless it is co-ordinated with and reinforced by fiscal policy.

Capital theory

Wicksell's theory of capital and interest evolved from a partial acceptance, along with a considerable reconstruction, of Böhm-Bawerk's capital theory, with the reconstruction placed securely within a Walrasian general equilibrium framework. From Böhm-Bawerk Wicksell adopted the heuristic quantification of heterogeneous real capital as a conceptually homogenized time dimension of production, Böhm's longish and lengthening 'average period of production', which in turn was derived from the classical quantification of capital as a real wages and rent fund of subsistence for advances to workers and landowners for the production period intervening between the start-up of production and delivery of the finished product, in agriculture usually a year. Wicksell expressed the near equivalent of Böhm's 'production period' more concretely as a two-dimensional time structure of production, which he referred to as the 'stratification of capital through time' (1936: 115–52; 1934: 144–218). That structure expands with net formation of real capital, usually first in its breadth and then in its height dimension and, later still, more in height than in breadth. Its mode of expansion had consequences primarily in positive growth of the national product and, also, in a gradually changing distribution of the national product as between owners of real capital and owners of all other factors of production.

Wicksell regarded capital goods as consisting organically of qualitatively 'saved up' (i.e. invested) inputs of optimally combined units of labour and land services. To be sure, producers of trucks, for instance, require inputs not only of labour and land services but also of services of some pre-existing capital goods. But since the latter can also be viewed as the products of older 'saved up' labour–land inputs, the entire stock of real capital can be regarded as consisting of past 'saved up' units of labour–land inputs.

Wicksell denoted labour per person by A and land per acre by B, the wage rate by w and rent rate by r, per unit of time paid for services of A and B on an uninvested basis in the production of consumer goods. These rates correspond to their marginal value productivity, and so we get units of $(Aw+Br)$. Similar A and B units employed in the production of capital goods become 'saved up' and when they are embodied in capital goods those goods must, for opportunity cost reasons, have a somewhat higher marginal value productivity than have the same kinds of units on an uninvested basis. That somewhat greater marginal value productivity of 'saved up' A and B units is the source of the return to capital, of interest on real capital, 'the marginal value productivity of waiting', and is expressed as $(Aw+Br)(1+z)$, z being the rate of interest. Investment of A and B 'saved up' units in capital goods can be for one or more periods or years. To bring an orange grove into production from planting the seedlings until they grow to yield marketable oranges takes at least seven years. Wicksell would have regarded this as a succession of seven annual investments of $(Aw+Br)$ units, each having a marginal value productivity which stands in a compound rate relationship to that of the first year's input. So the grove regarded as a capital good consists of 'saved up' labour–land units with a value of

$$(Aw+Br)(1+z) + (Aw+Br)(1+z)^2 + \ldots + (Aw+Br)(1+z)^7$$

The grove in this flow input–point output model requires annual maintenance and partial replacement for wear and tear of

$(Aw+Br)$ inputs, and it 'matures out' its product, oranges, in year 8 and subsequently in annual orange harvests, each of which has, *ceteris paribus*, a value of $(Aw+Br)(1+z)^7$. In other words, capital goods 'mature out' as products the value of their oldest annual 'saved up' $(Aw+Br)(1+z)^t$ input enhanced by its accrued marginal value productivity rate compounded for the duration in years during which that initial input has been invested.

The z marginal value productivity or rate of interest on real capital is determined at the margin of investment, i.e. by its magnitude for investments of shortest maturation terms, in this case for capital goods of a one-year maturity term.

One has to have at least this minimum of definitions and relationships as background to understand Wicksell's and 'Austrian' (e.g. Hayekian) capital theory, although some of its terminology and the graphic illustrations of its models all but disappeared from economic literature some decades ago (Wicksell, 1934a: 152–62; Hayek, 1941: 134 ff., 289 ff.; Uhr, 1960: 84–104).

The modest reward for regarding and/or reviewing these formulations and constructs is that a simple model based on them gives a clearer insight into the implications of height expansion in Wicksell's and in Austrian capital structures. We shall also arrive at a better understanding of why two central postulates of neo-classical economics have exercised such persuasive power over most of the economics profession from about the turn of the century until very recently. The postulates, most succinctly stated by Tatsuo Hatta (1987: 36), are that 'as the rate of interest falls, the capital/labor ratio increases ... and also as the rate of interest falls the output/labor ratio increases'. Neither of these relationships is very readily accessible in the non-Austrian approaches which define capital only in value terms as an aggregate of producer goods times their prices. Now for the promised simple model:

We have a small community the economic resources of which are the labour of 150 persons, each denoted by A and earning an annual wage of w, plus an equal number, 150, of acres of cropland, each of which is denoted by B and earns an annual rent of r, plus a structure of 100 different capital goods, ten with a three-year maturation term, thirty with a two-year term, and sixty with a one-year term. Hereafter let us refer to them as three-year, two-year, and one-year capital goods or just goods. Maintenance and partial replacement for annual wear and tear on this structure require that $100(Aw+Br)$ units of labour–land services be 'stored up' or invested in the production of capital goods for replacement. This leaves $50(Aw+Br)$ units for uninvested production of consumer goods, for which, of course, they use the services of the goods in the capital structure together with their own labour–land services as inputs.

At the margin of investment of $(Aw+Br)$ units in one-year goods, the net marginal value productivity rate, i.e. the interest rate, is 7 per cent with the yields of goods of longer terms in the capital structure standing in a proper compound rate relationship to that of one-year goods. For simplicity we assume that the annual wage and acre rent per one person and one acre is 1·0000, which equals the marginal value productivity per uninvested $(Aw+Br)$ input unit. Consequently this community generates a net national product of:

$10(Aw+Br)(1\cdot07)^3 = 10(1\cdot2250)$ for three-year goods
$$= 12\cdot250$$

$30(Aw+Br)(1\cdot07)^2 = 30(1\cdot1449)$ for two-year goods $= 34\cdot347$

$60(Aw+Br)(1\cdot07) = 60(1\cdot0700)$ for one-year goods $\ = 64\cdot200$

	110·797
$50(Aw+Br)$ uninvested $= 50(1\cdot0000)$	50·000

Total 160·797 = NNP

This net national product consists of 150(1·000) wage and rent income, and of 10·797 interest income. Their yields discounted at 7 per cent, the three-year capital goods have a present value of 3·214, and the two-year ones of 2·070.

At this point the community decides to 'broaden' its capital structure in all maturity terms by 10 per cent. When that has been done, there will be eleven three-year goods, thirty-three two-year ones, and sixty-six one-year capital goods. Annual maintenance and partial replacement of this structure requires $110(Aw+Br)$ inputs to be 'saved up', leaving $40(Aw+Br)$ units uninvested to produce consumer goods using the services of the goods in the widened capital structure. Since real capital has increased, with labour and land constant, the marginal value productivity of capital has declined, let us assume, by half (0·005) a percentage point across the board in all maturation categories to 6·5 per cent, while wages and rent have increased slightly from 1·0000 per $(Aw+Br)$ unit to 1·0500. Accordingly the marginal productivity yields of three-year goods have declined from 0·2250 to 0·2200, of two-year goods from 0·1449 to 0·1399, and for one-year goods from 0·0700 to 0·0650. But at these yields structure broadening has disrupted the proper compound rate relations between the yields, which should be $1 \cdot 0650^3 - 1 = 0 \cdot 2079$ on three-year, $0 \cdot 1342$ on two-year, and $0 \cdot 0650$ on one-year goods. The discrepancy between the across-the-board yields right after broadening and the proper compound yields would gradually be eliminated by trading between three-year and one-year goods to a common rate slightly higher than $0 \cdot 065$, perhaps to $0 \cdot 0665$ compounded to $0 \cdot 1374$ and $0 \cdot 2131$ respectively for the two-year and three-year goods. However, instead of such trading to adjust the yield rates, expansion in the height dimension of the structure will be undertaken. But first we must show the net national product situation as of the completion of the widening, keeping in mind that maintenance and partial replacement for each capital good is now at $1 \cdot 05$ per $(Aw + Br)$ unit:

$11(1 \cdot 05)(1 \cdot 2200) = 14 \cdot 091$ for three-year goods

$33(1 \cdot 05)(1 \cdot 1399) = 39 \cdot 498$ for two-year goods

$66(1 \cdot 05)(1 \cdot 0650) = 73 \cdot 805$ for one-year goods

---

$127 \cdot 394$

$40(Aw + Br)$ units
uninvested at
$1 \cdot 05$ per unit $\quad = 42 \cdot 000$

Total $\qquad 169 \cdot 394 = NNP$

This NNP consists of $150(1 \cdot 05) = 157 \cdot 5$ wage and rent income and of $11 \cdot 894$ interest income.

As compared with the pre-broadening situation, interest income has increased from $10 \cdot 8$ to $11 \cdot 9$. At the same time, with their yields at the current interest rate of $6 \cdot 5$ per cent, the present value of three-year goods is $3 \cdot 385$, and $2 \cdot 152$ for two-year goods, both higher than present values at a properly compounded yield of $6 \cdot 5$ per cent, which would be $3 \cdot 198$ for three-year and $2 \cdot 065$ for two-year goods. This motivates some members of the community to shift their investments more into three-year goods, and so height expansion starts, by undermaintaining some one-year goods and shifting their annual replacement into a fund-and-form that becomes the basis for forming additional three-year goods. This can be done in different ways, but it becomes clearer if we assume it is done over a four-year sequence.

In year 1 owners of three one-year goods decide to under-maintain them and transfer their replacements to begin investment toward three new three-year goods. The community then has eleven three-year, thirty-three two-year and sixty-three one-year goods, and now releases $3(Aw+Br)$ units to join the forty uninvested units. In year 2 the same procedure is followed. Three more one-year goods are undermaintained and their replacements shifted to investment in new three-year goods, and, with only sixty one-year goods left, three more $(Aw+Br)$ units are released to be added to the forty-three uninvested units. In year 3 the same thing is done. Three more one-year goods are taken out and their replacements shifted to complete the investment in three new three-year goods, leaving only fifty-seven one-year goods. The three-year goods will be ready to provide input services only from year 4 onward. Meanwhile three more $(Aw+Br)$ units are released to join the uninvested ones, which will then rise to a total of forty-nine. So in year 4 we have the following situation, with the yield relations between the various capital goods at proper compounding based on interest at 6·5 per cent:

$$14(1·05)(1·2079) = 17·756 \text{ for three-year goods}$$
$$33(1·05)(1·1342) = 39·300 \text{ for two-year goods}$$
$$57(1·05)(1·0650) = 63·796 \text{ for one-year goods}$$

$$120·852$$

$49(Aw+Br)$ units
uninvested at
1·05 per unit $= 51·450$

Total $172·302 = \text{NNP}$

This NNP consists of $150(1·05) = 157·5$ wage and rent income and of 14·802 interest income.

Consequently height expansion turned out to be profitable, as the following shows:

	Interest income	Net national product	Value of the real capital structure
Before broadening	10·8	160·8	110·8
After broadening	11·9	169·4	127·4
After height expansion	14·8	172·2	120·9

Interest income has increased steadily and so has NNP, while the value of the capital structure rose to a peak of 127·4 in broadening and then retreated to 120·9 in height expansion, despite the fact that net real capital was formed during height expansion. How? Owners of capital goods who over a succession of three years gave up, saved and invested income they would have had from three one-year goods per year to invest their replacements in new three-year goods. From the three one-year goods they undermaintained in year 1, they would have had an interest income of

$$3[1·05(1·065 - 1) = 1·11825 - 1·05 = 0·06825] = 0·20475$$

During the second year they gave up a similar amount of income while that given up in year 1 was left to increase in compound fashion based on the 6·5 per cent rate to 0·42273, and during the third year the income given up during the first year reaches a compound amount of 0·65490. Then in year 3 the sum of these 'savings' – invested in the three three-year goods comes to 1·28238. But account must also be taken of the fact that the new three-year goods, ready in year 3, produce income only when used in production, in year 4. Consequently owners of former one-year goods converted in this way into three-year goods, have to wait until the end of year 4 before they receive income from their investment in the new goods. That means that the value of income they gave up in the first year compounded, plus that of the second year compounded, and so on, comes to a cumulative value of 0·90249. Adding that to the earlier three-year amount of 1·28238 gives us a total of such saving-investing of 2·18487. For that amount, invested over a four-year span, the new three-year goods give their owners an income of

$$3[1·05(1·2079 - 1) = 1·2683 - 1·05 = 0·2183] = 0·6549$$

per annum. This is indeed a handsome rate of return on 2·1849 of savings invested, a return of 29·97 per cent, or 30 per cent in round terms.

Meanwhile the capital structure, which is now less broad (fifty-seven one-year goods) but greater in height (fourteen versus eleven three-year goods), has undergone a revaluation from a magnitude of 127·4 to 120·9. At the same time the annual wage-rent per $(Aw+Br)$ unit was held at 1·05 during height expansion, despite the fact that uninvested $(Aw+Br)$ units increased from forty to forty-nine by release from the capital structure. In strict logic one would expect this to have reduced the marginal value productivity and the wage-rent per annum per $(Aw+Br)$ unit to perhaps 1·015 or 1·020, seeing that that wage-rent was at the level of 1·000 when initially, instead of forty-nine, as now, there were fifty uninvested $(Aw+Br)$ input units using the goods in the capital structure to produce consumer goods. We shall leave that as a likely possibility and imagine that workers and landowners, by forming some kind of organization, a union or a producer co-operative, succeeded in staving off any reduction in the annual wage-rent from 1·05.

However, the important point in what follows is that there has been net real capital formation, with labour and land constant in both the breadth and height expansion. It was precisely in the process of capital formation that Wicksell discovered an exception to Thünen's law, his name for the marginal productivity principle. What he found was that, when real capital increases, other factors remaining constant, the social marginal productivity of capital does not equal (is smaller than) the rate of interest standing for the private marginal productivity of capital. On the other hand, if labour (or land) is increased, other factors constant, the social marginal productivity rate of labour (or land) equals the rate of wages (or rent).

The Wicksell effect

In an article (Uhr, 1951) calling attention to this phenomenon, I baptized it the 'Wicksell effect', never imagining that fifteen years later it would give rise to something like a doctrinal growth industry in the capital theory controversy between 'the two Cambridges'. We can only touch peripherally upon that subject here. The several issues raised in that controversy have by no means been settled. But at least some of them were resolved by attributing some paradoxical outcomes to the circumstance that real capital underwent a revaluation in the analysis. This may justify the model above, in which, as we have seen, such a revaluation occurs.

Wicksell wrote no fewer than four demonstrations of his 'effect', the partial wage absorption of real saving by which the social marginal product of increasing capital, assuming labour and land constant, becomes smaller than the rate of interest.[3] Initially he assumed stationary conditions for an economy with A labourers, land a free good, and real capital as real savings in the form of subsistence goods advanced as real wages, w, to labour for the production period, t, at an interest rate, z, corresponding to the micro-level marginal productivity rate of this capital. (Wicksell assumes a flow input–point output model in his early writings.) Under continuous production with 'real capital invested by install-ments' (1954: 121), the average investment period becomes $t/2$, so we get an equation expressing the annual product per labourer as:

$$p = w + wz\frac{t}{2} \tag{1}$$

With capitalists as entrepreneurs taking w as determined by the market, they reach output equilibrium for their firms by maximizing p, with respect to t, treating w as a constant, and thus by differentiation of (1) we obtain:

$$\frac{dp}{dt} = \frac{wz}{2} \tag{1.1}$$

Substituting this value of $wz/2$ in (1) results in:

$$p = w + t\left(\frac{dp}{dt}\right) \tag{1.2}$$

from which the solution for w as a residual between p and capital's share $t(dp/dt)$ is:

$$w = p - t\left(\frac{dp}{dt}\right), \text{ with } t\left(\frac{dp}{dt}\right) \tag{1.3}$$

determined relative to w so as to maximize z, the interest rate on the invested capital.

$$K = \left(\frac{A}{2}\right)wt \tag{2}$$

is the macroeconomic equation for aggregate real capital which is fully used up or demanded in advancing subsistence to the A workers at the w real wage rate for the production period.

Now some owners of real capital increase their net saving. This increases K by dK and output by dp, which, since p is a function of t, we write as:

$$\left(\frac{dp}{dt}\right)dt$$

But dK also increases the real wage by dw, and the production period by dt. The full effect of this increase in K is shown by the total differential of (2) with respect to w and t, as:

$$dK = \left(\frac{A}{2}\right)(wdt + tdw) \tag{2.1}$$

Next the differential of (1.3) with respect to t gives us:

$$dw = -t \left(\frac{d^2p}{dt^2}\right) dt \tag{1.4}$$

which is positive, for

$$\left(\frac{d^2p}{dt^2}\right)$$

is by nature negative, owing to diminishing returns to any factor increasing singly in combination with others held constant so that

$$-t \left(\frac{d^2p}{dt^2}\right) > 0$$

The social marginal product of the increase in capital is

$$\left(\frac{dp}{dt}\right) dt$$

multiplied by the number of workers, A, i.e.:

$$A \left(\frac{dp}{dt}\right) dt$$

Under the marginal productivity principle, 'Thünen's law', this social marginal product, divided by the increase in capital, which gave rise to it, gives us its social marginal productivity rate:

$$\frac{A \left(\frac{dp}{dt}\right) dt}{dK} = \frac{A \left(\frac{dp}{dt}\right) dt}{\frac{A}{2}(wdt + tdw)} = \frac{2 \left(\frac{dp}{dt}\right) dt}{wdt + tdw} \tag{3}$$

in the denominator of which we substitute the equivalent from (1.4) of

$$dw = -t \left(\frac{d^2p}{dt^2}\right) dt \tag{1.4}$$

to get:

$$\frac{2\left(\dfrac{dp}{dt}\right)dt}{wdt - t^2\left(\dfrac{d^2p}{dt^2}\right)dt} = \frac{2\left(\dfrac{dp}{dt}\right)}{w - t^2\left(\dfrac{d^2p}{dt^2}\right)}$$

where, as noted earlier, the second denominator term is positive. This social marginal productivity rate must now be compared with the interest rate, z, which we obtain by solving (1) for z, first by rearranging it to

$$z = \frac{2(p-w)}{wt}$$

and then by substituting the equivalent of w from (1·3) into this expression and simplifying it. That gives us:

$$z = \frac{2\left(\dfrac{dp}{dt}\right)}{p - t\left(\dfrac{dp}{dt}\right)}$$

in which the denominator equals w, and we have:

$$z = \frac{2\left(\dfrac{dp}{dt}\right)}{w}$$

Thus we arrive at Wicksell's discrepancy and find that:

$$\frac{2\left(\dfrac{dp}{dt}\right)}{w - t^2\left(\dfrac{d^2p}{dt^2}\right)} < \frac{2\left(\dfrac{dp}{dt}\right)}{w} = z$$

The social marginal productivity rate of capital is smaller than the interest rate. This would equally be the case if instead of K increasing by dK it decreased by $-dK$ (dissaving, partial capital consumption). Still, the social marginal productivity rate of capital would be less than the interest rate, because wdt would become negative, and so would tdw, as the marginal productivity of labour would decrease, given labour constant while capital decreases.

Wicksell attributed this discrepancy to two causes. First, real capital, unlike the other factors, is measured in a technical unit extraneous to its nature, measured as exchange value, while labour and land are measured in their own natural units. Second, and more important, the production (and consumption) of real capital, new additional real capital added to what was there before, takes time, during which capital, alone increasing, undergoes a revaluation, while the other factors if they increase can be applied to production immediately without any intervening construction period. By contrast, Wicksell said (but did not demonstrate) that there is no equivalent difference between the social marginal productivity rate of labour (or land) when it increases and the wage (or rent) rate. This can be shown as follows.

Let us use equation (1·2), and let labour alone increase by $dA = 3$ per cent, so that:

$$A_1 = (A_0 + dA) = 1{\cdot}03A_0$$

Let the initial production period $t_0 =$ two years, and initially the marginal products are:

$$p_0 = w_0 + t \left(\frac{dp}{dt_0}\right)$$

and we assume that the product of labour was $0{\cdot}9p_0$ and that of capital

$$0{\cdot}1p_0 = t_0\left(\frac{dp}{dt_0}\right)$$

The new production period will be somewhat shorter:

$$t_1 = \frac{t_0}{(A_0 + dA)} \quad = \quad \frac{1}{1{\cdot}03} \quad = \quad 0{\cdot}971t_0 \quad = \quad 1{\cdot}942 \text{ years}$$

Now let the marginal productivity of labour and its real wage decline 1 per cent, owing to the increase dA, and let capital's marginal productivity increase by an equivalent ratio, 1 per cent. Then:

$$w_1 = 0 \cdot 9 p_0 \, (0 \cdot 99) = 0 \cdot 891 p_0$$

but z, which was initially $0 \cdot 1 p_0$, has now increased to $0 \cdot 109 p_0$. Capital's share is now:

$$t_1 \left(\frac{dp}{dt_1} \right) = (p_0 - w_0) \, \frac{t_0}{A_0 + dA} = 0 \cdot 109 p_0 \, (0 \cdot 971)$$

$$= 0 \cdot 1058 p_0$$

Now the new annual product per labourer, p_1, must equal the sum of the marginal products of labour and capital respectively:

$$p_1 = 0 \cdot 891 p_0 + 0 \cdot 1058 p_0 = 0.9968 p_0 < 1 \cdot 000 p_0$$

before labour increases. The social marginal product of the extra labour is:

$$A_1 p_1 - A_0 p_0 = 1 \cdot 03 A_0 \, (0 \cdot 9968 p_0) -$$
$$1 \cdot 0000 A_0 p_0 = 0 \cdot 0267 A_0 p_0$$

This social marginal product of the additional labour divided by the dA increase in labour equals the marginal productivity-determined real wage rate, for:

$$\frac{0 \cdot 0267 A_0 p_0}{0 \cdot 03 A_0} = 0 \cdot 890 p_0 = w_1$$

except for a difference of $0 \cdot 001$ due to rounding decimals.

So the marginal productivity principle applies fully to labour (or land) with the social marginal product rate equal to the wage (or rent) rate, but for macro- or aggregate capital when it increases singly, other factors being constant, the social marginal productivity rate is smaller than the interest rate.

In his fourth and last attempt to demonstrate that the social marginal productivity rate of capital was less than the interest rate, in his article 'Real capital and interest' (*E.T.*, 1923, translated as appendix 2 of *Lectures* I, 1934: 258–99), Wicksell encountered unexpected complications and contradictions. The article was ostensibly a review of G. Åkerman's doctoral dissertation, 'Realkapital und Kapitalzins' (Stockholm, 1923). Åkerman had chosen the problem of extending capital theory, until then almost entirely focused on circulating capital, to the neglected area of durable capital goods and fixed capital. With great effort he worked up an analysis leading to a theory for determining the optimum durability of capital goods. In the process of that research Åkerman had uncovered conditions under which the Wicksell effect on aggregate or social capital would not occur. In substance what Åkerman was saying was that if we count as the real capital increment only the net new capital goods produced by the investment of labour and land inputs, and use the value of these 'concrete' new capital goods as the divisor of the output increment, the social marginal product, to which it gives rise, we would find 'Thünen's law' fulfilled; the social marginal productivity rate of capital would equal the interest rate. The reason Wicksell found a difference there, Åkerman inferred, was that Wicksell was dividing the social marginal product of capital by the real savings invested in it, including a part of those savings which had been absorbed in rising wage rates, before they could become capital goods, in the course of capital formation.

Because Wicksell used a different notation in the 1923 article from that used earlier in *Value, Capital, and Rent* and in *Lectures* I, it is necessary to define a few, a minimum, of them here. The social marginal value product of real capital is now denoted as $\Delta\Pi$, and the real capital increment that gives rise to that product is, as usual, stated by Wicksell as ΔK. But then there is Åkerman's definition of the capital increment he wants to use, one that is minus or net of any wage absorption of real saving, and it is denoted as:

$$\Delta K - K\frac{\Delta l}{l}$$

where l stands for the wage rate (the same as our earlier w), and the interest rate is denoted by ρ (our earlier z).

Wicksell took up Åkerman's problem of the optimal durability

111

of capital goods independently and incorporated into it some of Åkerman's formulations, mostly in arithmetical and tabular form, adapted to his own transcendental differential equations. His treatment showed that for many types of durable capital its durability can be increased to almost any desired extent by adding incrementally more labour input in its construction, and this can be done until the marginal cost of added inputs equals the value of the service-life extension they are estimated to secure. In the end, and after twenty-four major and many minor equations, optimal durability becomes an added feature of the height expansion of capital structures. Just as height expansion becomes profitable after wage rates have risen and then slows their further rise, so height expansion with goods of optimally increased durability reinforces the damper on wage increases, and in addition it reduces replacement costs, as replacements recur less frequently on more than on less durable goods.

Midway in his treatment Wicksell turned to Åkerman's denial of the Wicksell effect. But before taking up Åkerman's case he decided to consolidate his own model as a test of von Thünen's thesis in his equation (22), which he computed by using numerical values for $v=1/2$, $\phi(v)=1\cdot27$, and $\alpha=\beta=1/2$, values he had used earlier in his essay.[4] On that basis he found that his equation yielded:

$$\frac{\Delta\Pi}{\Delta K} = 0\cdot928$$

smaller than ρ.

At first this result did not surprise him, for he attributed it to partial wage absorption of saving. But then he began to have doubts about the generality of the partial-wage-absorption phenomenon. His work on increasing the height dimension of an expanding capital structure responding to wage increases argued for its generality. But then there were such events as recessions, during which capital formation is greatly curtailed but not reduced to zero. In a recession capital undergoes a revaluation and also structural change while the real wages of the employed tend to increase, with money wages falling and unemployment rising. This plus Åkerman's difficulties in determining optimal durability in the capital structure induced him to recompute equation (22) after making two changes. First he decided to make the capital exponent in the production function 'very small'. Arbitrarily I reduced that exponent from $\beta=1/2$ to $0\cdot1$, while the exponent for labour was raised correspondingly from $\alpha=1/2$ to $0\cdot9$. Using the same values for v and $\phi(v)$ as above, on recomputing we find that it yields the ratio:

$$\frac{\Delta \Pi}{\Delta K} = \rho 0 \cdot 476 \bullet \frac{1 \cdot 77}{0 \cdot 77} = 1 \cdot 0948 \rho$$

i.e. a ratio significantly greater than ρ.

At this point Wicksell decided to make a second change, to develop Åkerman's capital divisor purified from any wage absorption of savings, so he wrote Åkerman's ΔK divisor of the $\Delta \Pi / \Delta K$ ratio as:

$$\Delta K - K \frac{\Delta l}{l} = K \frac{\Delta K}{K} - \frac{\Delta l}{l} = K \frac{\Delta n}{n}$$

and then he made a simplification of equation (22) and stated it as equation (23), into which he had incorporated the purified Åkerman capital divisor. Computing equation (23) with the v and $\phi(v)$ values used above, he came to the conclusion that

$$\frac{\Delta \Pi}{\Delta K} = 1 \cdot 149 \rho$$

was not only greater than ρ but more so than in the previous case.

This surprised him even more and led him to conclude that these puzzling results 'presumably belong to the sphere of "dynamic" theory where we cannot confine ourselves to comparison of two equilibria but must also study the transition from one to the other' (p. 293).

On this basis he arrived at the very agnostic conclusion that the relationship of $\Delta \Pi / \Delta K$ to ρ was subject to considerable variation, depending on the value of β in the production function and on the magnitudes of v and $\phi(v)$, 'the life-extension function'. If v is very small, $\phi(v)$ will be very large and an upper limit to extension of duration is approached. But if v approaches unity, then $\phi(v)$ fades to zero, the opposite limit. As Wicksell put it, 'in both cases or limits, the right-hand side of equation 23 reduces to the value of ρ'.[4]

This was as far as Wicksell carried the analysis. He clearly intended to return to it, but for various reasons he never did, and not long after writing this article he died, in May 1926. However, it was the doubts about the applicability of the marginal productivity theory of distribution that his Wicksell effect had brought to light, and his own agnosticism about the scope and direction of that 'effect', that inspired Joan Robinson (1953–4) in her attack on neoclassical economics soon to be joined by Sraffa (1960). These writings in turn laid the basis of the capital theory controversy between the 'two Cambridges'. This is a subject we need not touch on. Had Wicksell lived he would undoubtedly have joined in the controversy, more on the side of Cambridge, Mass., than that of Cambridge, UK.

However, one remark seems needed. The Wicksell effect we have been discussing is now referred to as the Price Wicksell Effect, as distinct from another, the Real Wicksell Effect, a matter most succinctly explained by Mark Blaug:

> The Price Wicksell Effect involves a change in the value of capital stock, whereas the Real Wicksell Effect involves a change in techniques induced by a change in the rate of interest. A negative Real Wicksell Effect ... [brings on] 'capital revers-ing', less capital-intensive techniques being chosen at a lower rate of interest. The negative Real Wicksell Effect never appears in Wicksell because his standard assumption of contin-uous factor substitution effectively rules it out. (Cf. Robinson, 1953–4; Sraffa, 1960; Swan, 1965; Harcourt, 1972; Blaug, 1985: 561; Sandelin, 1980, 1989)

Public finance and social reform

Wicksell's major work on public finance was his *Finanztheore-tische Untersuchungen* (1896). It was preceded by a shorter work, *Våra skatter – hvilka betala dem och hvilka borde betala?* (Our taxes: who pays and who ought to pay them?), issued under the pseudonym Sven Trygg in 1894), which was highly critical of Sweden's system of taxation, based as it was mainly on regressive commodity excise and real property taxes, and argued for a broadly based progressive general income tax. Most of its analysis was incorporated in Wicksell (1896), which latter was presented in three parts: (1) 'Theory of the incidence of taxation (pp. 1–75), (2) 'Concerning a new principle of just or equitable taxation' (pp. 76–165), and (3) 'Sweden's system of taxation' (pp. 165–351, a histori-cal survey of Swedish taxes from about 1650 to the early 1890s). Subsequent to this work Wicksell wrote two tracts on taxation, half a dozen articles on various tax topics in *Ekonomisk Tidskrift* at intervals between 1899 and 1925, and during 1920–3 he served on a succession of parliamentary committees on taxation and finance, to the reports of which he contributed several chapters.

Still one is conscious that Wicksell never wrote a systematic work on public finance. Among other matters he barely sketched in *Finanztheoretische Untersuchungen* was his treatment of public debt, of deficit versus surplus budgets and their more or less regular co-ordination with business depressions and booms. However, there are two primary reasons why the book still merits attention both from a doctrinal history standpoint and from its potential application in economic policy, besides the fact that his work in *Finanztheoretische Untersuchungen* shows close linkages with his social reform programme, most of which was also expressed in his tract, *The Socialist State and Contemporary Society* (1904).

It was in Part II that Wicksell (1896) made two important contributions to economics, of which more presently. We omit any discussion of Part I on the incidence and shifting of taxes, because it offered little that was new or different from what contemporary writers such as A. Wagner, E. Sax, and L. Stein in Germany, J. C. Bullock and E. R. A. Seligman in the United States, or U. Mazzola and M. Pantoleoni in Italy had to say on the subject. Moreover, Wicksell's main concern in Part I was to refute the survival in Sweden of ideas borrowed from classical economics, such as the notion that taxes on wages and wage goods were always shifted from the workers to their employers. How come? Because at subsistence-level wages workers could not pay those taxes, and many of them would leave work in favour of poor relief, until employers, concerned about a shortage of labour, raised the wages offered to absorb any taxes on wages (1896: 163–4).

In his 'New principle of just or equitable taxation' Wicksell first of all extended the scope of the marginal utility principle, and with it the related benefit principle, not only to taxation but also to decisions about extending existing government functions, and/or adopting new ones, and to decisions about the allocation of government expenditure among the accepted functions; i.e. he extended its scope to the entire public sector. Second, and simultaneously, as J. M. Buchanan (1951: 173–8) was first to point out, he extended the marginal productivity principle to the many public-sector enterprises and services which can be financed at least in part, sometimes fully, by user fees for services or benefits conferred separately on individual citizens as distinct from collective, non-separable services extended to the public in general. Such user fees, sometimes called 'tax prices', said Wicksell, should be set or determined to equal the marginal cost per additional use of the public service or facility. In other words, fee-financed public services, which are 'public goods', should be offered to the public on a marginal-cost pricing basis, and he criticized the German authorities for setting fares on the State-owned Prussian railways so as to make a handsome profit for the exchequer. In the interests of the rational use of economic resources and in the interest of the general welfare, he argued that fee-charging public-sector enterprises ought not to be used as indirect means of taxation. If their services could not be fully financed at marginal-cost rates, as where the public enterprise is subject to increasing returns to scale, the difference ought to be financed from general taxation. And where the service, though separable, involves so small a marginal cost – pennies or less per additional use, as in the case of many a tollbridge – that it becomes uneconomic to collect a fee, then the service should be provided 'free', out of general taxation (1896: 126–38).

The foregoing refers to one of two methods (the other a broadly based progressive income tax) by which his principle of equitable taxation might be applied. Now we must look at the 'principle' itself. Before it could be adopted some important social changes would have to be carried out.

Before any genuine tax reform would be feasible the franchise, limited in Wicksell's day to upper- and middle-class men – the only people with sufficient income or property to qualify – would have to be widened. All adult citizens, male or female, should have the vote. Also, to guarantee political minorities a voice in parliament, the electoral system must be based on proportional representation (1896: 123–4). Workers and their wives would then be the political majority, naturally intent on reducing the great inequalities between upper-class incomes and their own, and on raising the level of the latter.

To this end Wicksell envisaged 'confiscatory taxation' would reduce, and eventually eliminate, forms of income and wealth the fairness of which 'appears doubtful [*Deren Recht zweifelhaft erscheint*]', which are regarded as 'unjust' (1896: 144–5). In this process the tax burden would be redistributed to bear upon the remaining incomes (the 'not unjust' ones) more equitably, at progressive rates, and in proportion to size of income as between workers and others in society.

Wicksell's notion of 'confiscatory taxation', like several other ideas of his put forward in *Finanztheoretische Untersuchungen*, was not worked out systematically. What he intended by it was evidently to reduce – ideally, to eliminate – by taxation the rent element in personal incomes, so that citizens' disposable income would represent 'earned' rather than a mixture of 'unearned' and earned income. How this was to be accomplished he did not indicate very clearly. Confiscatory taxes would be assessed on 'unearned increments in land value' after due allowance for any improvements the owner had made since acquiring the land, plus interest on such improvements and added to acquisition cost as the subtrahend from the higher current sale price or appraised value of the land, in determining its 'unearned value increment'. Confiscatory taxes would be levied not only on such land value increments but also on certain not very well defined monopoly gains, and on capital gains, on the amounts in excess of certain limits that individuals would be allowed to keep after the tax from inheritances and bequests, and, not least, on gains from inflation. In a different context at the end of World War I, during the course of which prices in Sweden had more than doubled, he urged that a commission be set up to administer restitution proceedings between creditors and the debtors who had paid off mortgages and other long-term debts in money of greatly reduced purchasing power.

As for the revenues brought in by 'confiscatory' taxes, Wicksell wanted them not to be spent on current government services but to be 'funded', i.e. invested in income-earning public projects and enterprises. Those revenues came from private capital investments, or changes in the value of capital investments, and to spend them on current government services would amount to a form of capital consumption, which was to be avoided. But if they were properly 'funded' they would yield a return, and as such 'fundings' accumulated with the passage of time the returns would in due course become large enough to sustain payment of a 'social dividend' to young persons as they reached the age of twenty-five. Such dividends (on his estimates, translated approximately into their current value or purchasing power, they might amount to a once-for-all social dividend of $7,000 per twenty-five-year-old) would enable young couples to set up their own home, or for one or both of them to acquire more vocational or professional education, and/or for them to start a business of their own. This rather visionary proposal – visionary because the returns from 'funded confiscation revenues' alone would be unlikely ever to suffice for the social dividend he had in mind (yet basic child allowance of $900 per year is now paid up to the age of sixteen) – reflects his deeply felt conviction, expressed in various contexts, that 'it is a mistake to believe, as is so often the case, that labour must live on its wages alone'. In other words, besides the primary distribution of marginal productivity wages as labour's income during its working life, he visualized a secondary distribution of pensions and other forms of social insurance characteristic of the so-called Welfare State to guard against the vicissitudes of life and to provide economic security in retirement.

117

Once the political and tax reforms alluded to above had been carried out, Wicksell assumed, the resulting distribution of income in the community would rest on a general (two-thirds or better), ideally on a unanimous, social consensus. Then it could be assumed that people would take a 'voluntarist' approach to taxes and the functions of government, regarding the former as the *quid* for the *pro quo* of the latter, in much the same way as an exchange of goods or services was regarded in the market place. Then, since incomes are subject to diminishing marginal utility, considerations of equity or relative equality of sacrifice require that taxes be assessed in proportion to ability to pay, i.e. progressively in relation to size of income, and that a broadly based, progressive income tax should become the chief source of revenue, so as to minimize the role of regressive excise taxes, the incidence of which, unlike that of an income tax, was substantially greater than the revenue they brought in.

Ability to pay is an excellent and equitable principle for distributing a given tax burden, but it is useless in determining (1) the total magnitude of government expenditure and the corresponding revenue or tax burden, or (2) the proportions in which a given total of public expenditure is to be allocated to the various functions of government. Decisions on such matters are essentially made in parliament on the basis of the benefit principle (or the marginal utility–marginal cost calculus) as applied indirectly on behalf of the population by its democratically elected representatives (1896: 85–7).

However, to avoid the tyranny of bare majority decisions over an almost equally large minority, Wicksell insisted that tax and expenditure decisions in parliament should be made only on the basis of 'qualified majorities' (by which he meant two-thirds or better majorities) and that expenditure decisions must be taken simultaneously with decisions about what taxes and how much taxation or what combination of taxes and public borrowing would be needed to finance the proposed expenditure. He would have allowed simple majority decisions in the following cases: (1) for financing the government debt and related government 'obligations' (mainly civil service and military pensions); (2) in situations where only two mutually exclusive alternatives were open and a third was not attainable (e.g. whether to set up a specialized research institute or not, with no near equivalent private or university institute capable of doing the job); and (3) decisions on the classification of government functions and correspondingly 'earmarked' revenues, as to kind but not amount for these functions (1896: 117–20).

It is not certain that the exemptions from qualified majority approval he was willing to concede were consistent with the other features of his budgetary tax and expenditure procedures, but we must leave that question in abeyance.

As D. Black (1955), among others, has pointed out, Wicksell's idea that government functions should be classified together with earmarked supporting revenues supposes a very complex and potentially difficult decision-making procedure if every one of hundreds or more alternative allocations is to be considered and voted on. That problem, like many others in the political arena, is likely to be settled more or less arbitrarily by attrition or fatigue. The much more important problem Black stresses is that:

> Inside Parliament Wicksell's principle, by requiring a high majority for an increase of expenditure and a very small minority for a reduction, would make increases of expenditure far more difficult and reductions far easier than with the normal requirement of a simple majority. The bias would be toward curtailment and reduction ... the principle would protect certain parliamentary minorities at the expense of the parliamentary majorities. (1955: 20–1)

There certainly is point in Black's criticism. Wicksell's insistence on qualified majority decisions would have played into the hands of recalcitrant minority parties and coalitions. How can this requirement of his be explained? As his career proves, Wicksell was anything but a social reactionary, and, while he was no social revolutionary, in his time he was rightly regarded as a radical social reformer. So his qualified majority requirement seems to contradict his own position and programme. At the practical level it does, but it has to be understood in terms of Wicksell's own character and in terms of another of his fundamental convictions. He regarded himself as a thoroughgoing rationalist, a character type common among intellectuals and academics. As such he was prone to consider other people, and most of his colleagues, as rationalists too, if not perhaps to the same extent as himself. Were his programme of political and tax reforms to be enacted, the resultant social structure and income distribution would rest, he believed, on a very broad social consensus. In such circumstances why should political minorities, guaranteed a role in parliament under proportional representation, act in an obstructionist and recalcitrant manner? Especially if it would not serve their own long-term interests?

Wicksell overestimated the rationality and underestimated the covetousness of most of his contemporaries. He was anxious to safeguard the rights and opportunities of 'the minority'. The minority he had in mind was not some small religious or utopian sect but the 'intellectual minority', always a minority in any population. He was convinced that it is largely due to the insights, the creative abilities, and the constructive criticism of intellectual minorities that we have made such progress out of the jungle as we can discern.

As a seer or a prophet Wicksell was by no means infallible, but in the main he was right on far more issues than on the few where he has been proved wrong. Now, some sixty years since his day, Sweden's standard of living has risen from comparative poverty at the turn of the century to one of the highest in the world. In addition, and contrary to Wicksell's urging, based on his fear of resource depletion, that the country's population be gradually reduced from about 5 million in his day to about 3 million, it has slowly increased to about 8·5 million, yet with a very high and rising standard of living *per capita*. This has been achieved together with and probably at least in part because of the gradual development from the 1930s onward of an efficiently administered cradle-to-grave Welfare State, which Wicksell visualized as one where labour need not be constrained to live on wages alone.

Notes

1   The first part of this chapter is based in the main on Gårdlund's excellent biography (1958), inclusive of its earlier version in Swedish (1956), the title of which may be translated as 'Knut Wicksell: a Rebel in the New Realm', where the 'New Realm' refers to new perspectives on social and economic relations emanating from continental Europe and the United States which reached Sweden and began to transform social relations there in the 1870s and 1880s. The Swedish version gives a somewhat fuller account of the environment and public attitudes against which some of the crucial events in Wicksell's career were played out. I have also relied on information provided in private correspondence with the late Professors Erik Lindahl and Emil Sommarin, and on a recent biography by a granddaughter of Knut and Anna, Liv Wicksell (1985).

2   There is a second version of the reason why *Value, Capital, and Rent* did not become Wicksell's doctoral thesis. The edition was small, and he found it difficult to obtain the number of copies required by the university regulations. See Gårdlund (1958: 159).

3   For the demonstrations see Wicksell (1892), 851 ff.; (1954), 120–30, 134–44; (1934a), 177–80; *E.T.* 25 (1923), translated as appendix 2 of *Lectures* I (1934: 258–99). Wicksell ran into difficulties with his demonstration when he applied it to durable or fixed rather than circulating real capital (see 1934: 293 ff.).

4   The nature of v, ρn, and $\phi(v)$ are explained in Wicksell (1934), appendix 2, in equation 5 (pp. 276, 288), and equation 9 (p. 278). Equations 22 (p. 292) and 23 (p. 293) are:

$$\frac{\Delta\Pi}{\Delta K} = \frac{1-v}{1+\beta(1-v)} \bullet \frac{v+\phi(v)}{v+\phi(v)-1}\,\rho \tag{22}$$

$$\left(\frac{\dfrac{\Delta\Pi}{\Pi}}{\dfrac{\Delta n}{n}}\right)\frac{\Pi}{K} = \beta(1-v)\frac{\Pi}{K} = \frac{(1-v)[v+\phi(v)]}{v+\phi(v)-1} \tag{23}$$

Chapter five

Gustav Cassel, popularizer and enigmatic Walrasian

Lars Magnusson

Among the first generation of Swedish twentieth-century economists and as a forerunner of the Stockholm school of economics Gustav Cassel (1864–1944) is commonly regarded as a second-rate figure, far behind Knut Wicksell and David Davidson, for example, in theoretical brilliance and originality. In effect he is regarded mainly as a popularizer, and consequently his undoubtedly great influence during his lifetime in the first place seems to have stemmed '... from his extensive writing and participation in public affairs' (Seligman, 1962: 561). A keen observer of practical economic matters, never hesitant in putting forward his views or inclined to doubt the validity of his own prescriptions, he was generally regarded during the 1920s and 1930s as a leading international expert, especially on monetary problems. According to one critical writer, Ben Seligman, he thus:

> ... exerted a remarkable influence not only on Sweden's monetary policy, but on that of other nations as well. A long flow of articles, reviews, speeches, pamphlets, and commentary came from his pen, most of them appearing in the Swedish newspaper *Svenska Dagbladet*. He wrote reports for the League of Nations, toured the United States lecturing on money, and offered his views to the House of Representatives' Committee on Banking.... Yet with the coming of the depression and the rise of the new economics, Cassel was soon eclipsed. At his death in 1944, his influence was virtually nonexistent. His economics, with its insufferable dogmatisms and self-esteem, simply had not met the requirements of the day. (1962: 562)

In his *History of Economic Analysis* (1972) Schumpeter seems to share the same critical opinion of Cassel as a theorist. In his view Cassel's economics was dated from the start and, above all, not nearly as original as the author tended to imagine. For example, according to Schumpeter, his theory of prices relying on a crude quantity theory of money was 'completely antiquated'. 'We may well use Cassel whenever we wish to find out what our own advance really amounts to' (1972: 1081). At the same time Schumpeter is ready to admit that Cassel presented his view 'extremely effectively', and as a popularizer of analytical economics he probably meant much to the lay public. Especially in Germany, where his textbook *The Theory of Social Economy,* first published in 1918, according to Schumpeter was 'exactly what German economists needed' at the time (1972: 1154). Moreover, during the 1920s Cassel was probably 'the most influential leader of our science' and 'rose to international fame during and after the First World War – chiefly as an expert on money and international relations and as an assiduous participant in international conferences on these subjects' (Schumpeter, 1972: 1154).

Thus as a theoretical innovator Cassel might not deserve more than a footnote in the history of economic thought. However, it is easy to lay too much stress on the innovators, to deal only with the successive improvements of the analytical apparatus, or the 'box of tools' – to use Schumpeter's words. Surely, to assess the impact of economics during the twentieth century, or to understand its position within social thought as such, one must look more closely into the more mundane course of development taken by economic pedagogy; study the second-rate figures, the ordinary professors, the influential propagandists and popularizers. To a great extent it was such people who got the message across to the lay public and became important as advisers to governments and politicians. Probably they also – by conveying some crude and simple principles – made academic economics of a less prescriptive and more abstract nature a much more influential science during this century than would otherwise have been the case. That the public have been so ready to listen to the prophecies of economists and accept their claims of access to a box of tools that could be practically useful may thus be due to a number of popularizers rather than to pure theoretical progress and intellectual brilliance (cf. Brannigan, 1981; Bloor, 1981; Knorr-Cetina, 1981; Stigler, 1982; Deane, 1983; Klammer, 1984; Whitley, 1984; Coats, 1985).

It is perhaps mainly in this sense that Gustav Cassel can still be of considerable importance, whatever may be said of his originality or innovative capacity. As was pointed out above, he was certainly one of the most influential economists of his time. He was without doubt remarkable as a teacher and as a popularizer. As such he most certainly paved the way for the Stockholm school in the

1930s and generally helped to make economics a prestigious and influential subject in Sweden from this period and onwards. And in his case theoretical elegance quite probably meant less than successful campaigning. Above all he was successful in presenting a rather analytical and hard-core version of economics to politicians with an increasing inclination towards social engineering as an essential tool for solving certain and so-called 'economic' problems.

Professional career

Gustav Cassel's academic and professional career was without doubt a success – but perhaps not as straightforward as one would imagine. Born into a well-to-do middle-class family in Stockholm, he started as a engineering student and took a doctoral degree in mathematics at Uppsala in 1894. While teaching mathematics in Stockholm he came to the conclusion that it was not the career for him and moved over to economics. Already from this early beginning he looked upon economics as a form of quantitative analysis, and his avowed ambition was to apply strict mathematical principles to his new subject. In 1898 it became possible for him to go to Germany as a *stipendiat*, where he studied economics and began to publish articles, especially in the journal *Ekonomisk Tidskrift*, founded by David Davidson in 1899. In 1901 he applied for a professorship in economics at Lund but withdrew when it became clear that Wicksell would get the Chair. However, 1904 saw his appointment in Stockholm, where he held a Chair in 'national economy and finance' until retirement in 1933.

During this whole period, besides his academic duties, Cassel was a keen participant in Swedish political debate. From the late 1890s until his death in 1944 he contributed regularly to the conservative newspaper *Svenska Dagbladet*. He also wrote pamphlets and books on political issues, for example the fierce attack against Swedish social democracy in *Socialism eller framåtskridande* (*Socialism or Progress*) which was published before the election of 1928 which was to prove a disaster for the Social Democrats. Although he was regarded as mildly radical early in his career, he undoubtedly became more conservative over the years. However, this does not seem to have deterred him from giving advice to any government that would listen. That he believed himself to be neutral as an expert quite above party politics seems quite clear. Especially in his autobiography, characteristically entitled *I förnuftets tjänst* (In the Service of Reason), he conveys the impression of a technocrat with an engineer's view of man and the social world.

Especially in the 1920s and early 1930s Cassel was often asked to sit on committees appointed by the government or the Riksbank (central bank) to advise on economic policy issues, monetary questions, etc. He was also a noted Swedish delegate to several international conferences during this period, organized, for example, by the League of Nations to deal with the severe economic and monetary problems after the First World War (Brussels, 1920; Genoa, 1922; and Geneva, 1927, as well as others). And as an active participant in the debate on the gold standard as well as a campaigner for price stability and a strong critic of policy against Germany (together with Keynes, for example) in the early 1920s Cassel became quite famous internationally (*Svenskt Biografiskt Lexikon*; Cassel, 1940, 1941; Myrdal, 1945; Giöbel-Lilja, 1948).

Cassel was also a prolific and extensive writer. However, most of his published work dealt with practical matters. His views on theoretical and methodological issues are presented mainly in his synthesis *The Theory of Social Economy* (1918, English edition 1923, 1932) but also in the much shorter *Fundamental Thoughts in Economics* (1925), and *On Quantitative Thinking in Economics* (1935). In an early treatise, 'Grundriss einer elementaren Preislehre' (1899a), he presented a theory of price and in 'Die Produktionskostentheorie Ricardos und die ersten Aufgaben der theoretischen Volkwirtschaftslehre' (1901a) he fiercely attacked production-cost theories of value in both Ricardian and Marshallian forms. In the early *The Nature and Necessity of Interest* (1903) he presented a critique of Böhm-Bawerk's *agio* theory of interest and instead argued for a basic supply and demand theory.

Further, his reputation as a radical stemmed from the publications *Das Recht auf den Vollen Arbeiterstrag* (1900) and *Socialpolitik* (1901) in which he argued that trade unions and a high-wage policy could be beneficial to economic growth through increased productivity, technical change (labour substitution), and increased aggregate demand. However, from the First World War and onwards his main interest lay in monetary theory and its practical applications. In this field he published several books and pamphlets, including *Dyrtid och sedelöverflöd* (1917), *Money and Foreign Exchange after 1914* (1922), and *The Downfall of the Gold Standard* (1936), as well as the influential memorandum for the monetary conference in Brussels in 1920, *The World's Monetary Problems* (1921). His main thinking may be summarized under four heads.

Value and prices

At the base of Cassel's discussion of the formation of prices and value lay a strong rationalist outlook and a specific conception of the scientific method as such. He was most sceptical about anything that he regarded as metaphysical. He saw it as the task of scientific economics above all else to root out such tendencies. The economic profession was still haunted by a 'worship of dogma', he stated in his *On Quantitative Thinking in Economics*.

> Loose and dim concepts, falsely stated problems, confused reasonings, representations not in touch with reality – in short, all sorts of dogmatic rubbish inherited from earlier epochs and accumulated for more than a century continue largely to determine the problems which economic science sets itself to study ... (1935: 3)

He presented himself – often in a pompous and self-important style – as a leading contributor to a necessary 'radical cleansing of economic science' as well as a laying the ground for 'a more satisfactory quantitative foundation' of the subject (1935: 5).

His own method he described as 'gradual approximation'. Simplification was the essence of theory and the first step in the scientific process. According to Cassel the economist must start out with some very general concepts and then gradually approach reality, 'real economic life'. He must at base have a simple theory which is logically consistent and so general 'that it is possible for us subsequently to introduce new elements into the theory without being forced to pull down the building already erected' (1935: 94). Against this background he insisted, for example, that the notion of 'marginal productivity' never could be the cornerstone of a general theory of distribution, as it relied on some rather special conditions, notably the 'principle of substitution'. Instead it must be based on the scarcity principle, as this was more general and did not rely on such restrictive premises. Cassel argued that factors of production would have a (scarcity) price even if the factors of production were technically fixed. Accordingly, 'the principle of substitution has only a secondary position as one of the supplementary principles' (1935: 124).

According to Cassel 'value' was a 'dim concept' of the first rank. Economics would be much better without it. It had no scientific content whatsoever, as it was impossible to define quantitatively or to give any concrete meaning to. Most important, it was impossible to measure 'different absolute values in a common unit' (1935: 30). For example, to define such a 'value' in labour units – as Ricardo and Marx had tried to do – was of course nonsense, according to Cassel. It was a roundabout method and relied on some very special assumptions (homogeneous labour, etc.). However, in Cassel's eyes a value theory based on marginal utility was not an improvement. Already in the early 'Grundriss', and later in subsequent works, he refused to accept marginal utility theory as a basis for price determination – as it had been presented by Wicksell, for example. According to Cassel economics must abandon any notion of utility as a cause of value. First, it had psychological and moral connotations. Second, it must be clear that any comparability of psychological satisfactions was impossible to establish; thus the whole concept of 'value' was meaningless. Nor could 'utility' be regarded in isolation from demand, which was determined by relative prices – hence the marginal utility theory was based on circular reasoning. In his characteristic way Cassel promptly states in *The Theory of Social Economy* that:

> Thus the introduction of the conception of marginal utility is of no material advantage, though it may at times be convenient to apply the term. In seeking to make this conception the basis of a whole economic theory by declaring marginal utility to be the determinant of price or 'value', a wholly untenable position has been taken up. The task of price, in accordance with the principle of scarcity, is so to restrict demand as to enable it to be satisfied out of the available stock of commodities. The demand for a commodity must thus be cut down somewhere by means of its price. Although the significance attached to the final satisfaction of the want is then equal to the price, this cannot possibly be construed to mean that this significance determines the price. On the contrary, the price determines the extent to which wants shall be satisfied, and accordingly, which is the 'final' or 'marginal' want. (1932: 83)

Although Cassel was not alone in this kind of critique at the time, according to Schumpeter (1972: 1067), his 'scrapping of everything behind demand functions' was 'the first uncompromisingly radical attack upon the whole structure of the utility theory of value made by an economist trained in mathematics'.

Thus criticizing both an 'objective' and a 'subjective' theory of value, Cassel states that a theory of prices must be based on 'sound quantitative principles'. He finds a solution in a kind of general equilibrium model of simultaneous equations that in content was a simplified version of Walras's model. Like Walras he takes as his standpoint the 'price-fixing' process as such and tries to show how all prices are determined simultaneously and thus decide the actual demand and supply. Thus, as Seligman (1962: 568) notes, price-fixing was the 'organizing principle rather than the outcome of market forces' in Cassel's model as well as in Walras's. In presenting his well known 'scarcity principle' Cassel particularly stressed that demand could not be established until the prices of goods had been determined and adjusted to supply. However, he was very reluctant to admit that he relied on Walras to any great extent. He mentions Walras in the early 'Grundriss', but in later works, including *The Theory of Social Economy*, omits any reference to Walras and instead talks of 'his' solution to the price problem. In fact, when he is presenting the equilibrium model here the only reference is to his own 'Grundriss' (Cassel, 1932: 137 ff.; cf. Myrdal, 1945; Seligman, 1962: 569; Schumpeter, 1972: 953).

Thus, according to Cassel, the scarcity principle was the basis of price determination. He argued that the fundamental reason why prices have to be paid is the scarcity of the different goods that people want to acquire. However, any description of price-fixing as a process where a number of buyers bid for a commodity which is supplied in a fixed quantity is not wholly correct. A buyer can fix his demand only when he knows the prices of all goods. The price-fixing process must therefore be a simultaneous process. Consequently it is quite meaningless to discuss whether prices are determined by costs or by demand. In effect it is to forget the process and look only to one side of it. In reality cost and demand are but two sides of the same coin.

Cassel found his own method advantageous for two reasons in particular. First, as we saw, it made it possible to abandon any notion of the metaphysical concept of 'value'. Second, it was true to his own methodological principle of 'gradual approximation'. Admittedly it was simple and functioned as a general principle in any kind of society, including a communist one, or in cases where free competition did not prevail. However, even more important was the fact that it could be used for any kind of price determination, including the factors of production. It was only proof of the lack of such universality that, for example, Ricardo – and his followers – had had to determine the rent price of land on a quite different basis from other prices: the differential principle. But, as Cassel insisted, given equal productivity on land its price would be based on scarcity. Or, to take another example, it was clearly a weakness of Böhm-Bawerk's theory of interest that he should have felt obliged to base it on a perceived lower estimation of future satisfactions as compared with those of the present. Rather, in

Cassel's view, interest could be treated like any other price with the help of the scarcity principle; paid for by 'waiting' or 'capital disposal' (see below).

Consequently, Cassel also rejected the use of marginal productivity as a basis for determining the distribution of income or for pricing the different factors of production – once again openly in opposition to Wicksell (cf. Gårdlund, 1956; Uhr, 1960: 32). According to Cassel, marginal productivity could never determine price because:

> Marginal productivity is not a given factor in the pricing problem, for the relative quantities of the various factors of production to be employed according to the principle of substitution can only be determined when prices are taken into account. Marginal productivity and price are, in fact, two completely similar unknowns in the pricing problem, and it is consequently impossible to present the one as the determining factor of the other. (1932: 110)

In *On Quantitative Thinking in Economics* he puts his objections more specifically. Here in a critique against what later came to be known as the 'Cobb–Douglas function' he first points out that marginal productivity can be constructed only 'in those cases where the amount of a factor can be varied continually'. However, in real life there are factors that are indivisible (for example, managerial services) and thus to base the price-fixing of factors of production on marginal productivity would be a violation of the principle of 'gradual approximation'. Second, it would be a mistake, in Cassel's view, to base a theory of distribution on the principle of substitution. Also when factors are technically fixed there is a price to be paid for the utilization of a factor dependent on its relative scarcity. Third, and in a way foreshadowing the Cambridge debate some decades later, Cassel points out that 'it is impossible to speak of the marginal productivity of any factor in the great social process of production except when the prices of the different factors are assumed to be known'. And further:

> If we consider the whole social process of production, the total product is a great mass of different commodities and services of the most varying nature and there is no technical possibility of expressing this mass as a measurable arithmetical quantity. Only if the different commodities and services have definitive prices may the value of the total product be expressed in terms of money. (1935: 125)

Thus, according to Cassel, distribution must be treated as part of the general price-fixing process, soluble only with the help of a system of simultaneously determined unknowns in an equation system. In this instance 'marginal productivity' is of no help, and if it is only another word for 'price' it is utterly meaningless. However, and not without some accuracy, he points out that this concept had its roots:

> ... in the endeavour to find an objective standard for a just distribution. This standard was sought in a kind of technical relation of cause and effect between activity and product. Since there is no such key to the problem, there can be no just distribution in this objective sense. The problem is essentially an economic one. (1932: 181)

Interest and steady-rate growth

In *The Nature and Necessity of Interest* Cassel at the outset presented 'the problem of interest' as an 'integral part of ... the general problem of prices' (1903: vi). Criticizing, as we saw, Böhm-Bawerk's *agio* theory in particular, Cassel argues that interest is simply a price paid for 'waiting'. He goes on to define waiting as 'the use of capital' – 'capital disposal' in later works – and as such an indispensable factor of production in all historical forms of production. Further, waiting can thus be measured 'by the product of a certain sum of money multiplied by a certain time' (1903: 90). In periods of economic expansion, due to external forces like the opening up of new colonies, war, etc., the demand for waiting increases and hence also the rate of interest, while in periods of contraction the opposite of course happens. Although he elaborates on this admittedly crude theory in later works he never really carries the analysis much further (Seligman, 1962: 570 ff.). In *The Theory of Social Economy* he largely repeats it and presents it as conclusive:

> Although it is best to leave forgotten the greater part of what has been written on the subject of interest ... it is, however, instructive to follow the main lines ... to be helped in our attempt to attain the conclusive solution to the problem. (1932: 185)

While dealing with rent Cassel approaches macroeconomic problems although he still stays within a static framework. Cassel himself regarded his 'discovery' and explanation of why the rate of interest in the long run tended to fluctuate between 3 and 4 per cent as one of his most important contributions – in his auto-biography he singles it out as a major innovation and maintains that the finding 'in the future will be necessary for any further investigation into economic dynamics' (1940: 163). It seemed especially important because Cassel thought that interest rates were the regulator of economic growth through the rate of capital formation – and this in turn was a function of the savings rate, 'the relative thriftiness of the people'. Thus, anticipating Harrod's famous growth model of some decades later, he defined the rate of growth of output as the propensity to save divided by the capital coefficient. Without any real evidence Cassel immediately went on to suppose that the degree of saving ($1/s$) would be approximately 20 per cent and with a capital coefficient of $6\frac{2}{3}$ per cent (estimated by a Swedish commission in 1908) he found an equilibrium rate of growth of 3 per cent (1932: 61 f.).

Further, Cassel supposed that in the long run interest rates were determined mainly by the supply of loan capital. Also, the degree of saving and consequently of capital disposal on the supply side was almost constant over time and 'passive in regard to changes in the rate' (1932: 246 ff.). On the supply side it is mainly the length of human life that decides at what rate people with capital want to put it to work:

> Why does the rate fluctuate between 3 and 4 per cent, and why can it not just as well fluctuate between 3 and 4 per mille? ... The length of life is one of the most important factors.... Men, at the age at which they have control of their own capital, cannot generally count on more than another twenty-five to thirty years of life, and will not, consequently, sacrifice much more than twenty-five to thirty-three years of returns to secure a perpetual annuity. (1932: 255)

However, if this may explain the minimum rate of interest – given a fixed savings rate – it can by no means explain why the rate could not increase *above* this level. Cassel offers no answer – partly of course because his treatment of the subject is totally static.

Theory of money

It is not surprising that the scarcity principle was applied also by Cassel to determine the value of money and thus the general price level. All through his extensive writings regarding monetary questions he took as his point of departure a quantity theory of money in which the price level was determined by the volume of money. He also tried to show this empirically by presenting quantitative series of stocks of gold compared with wholesale prices during the period from 1850 up to the First World War. His main conclusion was that there existed a clear functional relationship between these two variables. However, at the same time he emphasized that the general price level was effected by the *total* quantity of money, as the circulating amount was determined by the price level itself 'according to the daily needs of trade' (1932: 452). This total quantity could be regarded as given and not in itself affected by prices. And against this background the price of money could be regarded as determined by supply and demand like any other price.

As we shall be able to see more clearly further on, this reasoning lay at the basis of his views regarding inflation during the First World War, the deflation during the 1920s, and the great depression of the early 1930s. Thus, according to Cassel, the inflation during the war years was caused by an overissue of banknotes while the 1920s were characterized by too restrictive a money policy which caused deflation and eventually economic contraction and even depression.

However, to try and prove the accuracy of the quantity theory of money from series of nineteenth-century prices and gold stocks was rather bold, as these data can also hold for other interpretations (Phinney, 1933; Östlind, 1945: 73 ff.). Perhaps even more problematic was the use of data which suggested an annual increase in the gold stock of 2·8 per cent from 1850 to 1910, then linking this with the hypothesis of a long-run interest rate of 3 per cent in the 'uniformly progressing state'. Cassel proposed that price stability was assured by a certain relationship between economic growth and the growth of the gold or money stock. Like Wicksell in *Geldzins und Guterpreise*, Cassel could then assert that price stability was achieved when the interest rate – and thus also economic growth – was at its 'natural rate', i.e. 3 per cent per year. Hence at this equilibrium level there would be no natural reason for the general price level to change.

During the war years the high rate of inflation as well as the drastic changes in the rate of exchange between countries led Cassel to formulate the 'purchasing power parity principle', which first appeared in *Dyrtid och sedelöverflöd* in 1917. He argued that the exchange rate between two currencies basically reflected the internal changes in the currencies themselves. 'When two currencies have been inflated, the new normal rate of exchange will be equal to the old rate multiplied by the quotient between the degrees of inflation of both countries' (1921: 27; cf. 1917: 124 ff.). Although Cassel presented the purchasing power parity principle as his own invention it was clearly older, originating possibly with Wheatly (Seligman, 1962: 576). As has been pointed out, it also failed to give a complete explanation of the dramatic changes in exchange rates during the war years, as these were clearly also affected by balance of payments problems and other factors – pointed out in a Swedish context by Davidson, Wicksell, and Heckscher, for example (Heckscher, 1926: 25 ff.). However, emphasizing one factor and pressing it with great energy while somehow forgetting the others was quite in line with Cassel's general practice, as we have seen.

The theory of the trade cycle

While otherwise almost totally static in character, *The Theory of Social Economy* contains in its later chapters some attempts at dynamic analysis, especially when the author deals with the trade cycle. Cassel begins with an empirical investigation of the main features of past trade cycles. He suggests that it is the production of fixed capital which is most affected by secular cycles, while consumption goods are not markedly dependent: 'the alternation between periods of boom and slump is fundamentally a variation in the production of fixed capital' (1932: 552). Another marked characteristic is that the boom periods are dependent on an influx of additional labour from outside, especially from the agricultural sector. Indeed, this factor – the existence of a reserve army of labour – is one of the most important reasons why there are such distinct booms and slumps in the trade cycle. Thus a relatively underdeveloped economy is a precondition for trade cycles as such, and given a diminished reserve army with time, Cassel argued, the cycles would become less and less severe: 'the trade cycles are, to a very great extent, a phenomenon of the period of transition from the old to the modern economic forms' (1932: 573).

Further, according to Cassel, interest rates were the most effective regulator of the trade cycles as such. Low rates of interest during the slump led to a greatly increased output of fixed capital. This increase in its turn obviously led to a boom, which meant a shortage of capital and rising rents – as well as rising prices and wages – followed by a slump. Among the reasons why production of fixed capital should continue even though rents were rising Cassel specially mentions the length of the period of production, uncertainty about the future, etc.

133

In this context Cassel argues particularly against undercon-
sumption as a basis for trade cycles and crises. As we saw, it was
rather the other way round:

> The typical modern trade boom does not mean overproduction
> or an overestimate of the demands of the consumers or the
> needs of the community for the services of fixed capital, but an
> overestimate of the supply of capital, or of the amount of
> savings available for taking over the real capital produced.
> (1932: 649)

According to Cassel, Say's law was perfectly true: 'the total
income of the community is equal to the sum total of the
renumeration received by all those participating in the process of
production'. Anything else would be the product of 'charlatan
teachings' (1935: 66). In much the same way he rejected 'recent
monetary theory' (read Keynes) and its distinction between
investments and savings, which he seems to have perceived as
identical in essence (Cassel, 1935: 79). Once again he insisted that
the boom and following depression were in fact a function of too
little saving, not too much.

What then can be finally said in general of Cassel's theoretical
contribution to the core of economics? Perhaps some of his later
reputation as a one-dimensional and not very reflective and
innovative thinker stems from his self-esteem and habit of posing
as a great innovator – which he clearly was not, although he added
some new points and even helped to clear up some confusion,
especially on monetary issues. To some extent it may also be a
consequence of his general method and naive rationalism; his
interpretation of economic society as a mechanical apparatus in an
almost nineteenth-century sense. In this way Cassel tended to
present a picture of economic society which – in Schumpeter's
words – 'a physicist would have much less objection to ... than
most economists' (1972: 1101).

Thus it seems obvious that Cassel's role was not as innovator or
great theoretician. His strength lay rather in economic pedagogy,
in teaching, and as an inexhaustible promotor of the subject of
economics to the lay public and political society. It was typical that
Cassel should himself have stated in the Swedish preface to *The
Theory of Social Economy* that:

> It is the duty of the new science of economics to see that it uses
> its voice in order to increase its acceptability and respect among
> the 'practitioners'. Above all it must show in practice that there

is nothing as useful and practical as a good theory. (1934: 17)

That he saw himself primarily as a teacher who spoke with 'the voice of reason' seems clear from most of what he wrote. It also affected the way he presented his ideas. Hence he was always anxious that he would not be correctly understood and put much effort into being as simple and clear as possible. He was also very much influenced by political matters and practical issues of the day. Myrdal, for example, emphasized that:

Cassel's theoretical generalisations were heavily influenced by his ambition to understand and manage practical problems of the day. Hundreds of theorists have for example found it easy to demonstrate ... that Cassel's purchasing power parity theory is not generally true.... However, in a pragmatic way Cassel was right. After the first world war probably nothing was more important than to point out to politicians and bankers the need for money stabilization. And for that they needed such an approximative but in a sense very basic theory of the relationship between the price level and exchange rates. (1945)

As we saw, Cassel stated that it was an important part of the economist's task to make himself useful. Thus the question might be asked to what extent was it possible for Cassel to demonstrate the practical usefulness of economics and his own expert knowledge? Did he succeed in his ambition, and in that sense can he be said to have contributed to the growth of economics as an academic subject in Sweden from the 1930s onwards? The question is so clearly linked with the general economic history of the period, and to the achievements of economic policy in particular, that we have to broaden our perspective to assess Cassel's importance in this respect.

Economic policy in the 1930s

It seems clear that the role of the Swedish economists in public and political life increased markedly during the 1920s and 1930s. Without doubt Cassel here played a very important role. The background – especially with an emphasis on Cassel's role – can perhaps best be outlined in the following way, taking into account recent Swedish historical debate on this question.

To begin with, the manner and the means by which Sweden overcame the depression of the 1930s have of course been a hotly debated issue. However, two basic schools have emerged which emphasize different policy measures undertaken by successive governments in the 1930s. On one hand the view has been put forward that the expansionist financial policy pursued by the Social Democratic Finance Minister, Ernst Wigforss, was the main reason for Sweden's remarkable recovery in the early 1930s. In this context there has been argument about the extent to which Wigforss was influenced by Keynes or whether his policy of unbalanced budgets, increased public spending, initiation of public works, etc., had its roots in earlier social democratic or social liberal thinking (Lundberg, 1953; Landgren, 1960; Bergström, 1969; Steiger, 1971; Unga, 1976). Second – and of more interest in this context – a 'monetarist' view has also been promulgated which sees the scrapping of the gold standard in 1931 (by the liberal Minister Felix Hamrin), the stabilization of the krona, and the depreciation of the currency in the early 1930s as the main reason behind the recovery (Jonung, 1977, 1979a).

Foreign commentators in particular seem at the time to have regarded the stabilization of the krona as perhaps the main factor behind Sweden's success. Not surprisingly, of course, in his *Stabilized Money* (1935) Irving Fisher portrays Sweden as an example of successful money stabilization. In Fisher's view the monetary policy of 1931, when Sweden left the gold standard and instead of fixed exchange rates introduced a fixed internal price level, 'was the most important landmark up to this time in the history of stabilization' (1935: 408). Brinley Thomas, on the other hand – well informed on Swedish matters – presented a much more complex view and stated that the 'Swedish experiment' in reality gave no 'support to the naive gospel of price stabilization preached by Professor Fisher'. According to Thomas, the factors at work in Sweden were 'depreciation of the currency, public investment financed out of loans, the rapid revival in the demand for exports and the central bank's easy money policy' (1936: 233). However, Thomas seems also to have agreed that monetary stabilization played some role: although it could not of itself prevent a fall in production, income, and employment, it meant at least the establishment of confidence in the Swedish economy (1936: 232).

It is not the intention here to deal with these different interpretations in detail or to attempt to decide their relative importance in an objective sense. However, even if it is possible to disagree on its relative importance, it can surely be stated that the stabilization of the krona, along with depreciation and a fairly expansionist monetary policy, was one of the factors in the Swedish recovery of the 1930s. In a sense the change of monetary policy was also a landmark in the development of economic policy in Sweden. Above all it meant a breakthrough for a much more active monetary policy and especially a changed role for the central bank. It is also important in this context that price stabilization, etc., had been put forward by professional economists during the 1920s and 1930s, among them Wicksell and Cassel. Cassel also wrote the important declaration of 1931 on monetary policy which launched the policy of an internally stable krona (Jonung, 1977: 41). Thus to some extent the new policy was an application of ideas that an older generation of economists had propagated much earlier.

In the 1930s Stockholm-school economists like Lindahl, Myrdal, and Ohlin became known as promotors of a more active financial policy which they regarded as a more effective road to economic recovery than 'pure' monetary policies. However, they were heavily indebted theoretically as well as practically to the heritage of Wicksell – and Cassel. It is no coincidence that their first published works dealt mainly with monetary issues, i.e. Myrdal's *Prisbildningsproblemet och föränderligheten* (1927) and Lindahl's seminal work *Penningspolitikens mål och medel* (1930). Characteristically, also, in his early account of the Stockholm school Brinley Thomas (1936) prefers to discuss Myrdal and Lindahl in a chapter on monetary theory. He treats them as followers of a tradition leading back to Wicksell's famous 'monetary norm' first expounded in *Geldzins und Guterpreise* (1898). It was there, of course, that Wicksell first showed how it was possible to achieve a stable price level by keeping the real rate of interest at the same level as the lending rate (Thomas, 1936; Östlind, 1945: 89 ff.; Lundberg, 1953: 237 ff.; Uhr, 1960: 198 ff.; Jonung, 1977). To this recommendation he stuck throughout the First World War and into the 1920s. It must be the aim of policy-makers, Wicksell emphasized, to keep price levels stable, especially with the help of variable interest rates on loans. During the war years he also propounded a policy of gold exclusion in order to discourage any overissue of banknotes.

However, in his recommendation of a stable internal price level Wicksell was joined by other economists at the time, including Davidson (although he adhered to his own theory of price formation according to which prices should be allowed to fall at the same rate as productivity increased) (Uhr, 1975: 90 ff.; cf. Gårdlund, 1956: 299 ff.) and Cassel. Although disagreeing on many points Cassel and Wicksell at least shared the same view at bottom about monetary policy (cf. Gårdlund, 1956: 299 ff.; Heckscher, 1926). Thus, along with Wicksell, Cassel was undoubtedly the most outspoken advocate of a policy of price stabilization. In this sense Cassel, after Wicksell's death in 1926, only carried on where his older colleague had left off.

In 1931 the Swedish central bank was the first in the world to assert price stability as its central goal. Until then it had given priority to a stable exchange rate rather than a stable internal price level. Moreover it had been managed almost like a private bank and had taken scant interest in economic policy at large. During the war years the directors seem to have been more interested in selling off their large holdings of German marks than in keeping down the inflation of the krona. For this they were especially criticized by Cassel, who was undoubtedly their fiercest critic for many years (Heckscher, 1926; Lundberg, 1953: 261 ff.; Bergström, 1969: 15 ff.). Already in the first decade of the twentieth century he and Wicksell, like Davidson, had put forward suggestions for a more 'responsible' monetary policy which would aim to keep the price level as stable as possible, or at least, according to Davidson, to 'keep the monetary mechanism neutral to objective commodity value' (Uhr, 1975: 90).

Taking as his point of departure a crude quantity theory of money, Cassel as early as 1908 published a small book, *Riksbanken under krisen, 1907–1908*, in which he criticized the board of the central bank for being too passive during the acute business crisis of 1907–8 and attacked its general policies. In particular he blamed the directors for taking no measures to adjust interest rates to the 'real capital scarcity' prevailing at the time. By failing to increase interest rates in the years preceding the crisis they had let the boom get out of hand while in 1908 they had made the slump much more severe by not lowering the discount rate. Nor, according to Cassel, had the bank adjusted its note issue to the real situation and therefore money had become too scarce during the boom period (Cassel, 1908; cf. Cassel, 1940: 99 ff.). What Cassel of course was asking for was that the bank should adhere to the rules of the gold standard system and not act as if it had no responsibility for the economic situation as such or for maintaining equilibrium. In his memoirs Cassel said, 'It might seem unbelievable to a modern reader that the central bank was still in 1908 so weak ...'. The main problem was that it was run like a private bank and without 'clear and rational principles' (1940: 104).

It was during the First World War that monetary questions came to occupy Cassel's time even more than before. Increasingly he directed his attention towards the high inflation which had hit Sweden during this period, leading to severe problems, including falling real wages, adverse balance of payments, overinvestment based on too optimistic expectations, etc. (Heckscher, 1926; Östlind, 1945; Montgomery, 1946). In his work during this period Cassel strongly emphasized the role of the central bank in making the situation worse than it might have been even in wartime. At heart Cassel saw inflation as a reflection of the need to finance the war through an overissue of banknotes. Since Sweden was not a belligerent, she should not necessarily suffer inflation. It became a reality only because of the central bank's policies. Instead of taking measures to safeguard the internal value of the krona the bank had pursued a policy of stable exchange rates, which meant that the value of the currency must fall in proportion to foreign currencies (Cassel, 1917: 50 ff., 144 ff.). With low interest rates money became too cheap and investment as well as lending abroad soared – in a situation where there were shortages of goods. As the bank had no scruples about issuing new banknotes, inflation became inevitable.

As mentioned, most Swedish economists agreed with Cassel on these points, especially on the point that it had been a mistake to increase the supply of money when there was a shortage of goods. In 1918 Cassel, Davidson, Wicksell, and Brisman (a colleague of Cassel's and later Professor of Economics at Stockholm) were all appointed to different committees, on which they made proposals, among other things, for stricter regulation of lending abroad, raising the discount rate, etc. (Heckscher, 1926; Cassel, 1940: 230 ff.; Östlind, 1945: 99 ff., 113 ff.). Although it has rightly been stated that Sweden could scarcely have avoided inflation during the war, Heckscher's statement is probably accurate that an irresponsible money policy had made the situation much worse than necessary and that the central bank 'had followed no conscious policy whatsoever' (Heckscher, 1926: 21; cf. Östlind, 1945: 118 ff.).

While taking part in the various monetary conferences in Europe in the 1920s as well as making recommendations to different national governments on monetary and stabilization issues, Cassel argued in the Swedish context for a return to the gold standard (which came about in 1924) as well as for stabilization of the internal purchasing power of the krona. This was a policy Wicksell too supported. The central bank, however, was sceptical about returning to the gold standard and tying the Swedish currency to the dollar. By Cassel's own account he had to fight in the 1920s against the 'dictatorship of the central bank' and especially against its director, Victor Moll. He regarded Moll as incompetent and stubbornly attached to the old principle of 'splendid isolation' on behalf of the bank. Furthermore, in Cassel's view the inflationary policy of the war years had been pursued mainly for egoistical reasons (Cassel, 1941: 20 ff.; Péteri, 1984).

Thus during the 1920s Cassel had been heavily involved in debate about monetary problems. After 1929 he quickly came to the opinion that the crash and subsequent depression were purely monetary phenomena (1941: 235 ff.; cf. Temin, 1976; Jonung, 1979a; Saint-Etienne, 1984). Their ultimate cause was the depressive monetary policies pursued all over the Western world. It was made worse by the inflow of gold to the United States (and to a lesser extent France). According to Cassel the Federal Reserve Board had hoarded gold and not issued enough banknotes, which led to deflation – and a continued positive balance of payments in the USA. For the rest of the Western world, he concluded, this had made a slump inevitable (Cassel, 1936).

In Sweden one important consequence of the crisis had been that the country left the gold standard in September 1931, a week after Britain. In fact this step had been taken on the recommendation of Cassel, Davidson, and Heckscher. Basically, what the three economists had argued was that Sweden ought to establish a free paper currency and that the long-run aim of monetary policy should be to stabilize the internal price level (Jonung, 1979b). As already mentioned, Cassel also wrote the important monetary policy declaration which the Finance Minister, Felix Hamrin, presented to the Riksdag in 1931, corresponding closely to the recommendations so long urged by Cassel and other economists (Thomas, 1936; Jonung, 1977).

Thus it seems that the campaign waged by Cassel and others had been crowned with success. From 1931 price stability became an official object of economic policy. At last, too, the central bank seemed to have accepted its role as a national bank – something that Cassel had taken a lead in arguing for since the beginning of the century. Without doubt the rise and acceptance of the Stockholm school of economics during the 1930s must be seen also in this light. What Cassel and the others had so long been calling for seemed to have become the conventional wisdom. This implied, however indirectly, that they were equipped with a methodology which could be not only useful but necessary in a situation in which social engineering had become much more important than before. It is probably in this light that we should interpret Hugh Dalton's observation in 1935 that Swedish economists 'as a class ... have a better reputation than elsewhere' (Thomas, 1936: ix). In this respect Cassel undoubtedly played a very important role.

Chapter six

Eli F. Heckscher: the economic historian as economist

Rolf G.H. Henriksson

Eli F. Heckscher (1879–1952) is today known internationally among both economists and economic historians for contributions which are still important in their fields. His trail-blazing paper (1919), which set forth the central content of what was later called the 'Heckscher–Ohlin' model, is still a bedrock of research among economists in the theory of international trade, and his work on mercantilism (1931a) continues to be a point of departure in international historical research.

Heckscher is of course appreciated in Sweden for these contributions; however, his standing in Sweden is naturally based also on his many other scientific writings, most of which are so far available only in Swedish and are mainly contributions to economic history. There is therefore a tendency in Sweden to disregard Heckscher's accomplishment as an economic theoretician while his standing as an economic historian is high. To a Swedish economist his famous contribution to the theory of international trade stands, if not as a 'bolt from the blue', at least as a singular performance on a level Heckscher never reached in any of his other writings in economic theory. His monumental work in economic history, on the other hand, stands out not only because it was a pioneering contribution to the economic history of Sweden but also because it was a performance sustained throughout his life.

Heckscher's high standing in Sweden also rests on his non-scientific contributions. He was a prolific writer, boasting a bibliography (Heckscher, 1950b) of more than a thousand entries, where his economic theoretical and historical writings, in number at least, constitute only a minor part. Most of these writings were comments on and analyses of current problems where he applied his historical knowledge and theoretical acumen with such distinction and brilliance that he became a leading personality in the political and cultural life of his day.

Nor is his standing in Sweden a result of his intellectual

achievements alone. Economists today count him alongside David Davidson, Knut Wicksell, Gustav Cassel, and Gösta Bagge as one of the institutional founders of their discipline. The role he played for Swedish economic historians is in that respect an even more prominent one. Heckscher was the sole creator of economic history in Sweden as an institutionalized field. Its present-day organization, with autonomous departments of economic history separate both from departments of economics and from departments of history, is the result of a campaign he waged during the two last decades of his life (Hettne, 1980).

The task of presenting Heckscher as an economist obviously entails some difficulties of scope. It must, first of all, be clear from the above that even a brief chapter ought not to be confined merely to his accomplishments as an economic theoretician. It is imperative also to note his applications of economic theory in analysing the economic policy issues of his day. Furthermore an account of Heckscher as an economist must consider the entrepreneurial role he played in the institutional development of Swedish economics and the social life he was part of. To understand the power he exerted in his day it is also necessary to try and capture the major facets of his remarkable personality.

It also follows from the above that no satisfactory account of the economist Eli Heckscher can omit consideration of what Heckscher accomplished as an economic historian. He gave economic theory a central role in that field, to some extent foreshadowing the so-called New Economic History. However, his work in economic history is by no means easily reduced to that type of applied economics. It would be difficult to appraise him as an economist without exploring the particular methodological views he entertained concerning the relationships between economic theory and economic history.

This account will follow Heckscher throughout his career, mainly chronologically. The first section considers his encounter and early work with economic history and economics during his twenties, starting at the turn of the century. After that we deal with his thirties and forties, covering the decade of World War I and the 1920s. This was his main period as an economist, during which he held a Chair in economics and statistics at the Stockholm School of Economics. The following section offers a close-up of the events and circumstances of his transfer from that Chair to a personal research Chair in economic history at the age of fifty. Then we review the next two decades of his life which he devoted nearly exclusively to economic history. The final section deals with the last years of his life and briefly considers his legacy not only to economic historians but also to the economists.[1]

The emphasis throughout is on the economist but, as explained above, always against the backdrop of his major and eventually dominant efforts to adhere to his commitment to economic history and to carry out his research plans in that field.

Early work

When Heckscher entered the University of Uppsala in 1897 he was soon drawn into the circle of historians that had gathered around the magnetic father-figure of Harald Hjärne, and he made an early choice of history as a major in his licentiate degree. However, he was also early exposed to economics and made it a second elected field in his degree work, which also included political science.

At that time economics attracted particular attention among historians in Uppsala, partly owing to the notable presence of Wicksell, who, in his late forties after his fundamental theoretical contributions to economics, was studying for the law degree which university regulations required before he could be accepted to the position of *docent*.

Stimulus was also provided by the appearance in Uppsala of Sweden's first and only professional journal in economics, the *Ekonomisk Tidskrift*, edited by David Davidson. He held the Chair of economics in the Law Faculty at the university. Davidson himself, however, was apparently no great stimulus for people in his field. Heckscher appears to have been one of the very few who seriously pursued higher studies in economics under Davidson at that time.

The licentiate thesis

Heckscher's particular reason for studying economics seems to have emerged from his early choice of an economic historical topic as the subject of his licentiate thesis. In this thesis, presented in 1903 but not published until 1908, he dealt with the so-called Produktplakatet, the Swedish Navigation Act of 1724 which implemented the decree favouring Swedish vessels in the import and export of goods to and from the country (Heckscher, 1908b). The research for the thesis initiated Heckscher's two Faustian life ventures. This exploration of Swedish eighteenth-century trade policy was first of all the beginning of his great work on Swedish economic history which was to unfold as the predominant pre-occupation of the second half of his life.

Second, as a background chapter for the study of the Swedish

Navigation Act Heckscher started with a general survey of how similar trade policies had been proposed and enacted in other countries. In preparing this overview he presented it as a discussion of the workings of what Adam Smith had called the 'mercantile system'. In discovering this great theme in economic history Heckscher naturally had to absorb the extensive literature on it, which included Cunningham's and Schmoller's works. This had a decisive effect on his interest in the topic. It became his major line of research in economic history for the ensuing three decades, eventually leading to the two-volume work *Mercantilism* (1931).

Heckscher's studies in economics at Uppsala seem to have entailed only a minor absorption of economic theory. Davidson required, of course, that Heckscher should read the main classical authors, but since he himself had been introduced to the field before the neoclassical revolution began to spread he never converted to the new thinking. He was not the one to push Heckscher into contact with marginalism in any of its versions.

A methodological manifesto for economic history

The licentiate degree Heckscher earned in 1904 was an inter-mediate-level degree, which took seven years of full-time university studies. It was the year in which he turned twenty-five. Although the financial side of his further economic historical research for a while seemed somewhat uncertain Heckscher seems to have been firmly determined to go on to a doctorate in econ-omic history. The same year he wrote his first declaration or manifesto in the field of economic history, containing his well known 'plea for theory' in economic history research. It appeared in *Historisk Tidskrift* in autumn 1904 (Heckscher, 1904). It was a clear statement of the paradigm or the methodological part of the research programme he was to follow – with some revision – for the rest of his life. Stating the task, scope, and method of economic history, Heckscher had worked out a synthesis of the three disparate fields covered by his degree. The task was stated as the reconstruction of past economic life. Its wide scope covered not only the economic process and the state of the economy in the past but also the history of economic policy and the corresponding history of economic ideas.

The method he prescribed in this reconstruction was a combin-ation of the methods used in history and in economics. It combined the 'source-critical' approach in establishing facts and the theoretical approach of economics in interpreting them by applying economic theory in an essentially *a priori* or deductive way.

144

In this approach Heckscher arrived at a position which was the opposite of that of the historical school. Its main concern was to develop theory through induction based on statistical surveys and historical case studies. Like Wicksell, Heckscher rejected this inductive approach (Wicksell, 1904). However, while Wicksell rejected it because it was not a good method by which theory could be developed, Heckscher rejected it because it was not a good way to reconstruct the past.

Doctoral dissertation

While looking for a position Heckscher had a stroke of luck. He was approached by the Swedish State Railways, which were to celebrate their fiftieth anniversary by publishing a number of commemorative studies on various aspects of, and developments in, their history. This resulted in an assignment to undertake a historical study of the economic effects of the evolution of the railway system. He completed it in about two years, in 1905–6, and, somewhat revised, it was submitted as his doctoral dissertation in history at the University of Uppsala (Heckscher, 1907).

The railway study was mainly an economic statistical account, in which Heckscher did not notably heed his own plea for the use of economic theory in historical reconstruction. However, it was favourably reviewed by Wicksell (1907). Wicksell notes the great methodological difficulty involved in attempting to assess the effects of a factor in the process of economic development when nothing but what Mill called 'the method of concomitant variations' was applicable. He fully appreciated the straightforward empirical approach that Heckscher had used in answering what modern 'cliometricians' would recognize as a counterfactual question.

Fifty years before the modelling approaches of the so-called New Economic History there was, of course, no other method but to carry out a number of partial statistical explorations. Yet Heckscher still qualifies as a precursor of modern cliometrics. Although not attempting a total assessment of the significance of the railways in the economic development of the country, Heckscher's performance is nevertheless impressive, revealing considerable sophistication in dealing with many difficulties due particularly to the poor quality or even absence of data.

Heckscher under Cassel

The dissertation was evaluated high enough to earn him a position as *docent* in political economy at the University of Stockholm under Cassel. This appointment was not an entirely new position for him. He had worked as a part-time, unpaid assistant to Cassel since the autumn of 1904. Heckscher's main duty had been as head of a small library housed in a two-room office constituting the Institute of Social Science which Cassel had set up in 1903 while he was still only a *docent* at the university.

Initially there were only a small number of students. Most of the teaching was carried out by Cassel, who lectured about four hours a week. However, Heckscher too offered lectures. He seems to have been very successful in this, and attracted an audience far larger than the number of students who had signed up at the institute. Another activity at the institute was the seminars where Heckscher apparently played an important role, both as an organizer under Cassel and as a participant. Here he could draw on the experiences of his long period studying history in Uppsala. In this seminar work Heckscher probably also had the support of a younger student and 'comrade in arms', Gösta Bagge, later to become the second Professor of Economics at the University of Stockholm.

In 1907, when Heckscher was appointed *docent*, the university was endowed with a Faculty of Law, which led to the transfer of the economics Chair to the new faculty. The large number of law students enrolled in economics naturally strained the capacity of the institute. The task of catering to students of law was not particularly appealing to Heckscher with his mind set on economic history. He was also disappointed with his personal relations with Cassel. There had been a growing estrangement between them, no doubt due to purely 'chemical' factors beyond the control and goodwill of either. One of the disturbing things was Cassel's cavalier view that scientific work was its own reward even when it only entailed library attendance. They fell out when Heckscher, after two years' work, asked for financial compensation for his services to the Institute of Social Science.

Because of these developments Heckscher was probably not wholly disappointed when in 1908 he was sought out for the Chair in economics at the Stockholm School of Economics which was to be established the following year. Nor was Cassel unhappy about his departure. He actually actively endorsed the transfer through a letter of recommendation.

The Stockholm School of Economics, 1909–29

Heckscher's appointment to the Chair in economics at the Stockholm School of Economics was only to a very minor degree a result of Cassel easing him out. A personal relationship that was probably more important in the selection of Heckscher was his ties with the newly elected dean at the school, Carl Hallendorff, an historian from the Uppsala group to which Heckscher also belonged.

However, Heckscher had already made a name for himself. He had attracted particular attention on the board and in leading circles behind the new school through two public appearances in the beginning of 1908 (Heckscher, 1908c). The first was a widely publicized and acclaimed open debate challenging the socialists in February 1908. Here Heckscher revealed his considerable powers as an opponent of Marxist dogma. He stood up for economic science in combating the socialists and he convinced a broad public that he spoke as an authority.

His second appearance took place in the more exclusive circles of top-ranking bureaucrats and leading men in commercial and banking life who met regularly at the Swedish Economic Society. Early in 1908 Heckscher was the main speaker on the issue of how to set up a high-level public service degree composed of economics, statistics, political science, and other related fields. He presented a proposal (Heckscher, 1908a) worked out in a minor committee on which he had himself served as the secretary. No doubt Heckscher this time convinced key people in government as well as in academic circles and society at large that he was destined for a leading role also in the politics of academic reform.

Heckscher's main credentials, however, were of course academic. He had rapidly earned a reputation as a dynamic and engaging lecturer but his scientific research in economic history was also increasingly recognized. He had furthermore already made himself known as an accomplished writer not only on topics of history but also on current affairs. Yet he had not written anything on economic theory that would establish his competence as an economist by present-day criteria. However, such a performance was not then a prerequisite for a professorial Chair in economics. The science was not identified solely with theoretical economics. Both Wicksell and Cassel, for example, made a distinction between theoretical and practical economics. Cassel even recognized a third sub-field, generally referred to as descriptive economics, which included economic history.

Heckscher's Chair in economics was actually a Chair in economics and statistics, following the way in which economics chairs had been set up at business schools in other countries. The addition of statistics of course suited Heckscher. He had, as noted earlier, done much statistical research in his work on the railway study. He had also served for two years as secretary of the so-called Statistical Committee which carried out a major revision of official statistics and worked out reform proposals: Heckscher had played an important role as both a driving and a shaping force.

Conception of his 'real task'

Heckscher had succeeded in adhering to the economic-historical line under Cassel, even though it was his main period of initiation into economics. He had given a series of lectures on Swedish economic history. However, it was probably not until he joined the Stockholm School of Economics that he conceived of his *egentliga uppgift* (his 'real task') as to write an economic history of Sweden.

His specific plans evolved slowly. He turned thirty the year he was appointed to the Chair at the Stockholm School of Economics but he was close on thirty-five before the right moment appeared for an open 'declaration of intent'. We find such statements in his letters around the outbreak of World War I.

As Heckscher mentally committed himself to accomplishing the task of writing the economic history of Sweden he saw it as a life's work that could not be started immediately. There were some 'minor' uncompleted research tasks that had to be taken care of first. One such piece of unfinished business was the research on mercantilism which he had begun during his Uppsala period. This and other things would require a substantial amount of time, he thought. He planned to have cleared his desk for his 'real task' at about the time he turned forty.

Heckscher did not make much headway in his economic-historical research during the war. His teaching responsibilities at the Stockholm School of Economics were no sinecure. Although they were mainly of an introductory nature they were extensive. He also branched out and taught subjects outside his formal assignment such as business organization and economic geography. Furthermore, his lectures were indeed only formally elementary: he offered his students an introduction to his own research and studies, where he soon reached the frontiers of knowledge. However, his extensive teaching duties at the school were not the sole nor even the major explanation of why Heckscher was held up in his plans and research in economic history. Before the war he had become engaged in a number of extra-curricular activities, which increased and intensified as the war began.

Among these activities the most important was the co-editorship with his friend, the aforementioned Gösta Bagge, of the conservative periodical *Svensk Tidskrift*. This position, which he held throughout the war, put an increasing burden on Heckscher,

148

as Bagge frequently had to turn his attention to other important duties.

Of all the assignments Heckscher took on during the war the most demanding and time-consuming was his work for the War Planning Commission. He was its secretary for the first two years but was then promoted to become its executive head. In this position he had his first important experience of being close to the highest policy-makers in the country and was a confidant of Prime Minister Hjalmar Hammarskjöld for a number of years.

The fruits of wartime research

Heckscher was close on forty when the war ended and he had to recognize that his research plans in economic history of five years earlier had not got off the ground. He had done no work on the economic history of Sweden. Not even his attempt to complete *Mercantilism* had come very far. His main achievement in this respect was a study of *The Continental System* (1918a). The research for this study had begun in 1916. It was apparently an offshoot of a study he had published the year before on the Swedish war economy (Heckscher, 1915). The Napoleonic Wars offered a historical parallel with the World War.

Historical parallels were thenceforth Heckscher's favourite theme in his historical writings. However, the study is also interesting from a methodological point of view. It was a very conscious effort on his part to apply economic theory and an economic methodology to an historical study. In his study of the railways ten years earlier economic policy was not as prominent. Furthermore the use of theory to throw light on a question about the 'total' effects of something had not been attempted in the dissertation, where only the immediate, direct effects of the railways had been traced by means of a straightforward statistical covariation technique. Heckscher stressed this aspect of the study so much that he gave it the subtitle 'An *economic* interpretation' (emphasis added). Another notable study from this period where the counterfactual question is posed very clearly was the substantially extended edition of *Produktplakatet,* his study of the Swedish Navigation Act of 1724. It appeared in an anthology which also included a paper where he elaborated his new methodological stance (Heckscher, 1922).

With *The Continental System* Heckscher entered a phase in his approach to economic history where the use of economic theory was much more pronounced than before. However, it was a phase that was to pass, yielding towards the close of the 1920s to more modest claims in this respect.

While he undertook no other major studies in economic history during the war, he was responsible for several minor publications in economics. Some of them were assembled in a volume entitled *Svenska produktionsproblem* (Swedish Production Problems) (1918b). Most concerned policy issues with at least a tinge of history, but all were also applications of theory under the rubric 'Nothing is as practical as a good theory'. The volume was reviewed by Wicksell (1919) who pointed to various deficiencies, one of the most serious being Heckscher's treatment of questions of income distribution, one of Wicksell's constant concerns.

This review induced Heckscher to pen a reply. It appeared in the *Festschrift* for Davidson, a special issue of *Ekonomisk Tidskrift* (Heckscher, 1919). Here Heckscher used a model framework derived essentially from Wicksell's own theoretical writings to clarify the way in which foreign trade influenced the distribution of income. This was the paper in which Heckscher presented his famous statement of the so-called Heckscher–Ohlin model.

Having written the paper, he never really returned to the subject and seems to have more or less forgotten about it. The main reason is probably that he was off on a more Marshallian dynamic line of thought where he had abandoned the neoclassical trade model assumptions of fixed factor endowments and a given production function. There are also in Heckscher (1918b) anticipations of Salter's vintage approach in dealing with technical change.

The sabbatical

As the end of the war approached it opened an opportunity for Heckscher to disengage from a number of commitments that had occupied him during the conflict. He was able to give up his work for *Svensk Tidskrift* and for the War Commission. However, the most important step was that he was able to arrange sabbatical leave from the Stockholm School of Economics for the academic year 1918–19. Wisely he even moved away from Stockholm to ensure that he would not be interrupted in the decisive critical effort he considered he now had to devote to his economic-historical work in order to rescue his great plan.

Although the Stockholm School of Economics, the state of the Swedish economy, the Spanish flu epidemic, and other events of that year meant that he was not totally undisturbed, he was able to accomplish much of what he had planned. He devoted a major and probably decisive research effort to his work on mercantilism, enabling him to pursue most of the remaining work as a perpetual but secondary preoccupation during the 1920s. He also used his sabbatical year to work out a first major design for his project in

Swedish economic history. Although he does not appear to have made much progress on the archival work, it, too, was a decisive research effort.

The 1920s

Returning from his sabbatical retreat, Heckscher was again preoccupied with teaching and administration at the Stockholm School of Economics. He also took on new extracurricular assignments, most important of which was his work for the Ministry of Trade on the Tariff and Treaty Commission. Although he wrote only a minor part of the commission's report it bore the imprint of his views more than anyone else's (Heckscher, 1924b). Some members of the commission who disagreed with him therefore enlisted Cassel to write a minority report. Although Cassel was himself a liberal, he opposed Heckscher's views, which constituted a very strong plea for free trade.

The war had turned Heckscher's political views from moderate conservative to strongly liberal. This was probably why he resigned from the co-editorship of *Svensk Tidskrift*. He made a noted but somewhat belated declaration of his (new) liberal standpoints in a widely circulated pamphlet, *Gammal och ny ekonomisk liberalism* (Old and New Economic Liberalism 1921a). He was also enlisted by the liberal Swedish daily, *Dagens Nyheter* (the *Daily News*), which remained the principal outlet for his political views for the rest of his life.

One major undertaking which retarded his research on his main historical projects was his contributions to and editorial work on the volume on Sweden in the Carnegie Foundation series of studies of the history of the war. Heckscher wrote a major survey chapter and then an additional chapter on Sweden's monetary policy. Having completed a Swedish edition (1926), he put much hard work into revising it for the English edition (1930b).

This contribution was not solely a work of history. Heckscher incorporated in it his views on the theoretical issues of monetary policy. He commented in particular on Wicksell's and Davidson's contributions, and of course on Cassel's writings, which he criticized severely. However, the study did not meet with much recognition. When he bemoaned the fact to Keynes, Keynes retorted that publishing one's theoretical ideas in a study like that was 'to invite neglect'.

In retrospect it may be noted that Heckscher's ideas concerning monetary economics were not particularly innovative. He was a proponent of the modified 'quantity theory' developed by Wicksell, as were almost all Swedish economists, including even Cassel.

Heckscher's most noted articulation of his Wicksellian position appeared in a paper (1921b) on 'the effect of a too low rate of discount' which was published in the commemorative issue of *Ekonomisk Tidskrift* in honour of Knut Wicksell. However, it is noteworthy that later in life he renounced the position he adopted in that paper.

Heckscher's stance on policy issues is, however, quite interesting. He made several notable contributions to an intense debate among Swedish economists. These discussions had taken place both in the dailies and in periodicals but of course particularly in the *Ekonomisk Tidskrift.*

The Political Economy Club

The so-called Political Economy Club played a major part in Heckscher's life at this time (Henriksson, 1989). It was founded by Heckscher in 1917 partly in order to provide Wicksell with a forum. Wicksell had retired from his professorial Chair at Lund in 1916 and had returned to his native Stockholm. The club was a select scientific elite. It was very active and met regularly during the academic year to listen to talks by its members or by some invited speakers. Debates generally took place after each talk.

Wicksell was of course the centre of the club's activities until he died in 1926. Yet Heckscher should be recognized as not only the founder but also in many ways the dynamo of its life. The meetings were often held at his own house and he used to engage vigorously in the debates. Only one person was missing from these gatherings: Cassel attended the club only in the early years. The strained personal relations between Heckscher and Cassel were not the only reason: there were similar difficulties between Cassel and Wicksell.

With this club arrangement Heckscher may be said to have set the scene for an important 'oral tradition' in the transfer of Wicksellian ideas to the 'Stockholm school'. This tradition became particularly marked in monetary theory. Club members could absorb Wicksell's mounting doubts about his own model. The discussion sometimes ended with participants trying to persuade Wicksell that his model was right after all. Young economists, such as Ohlin, were probably much influenced by these discussions, which gave rise to ideas that were later developed further among the Stockholm group.

Heckscher continued to play an important role in the club even after Wicksell's death. In the late 1920s the club became the centre for the encounter between the elder economists led by Heckscher and the younger men, led by Myrdal. The efforts of the young to floor Heckscher on theoretical issues undoubtedly helped to shape their theoretical views. However, Heckscher too was learning.

They were all working in or reacting to the Wicksellian capital theory tradition, which, while emphasizing the Böhm-Bawerkian time dimension of capital accumulation, was also open to the contributions of Fisher and particularly of Knight. They all recognized the dynamic aspect as a primary one and, although they differed, they did so from a common base. Heckscher himself had developed an original approach for dealing with fixed capital in the process of technical change and economic fluctuations, and he presented his results to the club in 1922. They were later published in a paper on 'Intermittent fria nyttigheter' ('Intermittently free goods') in *Ekonomisk Tidskrift* (Heckscher, 1924a). Here he focused on the 'free good' character of fixed capital equipment, which in its early life incurred nil or very low current or operating costs, on a par with goods supplied by nature.

Heckscher's approach was in some degree an anticipation of that of Myrdal and Lindahl, who emphasized the role of expectations and uncertainty in capital theory. The main disagreements between Heckscher and the younger members of the club before the days of the Stockholm school were less theoretical but more ideological. Here Heckscher offered steadfast resistance. Although he absorbed the new message about the inadequacy of *laissez-faire* policy stances in the face of increasing unemployment he never surrendered to the new ideology, which, in his view, gave priority to decreasing unemployment at the cost of price-level stability.

The new economic theories

Heckscher withdrew from the club after the Depression mainly because of his growing commitment to economic history. He left the club in the hands of Ohlin, who made it a battleground for the internal feuds of the Stockholm school. From this point on, Heckscher took no part in the 'transactions'. However, he continued his political-ideological criticism of the Stockholm school. After the year of the *General Theory* (1936), his critique also naturally included Keynes. Heckscher rejected the budgetary policy proposals of Keynes and the Stockholm school primarily because of the danger that an expansionary fiscal policy would have a political ratchet effect.

However, he was also critical of the new economic theories. He was never convinced of the stability of the consumption function and actually shared many of the negative views of Keynes held by the Stockholm school. But he was also opposed to the sequential analysis of the Stockholm school for methodological reasons.

According to his own capital theoretic approach, it was not the right way to deal with issues of dynamics. Heckscher's theoretical views gave him a different outlook on the unemployment problem.

The spectacular switch

In terms of output the 1920s (i.e. Heckscher's forties) were again for him a decade mainly as an economist rather than as an economic historian. Perhaps Heckscher did more hard work on his 'real task', the economic history of Sweden, than meets the eye in terms of published reports, but little appeared in print. However, important preparatory work was being done at least in the early 1920s. This is proved by the fact that in autumn 1922 he gave a major series of lectures at the University of Stockholm on the economic history of Sweden. A few publications further reveal that he had begun research on the sixteenth century. But the second half of the 1920s seems to have meant a new delay in this historical research.

Approaching his fiftieth birthday in 1929, Heckscher seems to have reached a 'now or never' state of mind, and he pursued his historical research much more resolutely than before. He was able finally to clear the slate by completing *Mercantilism* (1931a) and within a few years German and English translations had been published.

In the same year Heckscher also published a survey of the industrial revolution. It was essentially a summary of the lectures which he had given on the topic during the years since his period under Cassel. This work, entitled *Industrialismen* (1931b), was thereafter revised several times and became a standard text in Swedish universities well into the 1970s.

However, he realized that he would not be able to complete his work on the economic history of Sweden unless he cut down on all the other commitments that intruded on his time. He was able to accomplish this through the initiative of setting up the Economic History Institute under the joint auspices of the Stockholm School of Economics and the University of Stockholm. How he did it and how events unfolded to render him also a personal research Chair in economic history is a story in itself, full of dramatic turns of event and too complex to be related here. Only the peak incidents can be noted.

The deanship incident

When all the preparations for the Economic History Institute had been made and cleared Dean Hallendorff unexpectedly died in spring 1929. The arrangements were completely disrupted, owing to Heckscher's suddenly revealed aspirations to succeed Hallendorff as dean of the school. But he was denied the position. It was probably the biggest shock and taste of defeat in his life. However, a solution was worked out whereby Heckscher would be offered a personal research Chair in economic history at the Economic History Institute, with no teaching obligations but notably with the right to teach if he wanted to.

The question of why he was denied the deanship is an interesting one. Heckscher had put his heart and all his extraordinary energy into his duties at the Stockholm School of Economics. He established the high standards reached in economics teaching at the school. He was an engaging lecturer and a dynamic seminar leader. For all this he was, of course, generally respected and admired. However, his pedagogic zeal was not always admirable in the eyes of students and colleagues. Heckscher could be sarcastic, when the 'revealed intelligence' of a student did not measure up to what could be expected of a student at the college. Passing an oral examination could be an ordeal. He did not hesitate to 'rescue' intellectually underprivileged students from spending precious time and money on studies they were not suited for, and he readily told them what he thought about their prospects: for example, Mr So-and-so might make a good bishop, a Prime Minister or something of the sort, but he would never become a good economist.

The statistical record indicates that only 0·5 per cent of the students passed with distinction. Those who obtained the highest grade from Heckscher became legendary figures in the school. In economic circles at large it was a more highly regarded achievement than becoming a professor, chief executive, or high government official. Two of the students in this very select group were to become leading names in the so-called Stockholm school. One was Bertil Ohlin, the other Alf Johansson.

Heckscher later admitted that the decision not to give him the position was a good turn. The pain he felt was soon replaced by gratitude at having been spared the responsibility and thus enabled him to devote so much more time to historical research.

Remaining ties with the Stockholm School of Economics

Heckscher did not entirely avoid further duties at the Stockholm School of Economics. The new dean who had been elected in his stead fell victim to a severe illness and Heckscher was called in to serve as acting dean. Nor was he entirely relieved of teaching duties. His engagement in these activities led to another dramatic event at the school with even more severe consequences than the deanship incident.

As his successor Heckscher had chosen his most successful and outstanding student, Bertil Ohlin. Ohlin more than once took extended leave of absence to attend to his research and extra-curricular commitments, and was off for some time with a chronic eye affliction. Heckscher was generally called in to take over Ohlin's duties. He grew increasingly annoyed at Ohlin's seeming lack of a sense of responsibility for the teaching obligations of his Chair. Eventually there was a severe personal breach between them on account of it. Besides the resentment he felt, he was also hostile to Ohlin's Keynesian stance on economic policy and perhaps also to the dynamic approach in economic theory of the Stockholm school, where Ohlin held a central position.

The Economic History Institute, 1929–49

As the effects of the stormy incidents receded, Heckscher soon became absorbed by his research into the economic history of Sweden, turning to it with renewed vigour and determination. Within little more than five years two large volumes appeared covering the sixteenth and seventeenth centuries (Heckscher, 1935–6). He then went on with work on the eighteenth century. However, the results were now slower to appear. He published a number of papers in the late 1930s revealing that he had made a good start but his work on the eighteenth century was not completed until 1949. Three years before he died two monumental volumes testifying to his labours appeared (Heckscher, 1950a).

The main reason why his study of the eighteenth century took so long was basically the sheer magnitude and difficulty of the task. But other obstacles contributed to the delay. Despite his resolve he could not avoid all involvement with his former field of economics. He could not completely divert his attention from issues of economic policy as well as more general public issues in which he used to engage.

Remaining ties with economics

Having left his teaching post in economics, Heckscher gradually lost contact with theoretical discussion in that field. He was able to follow certain lines of development, and having, as noted earlier, something of a theoretical approach of his own, he retained some capacity to criticize developments in macroeconomics. He admitted that most other advances, especially the more technical ones such as econometrics, left him behind. Not surprisingly, he viewed the move towards greater technicality with scepticism. He never relinquished the right to pass methodological judgement on what he saw. In matters of practical application of theory he retained supreme confidence in his judgement.

His detachment from economic teaching and research meant, of course, that he was also losing contact with important institutional developments. He remained on the faculty board at the Stockholm School of Economics, which gave him an 'inspector's' overview of how the teaching was conducted, but he was no longer in the forefront as younger men took over. Furthermore much of the institutional context of economic research moved out of his reach when in 1931 he left the Political Economy Club and Ohlin took over. However, he preserved at least some supervisory powers over economic research, as he was appointed member of several boards which distributed funds for that purpose.

His admission to the Royal Swedish Academy of Science, where he had to collaborate with Cassel and Davidson, was an important appointment. His energetic hand on the reins tightened them abruptly, and grant recipients were surprised to find stern deadlines imposed. In some cases Heckscher even asked for repayment. One of those who felt the new regime most severely was Lindahl, who was very frustrated by Heckscher's request that he should fulfil the conditions of the grant he had been given.

A similar position was that of executive secretary to the Palme Fund, which not only funded individual research projects but supported student societies and other institutions in the field (Henriksson, 1979).

Ekonomisk Tidskrift

One of the institutions that received financial support from sources partially under Heckscher's control was the *Ekonomisk Tidskrift*. After the death of Wicksell the journal had begun to lose its position as a key vehicle of scientific discourse among Swedish economists. Publication lagged more than a year behind schedule during the Depression years. This was intolerable to Heckscher, but for a long time there was little he could do because Davidson refused to accept assistance. He was financially dependent on his position as editor. However, by mobilizing his considerable diplomatic and persuasive powers Heckscher was at last able to negotiate the transfer of the journal to a new editorial board in 1938. Through his influence with various financial sources Heckscher had been able to organize a buy-out. Upon the receipt of a sizeable honorarium, Davidson, then eighty-four, retired from the editorship which he had held entirely on his own for four decades.

Continued economic policy activity

What was apparently most difficult for Heckscher was to refrain from becoming involved in economic policy. The Depression years exacted a fair number of official engagements from him. The currency crises in the autumn of 1931 in fact entailed quite intensive participation in the shaping of policy as an analyst and adviser. Heckscher was one of the first to react to the drastic worsening of the Swedish gold and exchange reserve position in late summer that year (Henriksson, 1987b, 1989). On his own initiative he had set up an *ad hoc* emergency group to analyse the rapid shifts in Swedish foreign exchange reserves during the weeks prior to the final decision to suspend the gold standard. During the dramatic week when the suspension decision was taken he also performed an important advisory role to Ivar Rooth, the head of the central bank. He thereafter influenced the monetary policies of the bank for quite some time.

The 1931 currency crisis was probably the moment in Heckscher's life when his influence on economic policy was the greatest. He responded to the need to take quick action in the swiftly changing economic crisis when politicians were overtaken by events. As an 'explosive' personality with a great capacity for work and an ability to grasp the essentials of a critical situation faster than most, he rose to the occasion almost to the point of taking over the leadership. However, his influence waned as the situation calmed down and politicians and others caught up with events. His impetuous and powerful personality did not fit in with the slower processes of bureaucratic political machinery. He had actually realized as much very early in life.

Committee work almost relinquished

Heckscher's determination not to become too involved in the policy issues raised by developments in the economy seems to have prevailed in at least one important respect. From the 1930s onward he resisted all extensive engagements in government or parliamentary committee work. This was evident during the Depression, when the unemployment issue stood at the forefront.

Heckscher had a lively interest in this question. He had analysed the problem both as an aspect of his capital theory approach and as a policy issue. His analyses had been developed particularly in the 1926 Unemployment Committee, dealing with the question of unemployment insurance (Heckscher, 1928). One of the results of that committee was the realization that it was necessary to find out much more about the phenomenon of unemployment empirically and theoretically and that fuller investigation was needed before any proposal about unemployment insurance could be put forward.

Hence on Heckscher's suggestions such an investigation was initiated with the setting up of the 1927 Unemployment Commission. It was to present a large number of published reports, the last in 1935, and a much larger number of internal reports which were never published (Uhr, 1977).

Fortunately for Heckscher's historical research, he avoided direct involvement in the work of the commission. Instead his old friend Gösta Bagge was appointed as a key member representing what economic theory and the older members of the economic profession had to say on the issue. However, when Bagge's report appeared Heckscher was a keen observer and commentator. He also influenced the commission's later work. Heckscher had good contacts with the secretary of the commission, Dag Hammarskjöld, who had been a member of the above-mentioned *ad hoc* group Heckscher had assembled to deal with the currency crisis.

Shaping and stirring public opinion

Heckscher's efforts from the 1930s to withdraw from all economic policy issues included not only the direct involvement mentioned above but also the less direct involvement of attempting to influence public opinion. It was not easy for him to hold back on this front. He was a prolific writer and public speaker who took considerable pride in his ability to deliver public addresses and 'messages to the nation'. From his earliest years he had stood up in defence of truth and justice, and had taken a swing at trade unions as well as at employers when they acted against the public interest. This habit of speaking his mind had made powerful interest groups wary of him and he paid the price by incurring some very personal antipathies in such circles.

In 1918, in an 'eyeball-to-eyeball' confrontation, he made an enemy of Marcus Wallenberg, the head of the Wallenberg family, by supporting a paper in *Svensk Tidskrift* which criticized the fact that representatives of high finance held government posts, giving them an opportunity to exploit their position to further their own interests. The author of the paper was Gösta Bagge, but Heckscher refused to reveal his name because it was published as a leading article for which the editors were jointly responsible (Henriksson, 1979, 1988).

His public protests sometimes even turned into demonstrations which could transcend the boundaries of symbolic action. Thus in 1905 he could be seen participating in street cleaning operations in

Stockholm in his role as organizer of a 'civil guard' campaign to break a scavenger union strike.

His forceful writings stirred not only public opinion but sometimes 'public action' too. He attracted nationwide attention in 1920 when he admonished the public in a newspaper article to present their notes at the central bank for redemption in gold. Inflation had reduced the worth of bank notes below their official gold value. Heckscher thought the public demand for gold would force the central bank to raise the rate of interest and thus counter inflation (Henriksson, 1979, 1989).

Although there was no real panic the next day, a long queue of people formed outside the bank to exchange their notes for gold. Little gold was exchanged before a parliamentary decree released the bank from its obligation to redeem the notes in gold but, soon after, the bank raised the rate of interest. This victory was a public triumph for Heckscher.

So was a radio speech he made after the Kreuger crash in 1932. In a convincing analysis he showed how little significance the crash had for the real state of the economy, thus helping to calm a rather hysterical public opinion.

Ideological warrior

It seems as though Heckscher was fairly successful in controlling his impetuous temper after he reached fifty, at least he thought so himself. He was less successful in resisting the force of his inbuilt moral imperatives when ideological issues arose. He held a great record as an effective critic of the totalitarian left. His early battles with Marxists before and during World War I have already been mentioned. He went on to help suppress whatever revolutionary fervour remained. However, he was perhaps more active still in criticizing the tendency towards central planning which he thought he detected even on the democratic left in the inter-war and post-World War II periods.

He had a great influence on many leading Social Democrats, reducing the tendency for that party to resort to price controls and the regulation of economic life. His influence was probably strongest in the 1920s but it continued even thereafter. In his criticism from the 1930s onward he often had to take on his younger colleagues Gunnar Myrdal and Alf Johansson, who were at that time lining up with the political left.

The open contest with Myrdal over economic policy began in the autumn of 1931. An attempt by the economists in the Political Economy Club to issue a joint statement on economic policy failed because Heckscher could not accept the draft written by Myrdal.

Heckscher instead wrote a statement of his own and had it published in record time (Heckscher, 1931c). However, Myrdal felt overrun by Heckscher and in response to the latter's publication had his own statement (Myrdal, 1931) rushed to the printer so fast the public probably did not know which was published first. Myrdal then remained the favourite target for Heckscher's criticism of the economic policies which emerged after the Social Democrats had assumed office in 1932. He fought Myrdal not only on the new Keynesian policies but also on the social policy proposals of the Social Democrats, where Myrdal was a leading ideologue (Heckscher, 1934). A major exchange occurred in the press in 1934 when Myrdal made a big splash in the media over the population question (Myrdal and Myrdal, 1934). In this inflamed tournament both contestants were assisted by their wives.

Heckscher's public criticism of Johansson came later. It was part of Heckscher's last campaign on a matter of economic policy. Johansson was once, as mentioned, an outstanding student of Heckscher's at the Stockholm School of Economics. In the 1920s he had been close to the Heckscher family and, renting a room with them, was treated almost as a son. He greatly disappointed Heckscher in the early 1930s particularly by failing to complete a dissertation in economic history which Heckscher had exhorted him to do. Instead he wrote a dissertation in economics in line with the Stockholm school theory (Johansson, 1934) of which Heckscher severely disapproved. Together with Myrdal, he joined the Social Democratic ranks.

Heckscher, however, staged no 'public burial' of Johansson until after the Second World War, when Johansson became the Social Democratic front man for a socialistic building and housing policy. Ailing and overworked completing his *Economic History of Sweden*, Heckscher proved that he was still able to 'blow his top'. Yet, although a 'renegade', Johansson never lost out with Heckscher the way Ohlin did.

The Swedish Economic Society

Heckscher's contributions to policy debate since the early 1920s had appeared mainly in the daily press. However, some of his most interesting and important outbursts found expression in the exclusive Swedish Economic Society mentioned earlier. Before he died he held an historical record as the most active participant in its public meetings.

Some of Heckscher's great contests with Myrdal and other members of the Stockholm school took place in this society. Naturally the issues taken up were the narrower economic policy questions, addressed to the more sophisticated expertise of the members. However, Heckscher had the ability to raise the level of discussion to the heights of general principles.

The Nordic Economic Meetings and the language question

The Swedish Economic Society was a partner in an unofficial effort at Nordic co-operation, the main activity of which was the so-called Nordic Meetings, which took place about every third or fourth year between the wars. Finland was to host a meeting for the first time in 1929. However, the Finns wanted Finnish to be one of the conference languages, a proposal which was rejected by the other countries, and no meeting took place.

Heckscher played a central role in this deferral of the Finns, who did not host a meeting until 1938, some years after Heckscher had resigned as chairman of the Swedish Economic Society.

Heckscher's main objection to Finnish as one of the official conference languages was of course a practical one. However, he also had an aversion to Finnish nationalism, many manifestations of which seemed to him absurd. Its most extreme embodiment, the so-called Lappo movement, reminded him of German Nazism, which he hated perhaps more than anyone else in the Nordic countries (Henriksson, 1979).

As a Jew he realized what Nazism stood for, but the breadth and depth of his historical vision made him sceptical even of the Zionist movement. He was a strong opponent of the establishment of an independent Jewish State in Palestine. He foresaw what a precarious position such a State would be in and what a threat it would create to world peace. In his declaration on the issue he said that he was above all an internationalist and citizen of the world, a Swede second. He held his Jewish identity only in third place.

Overwork

Heckscher always worked at an exhausting pace. The hardest work, as mentioned earlier, was the slow ploughing through and processing of the eighteenth-century records to gather as much quantitative information as possible. Pushing on relentlessly with that work, relinquishing few of his social and other obligations such as maintaining a voluminous correspondence, allowing himself no vacation, no weekends off, and only a minimum amount of daily rest, Heckscher overstrained himself. Turning sixty he began to have spells of dizziness and momentary blackouts; he suffered a severe collapse early in 1942.

After this he had a brief period of rest but upon returning to work was even more anxious to catch up on lost time. Only after another collapse in 1943 did he heed the warnings; but now he had had a more serious setback, and could never again return to his old pace of work. Yet he continued heroically throughout the remainder of the war and after it pushed on for another five years in the same way. When in 1949 the work was finally completed, two major volumes were published – every page a piece of pioneering work accomplished by overwhelming effort (Heckscher, 1950a).

A martyrdom? Not entirely. Heckscher was a work addict. He had generally enjoyed sustained work. His collapses were partly due to physical exhaustion, because he could barely refrain from work even to eat or sleep. Being early a legend, he enjoyed the reputation of an extremely early riser. Nothing pleased him more than to be caught working before six o'clock in the morning.

It is evident that Heckscher had no realistic notion of his physical state. In his earlier years one of his legendary habits was to take brisk walks on the coldest days of the Stockholm winter without hat or coat. He thought that high-speed 'locomotion' would generate sufficient heat within to prevent any chilling of the body's 'exterior extensions'. He nourished the idea that he was destined for a long life.

Economic history as an independent field

According to general rules in Sweden at the time the retirement age for a professor was sixty-five. Heckscher passed that milestone in 1944 but was able to arrange a five-year extension and did not really retire from his Chair until 1949. Of course the extra time was needed to complete his work, but it was also needed in order to arrange for his successor. It should be recalled that Heckscher's was a personal research Chair with no teaching obligations.

The story of how Heckscher proceeded to establish the discipline of economic history is a long and complex one (Hettne, 1980). Suffice it to record here that in 1937 he quite successfully initiated an economic history seminar and organized lectures, etc., i.e. almost everything that was required for a Department of Economic History.

A decade later a sizeable number of licentiate and even some doctoral degrees had been granted, guaranteeing the continued existence of the discipline in Stockholm. Heckscher picked Ernst Söderlund as his successor from among this group. Finally, teaching positions were created in economic history in all Swedish universities. Here, too, Heckscher was generally successful in seeing men of his own preference appointed.

The Royal Swedish Academy of Sciences

During these years when he was pushing for the establishment of economic history as an autonomous subject, separate from economics and history, Heckscher seems to have cultivated good contacts with the youngest generation of economists emerging at that time, particularly the group that took over the *Ekonomisk Tidskrift* from Davidson. However, he also kept up some contact with the older generation through his position in the Royal Swedish Academy of Sciences. As noted earlier, here he had to collaborate with both Cassel and Davidson, among others. They got on well, it appears. They even agreed on granting Keynes the highest honorary distinction the academy could offer in economics before the days of the Nobel Prize in that field. This award, the Söderström Gold Medal, was, however, given to Keynes not in recognition of his *General Theory* but for his earlier work, especially in international finance.

However, on Davidson's death Cassel and Heckscher began to have disagreements about who should fill the empty Chair. Cassel favoured Myrdal, and Heckscher favoured Lindahl. No one could force the other to yield an inch. In consequence the majority of the members of the committee settled for a compromise. Gösta Bagge was elected, but Heckscher apparently voted against him. In the Bagge literary remains there is a little congratulation note where Heckscher tells Bagge that he had never before been so happy at having been outvoted.

The Heckscher legacy

Heckscher stayed on as the leader of the Economic History Seminar in Stockholm until 1949, when he finally stepped down to let Ernst Söderlund take over. He reached seventy the same year and was at last finished with his study of eighteenth-century economic history in Sweden. However, to Heckscher his work thus far on the economic history of Sweden was still incomplete. Perhaps following his original plan, he now wanted to write a sequel covering the nineteenth century. There were many other items on his agenda; one was a survey of Western pre-industrial economic history, starting with antiquity but with the focus on the Middle Ages. He also had plans to write an assessment of the state of economics as it had developed under the new Keynesian regime.

He never made much of a start on any of these projects. When he died at the end of 1952 he left such new beginnings and other unfinished work as a bequest to Swedish economic historians.

However, it was by no means the whole bequest. The Heckscherian legacy also had an important methodological dimension, with a special message for economists.

Methodological message to the economists

The economist could assist in the construction of a picture of the past. But it was important to understand the limitations of theory in this respect. It could not, according to Heckscher, be used in the reconstruction of a series of events in time as an endogenous economic process. It was helpful only in sorting out how events and facts were interrelated in a situation of 'stationary' or 'steadystate' recurrences.

The task of explaining the dynamic causal relationships between events in an unfolding historical process required sociological or other non-economic theories, if indeed any theory could ever do that. Economic theory in particular could not, being inherently static. Economic theory, then, was applicable to historical interpretations and reconstructions only as an inquiry into how the basic economic functions of a system were resolved institutionally. It offered no explanation of how those institutions changed. To explain this was the task of economic historians, and they had to do it without much help from economists.

In rejecting all evolutionary deterministic theories of history Heckscher also rejected all so-called 'economic' interpretations, such as the one associated mainly with the Marxist school. He would undoubtedly have been more open to the so-called New Economic History. However, it is not likely that he would have endorsed its later neo-institutionalist tendencies.

Heckscher's farewell to the economists

Heckscher made his farewell appearance at the Swedish Economic Society in 1952, on the occasion of its seventy-fifth anniversary. He gave a lecture to an audience that listened intently and was deeply moved, realizing that it might be the last time Heckscher had the strength for such a performance. He surveyed – without a draft or supporting notes, in exactly the time allotted to him – the history of Swedish economic discussion (Heckscher, 1953a).

The theme of his lecture was the one he had developed in *Mercantilism* (Heckscher, 1931a). He argued that economic thought and conceptions of the state of the economy had evolved more or less independently of the actual state and evolution of the economy. His thesis was that ideas developed independently of the material base. It was a denial or reversal of the Marxian thesis which claimed the opposite.

Heckscher's own physical appearance at the time was living proof of the – at least temporary or Pyrrhic – victory of spirit over matter. As related earlier, his life was one of austere intellectual labour, and he had literally sacrificed his health to a regime of work that can only be called brutal to his well-being. He articulated his addiction to work by referring to leisure as a state of painful 'vegetation' which he avoided by always having some 'knitting' at hand. His greatest pleasure in life was work; not, of course, any type of work, but work that was morally sanctified. 'Non propter vitam vivendi perdere causas' was the Latin sentence in his *ex libris*: the only life worth living is the moral life.

Science and politics

Heckscher's career was devoted to two fields, economics and economic history, and it may be said that there was a 'creative tension' between the two which to a considerable degree explains his great productivity and outstanding performance in both.

However, his life revolved mainly round the Weberian polar axis, between science and politics. It appears that he arrived at a better synthesis of opposites here than with the two sciences. Heckscher retained his political-ideological premise in his scientific work, while there was always a scientific dimension in his political-ideological stance. This harmonic unity of opposites was clearly expressed when he rose to the defence of academic freedom – as he did frequently. He protested against the attempts from private as well as public quarters to influence teaching and research. Heckscher was no defender of ivory-tower research, however. On the contrary, he wanted teaching and research to serve the interests of society, but he held the view that what was best for society in this respect was best judged by the grass roots in the ecclesiastical hierarchy. While science had to be protected from undue political influence, the scientist had not only the right but the obligation to take a stand on political issues. Heckscher thought that scientific knowledge could shape political disagreements so that the objective facts could be agreed upon and the real clash could be about values.

This view had practical implications. The scientist ought to preserve his academic independence and should not sell his labours to interest groups or even public agencies. The absorption of scientists into government and the corporate world was a danger, Heckscher believed. Economists in such positions might monopolize all influence by shifting public debate, and keep academic scientists from information and advisory roles. The result would be harm not only to the interests of society but to science itself, which needed to keep in touch with the real issues outside academia.

Note

1 In Sweden there are a considerable number of writings and commentaries on Heckscher and his work, but so far no major biographical account has appeared. There are also a few English-language accounts. The most authoritative, but unfortunately all too brief, is the obituary by Söderlund (1953). A perceptive but equally brief assessment is Ohlin (1968). More recent and more extensive presentations have been given by Uhr, most recently in the *New Palgrave* (1987); his 1979 paper contains a useful bibliography. Still the best account of Heckscher is Montgomery (1953). Montgomery pays more attention to Heckscher as an economic historian than does the present brief presentation which, for example, omits any reference to Heckscher's best seller of 1941 which was a preliminary and a short version of *Sveriges Ekonomiska Historia* (1935–6; 1950a). It has been translated into English by Göran Ohhn, with a foreword by Alexander Gerschenkron (Heckscher 1954).

Chapter seven

The Stockholm school and the development of dynamic method

Björn Hansson

Introduction

Interest among English-speaking economists in the development of economic theory in Sweden during the period after Wicksell's death was heightened by Ohlin's article in the *Economic Journal* (1937) where the existence of a 'Stockholm school' was mentioned for the first time. After most of the major works belonging to the Stockholm school had been translated in the late 1930s a consensus arose on the nature of the contribution of the Stockholm school, which has been aptly described by Winch: 'Swedish economists, building on a Wicksellian foundation, developed a body of analysis which is separate from, but parallel to, that associated with the name of Keynes' (1966: 170).

However, studies of the Stockholm school have concentrated on the macroeconomic theory and economic policy of the school and its relation to the Keynesian revolution. In fact the relationship between the works of Keynes and those of the Swedes has been obscured by the concentration on these issues. The aim of this chapter is to analyse the Swedish school from a different angle: the development of dynamic method which is considered the *differentia* of the Stockholm school.

For the first ten years, 1927–37, one can speak of a school in the strict sense, since there was an interrelated development of a common theme among its members with very little influence from outside Sweden. After Lundberg's *Studies in the Theory of Economic Expansion* (1937) it is evident that the works to quite a considerable extent took into consideration what had been done abroad as far as the dynamic method was concerned.

Propositions and hypotheses

The first proposition is the existence of a distinctive school, the 'Stockholm school', between 1927 and 1937; the school included

168

Myrdal, Lindahl, Lundberg, Hammarskjöld, Johansson, and Ohlin. A 'school' is here defined as an interrelated development of a common theme among its members. The common theme which defines the school is the explicit attention to and development of dynamic method. 'Dynamic methods' refer to notions such as temporary equilibrium, disequilibrium sequence analysis, etc. The discussion of dynamic method is not a methodological discussion in any philosophical sense, like, for example, the advantages of a deductive and an inductive method.

Their development of dynamic method is an original contribution. Although some elements of their work were discovered independently elsewhere, e.g. intertemporal equilibrium, there is no evidence that the Swedes, once the school had started to develop, were influenced in any significant way by other contemporary economists. The only comprehensive analysis of non-Swedish attempts to develop dynamic methods is to be found in Lundberg's dissertation of 1937, and his comments are mainly of a critical nature.

The second proposition is that after the founding years the interest in dynamic methods persisted in Sweden (although Bent Hansen is of Danish extraction). Hence the analysis of the development after 1937 is still concentrated on the contributions which concern the dynamic method, but these contributions are no longer isolated from foreign influences. It is therefore not possible to speak of a school in the same strict sense as for the initial period. The analysis includes contributions which relate to the ideas of the Stockholm school, but the works must contain something original from the point of view of dynamic method. This chapter looks only at a sequel to the Stockholm school from this limited perspective and it is not at all excluded that the school may have had an important influence in other areas. Both Ohlin and Lundberg, for example, wrote long tracts on economic policy which were obviously based on the old approach.

From our main propositions follow three secondary hypotheses. (1) It is commonly thought that the 'Swedishness' of the Stockholm school arose from their presumed Swedish ancestry: Wicksell and Cassel (cf. the quotation from Winch above). While this may be true of macrotheoretical issues, it is shown in this chapter that their influence on the distinctive feature of the Stockholm school, the dynamic method, is negligible. It is even the case that the cumulative process as developed by Wicksell was not the immediate starting point of the Stockholm school. (2) The nature of the relation of the Stockholm school to the Keynesian revolution, i.e. the principle of effective demand, has been a long-standing puzzle in the history of economic thought. We hold that there was no influence either way as far as the principle of effective demand is concerned. The question to be answered is rather whether the Stockholm school developed the principle of effective demand independently. It is shown in this chapter that although the Swedish analysis contains elements which are similar to the principle of effective demand, e.g. the rate of interest does not always equilibrate saving and investment, this principle is always used within a disequilibrium framework. (3) There is a widespread view among some historians of thought that the Stockholm school more or less suffered a sudden death after the Keynesian revolution. Our exposition of the second proposition shows that this is not a well founded view.

An outline of the chapter

This section is intended to give a schematic outline of the chapter and to provide the reader with an overview of the main steps in the development of dynamic methods. Before the actual analysis of the school I give a brief biographical sketch of the main members. The section on the analytical framework gives a classification of the different dynamic methods developed by the Swedes. It is possible to divide the period under consideration into four separate stages, where each stage is characterized by a specific dynamic method.

The first stage is represented by Myrdal's dissertation (1927), which shows how anticipations of an uncertain future are an independent part of the data which is supposed to determine a 'long-run' equilibrium position. The crucial factor for the further development of the Stockholm school was the treatment of anticipations and uncertainty as part and parcel of the theoretical core, and their placement on the same level as preferences, technical conditions, and given resources.

Lindahl's construction of intertemporal equilibrium (1929) constitutes the second stage. This concept grew out of a critique of comparative statics as a tool for handling dynamic problems, and its aim was to describe the traverse between two equilibrium positions. It seems that one of the reasons why Lindahl gave up his method was that he realized that it could not tackle imperfect foresight in a meaningful way. This weakness provided the rationale for the next stage, temporary equilibrium, whose object was to analyse cumulative processes. However, intertemporal equilibrium as well as temporary equilibrium are examples of an equilibrium approach. Both Lundberg and Myrdal criticized this approach, since it could not explain the link between consecutive periods. Thus Lindahl was not really portraying a process over time.

The last stage culminates in 1937 with Lundberg's disequilibrium sequence analysis, but this notion is preceded by a long and protracted development. Myrdal was again the one who pushed the development in the right direction with the publication of *Monetary Equilibrium* (1932), which laid the foundation for the disequilibrium approach with the notions of *ex ante* and *ex post.* Hammarskjöld's idea of windfall profit as a link between periods gave the first, though incomplete, formal sketch of a sequence analysis. It will be shown that Ohlin's work in 1932-4 made a direct contribution not to the development of dynamic method but to macroeconomic theory. Lindahl finally came back on the scene with two works in late 1934 and early 1935 respectively. Building on Myrdal and Hammarskjöld, he formulated the first proper algebraic expression of a single-period analysis, which exhibits how incongruent *ex ante* plans lead to determinate *ex post* results. Lindahl also discussed the problems in building a sequence analysis which assumes that there is equilibrium in each period. In this respect Lundberg went beyond Lindahl, since his sequence analysis builds on disequilibrium within the separate periods. However, Lundberg's analysis is still an equilibrium process, since it presupposes routine behaviour, which is represented by the assumption of constant response functions over the process.

After the analysis of the Stockholm school proper follows the development of dynamic method when the influence from abroad is apparent. This part begins with Lindahl's reaction to Keynes's *General Theory*, which shows that his critique of Keynes's static method is based on his own period analysis. The next section analyses the notion of quasi-equilibrium which was developed by Bent Hansen in his dissertation of 1951. Recursive and independent models are notions that were used by Ragnar Bentzel and Bent Hansen in their analysis of recursive systems. The last development of dynamic method is Faxén's idea of strategic equilibrium, which is an application of sequence analysis to oligopolistic conditions. We finally attempt an assessment of the contribution of the Stockholm school to economic theory.

Biographical sketches

The short biographies which follow are intended only to give an outline of the professional career of the most important members of the Stockholm school.

Dag Hjalmar Agne Carl Hammarskjöld (1905-61) came from a family with a long and distinguished tradition as civil servants; his father, Hjalmar Hammarskjöld, was Prime Minister (1914-17). Hammarskjöld took his Ph.D. in 1933 at the University of

Stockholm (Hammarskjöld, 1933) and then taught economics at Stockholm (1933–6). He later rose rapidly as a civil servant in the Ministry of Finance (1936–45) and as chairman of the Board of Governors of the Bank of Sweden (1941–8). Before being elected Secretary General of the United Nations (1953–61) Hammarskjöld had been chairman of Sweden's delegation to the General Assembly. He died in an air crash in Zambia and in 1961 was posthumously awarded the Nobel Peace Prize.

Erik Filip Lundberg (1907–87) took his Ph.D. at Stockholm in 1937 (Lundberg, 1937). In the same year he became the first director of the Government Economic Research Institute, the Konjunkturinstitutet (1937–55). He was also Professor of Economics at the University of Stockholm (1946–65) and later at the Stockholm School of Economics (1965–70).

Erik Robert Lindahl (1891–1960) obtained his Ph.D. at Lund and the title was *Die Gerechtigkeit der Besteuerung*. The dissertation was to a great extent based on Wicksellian ideas, and Lindahl had contacts with Wicksell but was not a student of his. In 1932 Lindahl became professor in political economy at the Göteborg School of Economics and Business Administration, and he had later on Chairs at Lund and finally Uppsala. Lindahl was the only member of the Stockholm school who had a purely academic career.

Gunnar Carl Myrdal (1898–1987) was Gustav Cassel's favourite pupil. He took his Ph.D. in Stockholm in 1924 (Myrdal, 1927). Myrdal had a distinguished career in academia, international organizations, and politics. He was professor at the University of Stockholm (1933–50, 1960–7); General Secretary of the United Nations Economic Commission for Europe (1947–57); a Social Democratic Party member of parliament (1935–8, 1944–7) and served as Minister of Trade and Commerce (1945–7). Myrdal was prolific on economic theory and policy in the 1920s and 1930s but after that period he hardly wrote anything on those subjects. However, in the 1950s his interest turned to development problems, which culminated in the three-volume work *Asian Drama* (1968). In 1974 Myrdal shared the Nobel Prize for Economics with Friedrich von Hayek.

Bertil Gotthard Ohlin (1899–1979) took his undergraduate degree at Lund but then left for Stockholm. His Ph.D. was on international trade, *Handelns Teori* (*Theory of Trade*, 1924), with Gustav Cassel as the supervisor. In 1925 he obtained a Chair in Copenhagen, then he succeeded Eli Heckscher as professor at the Stockholm School of Economics (1929–65). From the 1940s his activities as a politician took up most of his time; he was leader of the Liberal Party (1944–67) and a member of the Cabinet (1944–5). In 1977 Ohlin and James Meade received the Nobel Prize in Economics for their contributions to the theory of international trade.

Analytical framework

This section attempts to construct a classification which is fine enough to distinguish between the different dynamic 'methods' developed by the Swedes. The classification builds on an analytical framework which draws on the ideas of the Stockholm school. This is most obvious from the fact that our examination of different dynamic methods uses 'sequence analysis' as the point of reference.

Sequence analysis as the point of reference

The different dynamic methods are considered here as separate analytical terms, which are applied to a theoretical explanation of dynamic processes. The latter term is here used only in a descriptive sense to denote ongoing changes in prices and/or quantities. It is in this descriptive sense that we shall speak of cumulative processes, a term which includes the cumulative process associated with the name of Wicksell but is not restricted to his version.

Our classification is based on the concepts developed by the Stockholm school for the purpose of sequence analysis. Sequence analysis, which is just one type of dynamic method, is related to that particular economic object where the timing of economic events is of paramount importance. A sequence signifies here a recursive model where the outcome at the end of period t, i.e. at the point of time $t+1$, is completely determined by the actions undertaken during the period, and the actions in their turn are derived from the plans formed at the beginning of the period, i.e. at the point of time t. Furthermore the results of period t are linked in a determinate way, fixed at the point of time t, with the plans for period $t+1$. Hence, following this procedure, it is possible to determine the outcome for some periods ahead in time. The irreversibility of the sequence analysis refers to the fact that a unilateral dependence over time is used in this analysis in contrast to a mutual interdependence (Svennilson, 1938: 4). However, even sequence analysis belongs to the class of equilibrium processes, since routine behaviour is represented by constant expectation functions. It is therefore a variant of our general notion of equilibrium: 'It is the invariance of behaviour [routine behaviour] over a certain period which gives significance to the concept of equilibrium' (Hahn, 1952: 803).

The central idea in Swedish sequence analysis is the notion that a plan epitomizes economic behaviour, which means that all economic actions are directed towards fulfilment of plans based on expectations of the future and that the plans will be revised in the light of the actual results. This provides for the discontinuous character of sequence analysis, in the sense that the continuous flow of actions, in realizations of plans made at an earlier stage, will sooner or later be interrupted because of incongruent plans, which will lead to the formation of new plans. Hence the crucial role of expectations, since they represent the connection between preceding events and the new plans.

Sequence analysis may be said to be made up of two separate parts, namely, the single-period analysis and the continuation analysis. The first is concerned with an analysis of what is going to happen during a single period, showing how certain *ex ante* plans at the beginning of the period lead to determinate *ex post* results at the end of it. The second part analyses the effects of the *ex post* results in the current period on the plans for the subsequent period. It is obvious that both parts are necessary components in a sequence analysis, since the latter is supposed to determine a process spanning several consecutive periods. However, it is interesting to notice that Myrdal (1939) laid the foundation for the single-period analysis without mentioning continuation analysis.

The static method

The static method, which refers to a stationary society – the type of society represented roughly by an unchanged supply of factors of production (Wicksell, 1934: 7; cf. 207) – deals in particular with the conditions of static equilibrium: 'the static aspect of the problem of equilibrium, i.e. the conditions necessary for the maintenance, or the periodic renewal, of a stationary state of economic relations' (ibid.: 105). It may seem odd to include the static method among methods which are supposed to explain dynamic processes. But the static method is related to a particular dynamic process, namely where prices, relative prices as well as the general price level, do not change while quantities may change in a regular manner as in the case of proportional growth.

Examples of this method are stationary state and proportional growth models. Stationary state could be interpreted in sequential terms, as saying that the *ex post* results of the previous period lead to such *ex ante* plans for the current period that the same *ex post* result will be determined for this latter period, and so on (Lindahl,

1954: 27), which means that the process has a reiterated character. In the proportional growth model several quantities are changing from period to period, but the change between two consecutive periods is uniform and equal to the common growth rate. Hence the *ex post* values for the former period will initiate such plans for the current period that the plans are uniformly expanded by the given growth rate, and the *ex post* results of the current period will then stand in the same relation to the *ex ante* plans of the subsequent period, and so on.

The proper use of the static method has generally been for comparisons between stationary states or proportional growth paths, where the actual transition between two equilibrium situations is not taken into account (ibid.: 152), i.e. comparative statics (Robbins, 1935: 101; Lindahl, 1942: 46).

One may say that plans and the realization of plans play no significant role in the static method, in the sense that the determination of the equilibrium conditions for the stationary state is achieved without any reference to plans. That is to say, it is implicitly assumed that plans and expectations are fulfilled, which is the same as saying that anticipations are not part of the data determining the equilibrium. In this method plans and expectations have instead been reserved for the analysis of disturbances around the equilibrium level, like the difference between the normal rate and the money rate in the cumulative process. But this analysis is completely separate from the determination of the equilibrium level itself. Hence 'dynamics', even as recently as the 1920s, referred basically to a qualitative account of how disturbances might arise and work themselves out through credit cycles or trade cycles. Dynamics therefore came to belong to that part of economics related to the so-called 'Theory of Money and Credit', intended as vol. II of 'Economic Principles', while vol. I was 'Value Theory', which analysed the determination of conditions of equilibrium.

Intertemporal equilibrium

The next method is intertemporal equilibrium, involving a sequence of periods which are different from one another. The outcomes of all periods are determined at the beginning of the process by the existence of complete future markets or perfect foresight. This method does not really portray a sequential process, since it makes no sense to say that the plans and outcome of the current period determine what is going to happen in the subsequent period, as the relative price exchange ratios and quantities are determined simultaneously for all periods before the process starts (Lindahl, 1954: 27). Hahn (1973: 16) seems for similar reasons to consider this equilibrium notion to reflect an inessential sequence.

What is the object of this dynamic method? Hayek (1941: 21) holds that the notion may 'help to explain real events', since it tells whether the plans of the different individuals are mutually consistent and may therefore be realized, or 'whether the present situation carries the seed of inevitable disappointment to some, which will make it necessary for them to change their plans' (ibid.: 22, 28; cf. Hahn, 1973: 7).

Temporary equilibrium

Temporary equilibrium determines the complete outcome only for a single period, and it is implied that equilibrium rules only for the current period. However, anticipations for the first period as well as for the forthcoming periods are included in the current plans, owing to the existence of capital goods. But there is no necessity that equilibrium will exist for the forthcoming periods, in the sense that the plans for those periods, made up at the beginning of the current period, will be consistent. Hence the temporary character of this equilibrium.

A continuation theory can be constructed from this method by assuming a string of periods all in temporary equilibrium. However, such an analysis is almost identical to intertemporal equilibrium, since it must be assumed that the plans are from the outset consistent over all periods. That amounts to the existence of perfect foresight, since no prereconciliatory procedure, except for the first period, is supposed to take place. Owing to the lack of proper continuation theory, this method has instead fallen back on a procedure which is akin to comparative statics, which in this case means a comparison of alternative temporary equilibria (Hicks, 1965: 65). This method is therefore most suitable for analysing an economy which has few, if any, futures markets, i.e. a spot economy (Hicks, 1946: 136; 1956: 144–5). Temporary equilibrium has been used to analyse Marshall's fish market, which is Hicks's flex-price example (Hicks, 1965: 52–4), while Lindahl's case is more akin to Marshall's short-period equilibrium, since both production and sales are in equilibrium.

Disequilibrium methods

Finally we have the disequilibrium method, which can analyse single periods out of equilibrium and which signifies that the *ex ante* plans are not consistent but the *ex post* values are equal. This method implies two different versions of continuation theory:

equilibrium and disequilibrium sequence analysis. However, the equilibrium sequence analysis, although it starts out from a single-period analysis which allows for disequilibrium, i.e. *ex ante* plans must not be consistent, as a continuation theory assumes that each period is in equilibrium. Hence this version is akin to intertemporal equilibrium (Hicks, 1946: 132). In the disequilibrium sequence analysis the process is represented by an array of single periods which are not in equilibrium, but there are constant rules of conduct which determine how the *ex post* results from one period influence the *ex ante* plans for the subsequent period. These rules guarantee that the disequilibrium sequence analysis is still an equilibrium process. But it is only a question of the maintenance of equilibrium for a short period of time, since the rules, at least in the case of expectational disequilibrium sequence analysis, cannot be assumed to stay constant for more than a few periods.

This method is the first with a meaningful sequential character to it in the sense that both cause and effect are involved. Hence it is no longer a case of 'mutual interdependence between all phenomena but a unilateral dependence of the succeeding event on the preceding one' (Hayek, 1941: 17). According to Hayek, the latter is the hallmark of real processes in historical time, i.e. what he calls 'a chain in historical sequences' (ibid.). We have thereby come as 'close' to the 'real world' as is possible in a theoretical analysis. Consequently this method takes as its object a 'real world' where the sequential relations between the formation of plans, actions, and the revisions of plans are of ultimate importance, which of course is a characteristic of plans and actions in real time.

Disequilibrium sequence analysis can finally be divided into a mechanical and an expectational varity. Mechanical disequilibrium sequence analysis has a mechanical character in the sense that expectations are formed endogenously, i.e. there is a strict and stable relation between expectation and earlier events, and there is no case for revising the expectations due to the accumulated information. This varity is akin to models in mathematical dynamics, that is to say, systems of difference equations, where the analysis considers the existence, uniqueness, and stability of the model. Expectational disequilibrium sequence analysis, on the other hand, allows for the fact that unfulfilled plans generate information which after a while will lead to a revision of expectations.

The method of expectations

> The 'method of expectations' is the introduction of expectations as explicit variables in a formal 'equilibrium' theory. (Hicks, 1973: 143 n. 11)

This section analyses Myrdal (1927), where he includes anticipations as part of the data, which are the immediate or primary determinants of price. We denote this idea, following Hicks, as 'the method of expectation'.

Myrdal's dynamic method

In this section we first look at the particular sense in which Cassel's version of dynamic method could be considered as a springboard for Myrdal's own construction. It is then shown how Myrdal developed ideas, which he probably got from Knight, to construct a dynamic norm which is different from the static norm.

For Cassel the dynamic problem was to gauge the influence of the outside factors on the immediate determinants, and after that the pricing problem is solved in the traditional way, namely as a system of simultaneous equations. It is crucial to notice that Myrdal related his own purpose to this idea by arguing that it is necessary to include, in the theoretical determination of an equilibrium, 'the anticipated consequences of "the effect of certain movements and changes" as more or less probable possibilities' (1927: 7 n. 4). Hence the direct spur to the dissertation seems to have come from what Myrdal considered to be Cassel's incomplete handling of the dynamic problem, since the latter had left out the problem of including the 'continual changeability' which for Cassel was the main complication in the dynamic case (Cassel, 1929: 18–19). The origin of Myrdal's construction may therefore be characterized as a theoretical attack on a problem which was mentioned by Cassel but to which he provided no solution.

The influence on Myrdal's particular way of attacking the dynamic problem has probably emanated from Knight, since in his *Risk, Uncertainty and Profit* (1921) a future change could be foreseen and so included in the economic calculations (Myrdal, 1927: 9; Knight, 1921: 35 ff.). Myrdal's difference from the latter is that Knight did not try to establish a long-run equilibrium which included anticipations as a datum (ibid.: 108). However, this was done by Marshall, and in his *Principles of Economics* (1920) risk was a part of the supplementary costs (ibid.: 25 n. 4; Marshall, 1920: 337, 400), but Myrdal criticized Marshall for assuming that the anticipations were fulfilled in the long run and the factor of change thus disappeared (ibid.: 26; Marshall, 1920: 360, 424 n. 1). The point in Myrdal's method is to put the 'anticipated consequences', or, as he usually calls them, the 'factor of change', alongside the other immediate determinants. The factor of change implies that 'the changes whether they are completely foreseen or not exert their effects on the economic process long before they actually take place' (ibid.: 9; cf. 7). Such effects are possible because 'price formation takes place in human minds' (ibid.: 8; cf. 33). The main reason for bothering about such effects is the fact that 'means of production are permanently bound, so they could not be moved or adapted at all, or only with costs, to new circumstances of price formation' (ibid.: 17).

The dynamic norm

The new determinant specific to the dynamic theory, i.e. the anticipation of changes, implies that the dynamic norm will be different from the static norm:

> a normal price formation within a dynamic situation is not the price formation, which under similar circumstances would exist, if it could be anticipated with certainty that no new primary changes will from now on take place.... Or, expressed in a different way: the equilibrium price of the dynamic economy is by no means the price which sooner or later would be realized if the reality became static. (ibid.: 7)

This is a criticism of J. B. Clark's dictum that 'the static forces set the standards, and the dynamic forces produce the variations' (as quoted and italicized by Myrdal from Clark, 1899: 31; ibid.: 9). According to Myrdal, who in his turn referred to Knight, Clark did not realize that 'the disturbances that progress causes' (as quoted by Myrdal from Clark, 1899: 29, ibid.) could be incorporated as anticipations into a theory which would still satisfy the conception of a long-run normal. Hence Myrdal's opinion on dynamic theory came out clearly in his reformulation of Clark's saying: 'static and dynamic forces set the standard, and the dynamic forces produce the variations' (ibid.: 10).

This idea that the equilibrium price of the dynamic theory has an existence of its own, and that it is different from the static equilibrium price, must be considered the most important proposition in Myrdal (1927). Static theory is therefore not a proper approximation to reality, since the static prices are in general not the normal in relation to the actual prices. Nevertheless, it cannot be thrown overboard, because it still forms 'a theoretical framework for a more sophisticated and deeper analysis' (Myrdal, 1927: 27; cf. 6), in the sense that it functions as a starting point for dynamic theory. In this context Myrdal naturally opted for Cassel's version: 'Professor Cassel's static theory of price formation has been the genetical and logical starting point from which I have tried to study the dynamic problem' (ibid.: vii).

Objective and subjective risk

The notion of objective risk is 'objective' in the sense that all irrational factors of the entrepreneur's mind have no effects on his estimation of risk (Myrdal, 1927: 98). However, the important point is that the risk is objective, or logical (Keynes's term), in relation to the individual entrepreneur's given experience (Keynes, 1921: 4).

The anticipations are now 'correct', thus ensuring that a dynamic equilibrium exists in the sense that if entrepreneurs always acted according to the objective risk, their anticipations 'would on the average be realized according to the law of great numbers, if the single entrepreneur had a sufficient number of opportunities to test them (Myrdal, 1927: 96). This connection between anticipations and outcome is 'obviously regulated by the law of large numbers' (ibid.: 118). Thus the connection does not hold for a single act of a single entrepreneur, but only for the aggregate anticipations and the aggregate results of several entrepreneurs over a period of time (ibid.).

If we now abandon the assumption of objective risk, which means that we take at face value the fact that the estimation of risk is 'completely subjective and specific to the person and for the moment of time' (ibid.: 102), then an 'irrational' moment or 'emotive' factors can 'be expected to have a directly disruptive inference on the intellectual, i.e. a non-emotional process' (ibid.: 183). The inclusion of 'emotive' factors has the effect that 'we annihilate the connection broadly speaking between the anticipations and the results' (ibid.). However, this new factor is not part of the *ex ante* investment calculation, since it is 'concealed during the process and it first emerges in the entrepreneurial results' (ibid.: 188).

Myrdal devoted only a couple of pages to this issue and he gave no hint whatsoever as to its consequences for his equilibrium construction. But this new factor seems to overthrow the whole idea of a long-run equilibrium. It implies that the anticipations are not congruent, which means, in turn, that endogenous changes have to ensue, so that a long-run equilibrium cannot exist.

Myrdal's critique of Marshall for assuming that the anticipations were fulfilled in the long run appears, therefore, to be misplaced. In fact this is a proof of the inherent difficulty of including antici- pations among the data for determining a long-run equilibrium. Myrdal does not seem to have been aware of the problem, and this probably shows that his dynamic method is inconsistent as long as it is supposed to determine a long-run equilibrium.

These complications due to the non-existence of objective risk may be one of the reasons why Myrdal (1939) never mentions long-period norms.

The development of intertemporal and temporary equilibrium

The subject of this section is Lindahl's development of inter- temporal and temporary equilibrium in 'The place of capital in the theory of price' (1929) and 'The rate of interest and the price level' (1930) respectively, where both methods are examples of an equilibrium approach (Lindahl, 1939). It shows that intertemporal equilibrium grew out of Lindahl's critique of comparative statics, while temporary equilibrium evolved in a response to certain weaknesses in intertemporal equilibrium. Temporary equilibrium was applied to the analysis of the equilibrating mechanism between saving and investment during a cumulative process. This mechan- ism looks akin to Keynes's principle of effective demand, but this is only true for the cumulative process itself.

The aim of Lindahl's analysis

Lindahl's aim was to analyse the effects on the price formation 'due to the existence of a time factor in production' (1939: III, 271), and he showed how capital goods can be included in the determination of a static equilibrium (ibid.: 301–9). But at the same time he was critical of this solution, since the static method postulates an equilibrium situation with determinate relative prices as already existing, which implies for the relative prices 'that the values in question are a necessary condition for the continuation of the stationary state, but not that they are a necessary consequence of certain given functions concerning supply, demand, etc.' (ibid.: 310–11). The point is that the dynamic process itself may in- fluence the new stationary state. Lindahl's object now is to find a method of analysing this type of dynamic process.

However, he showed first that comparative statics was not a suitable method for handling the problem, since comparative statics 'solves' the problem by actually circumventing it in the following way: 'a comparison between independent stationary

181

communities which are conceived to exist in isolation and which, in respect of the factors determining prices, show both resemblances to and differences from each other' (ibid.: 311).

It is this flaw in the comparative static method which explains why Lindahl developed intertemporal equilibrium as a formal attack on the dynamic problem. Hence intertemporal equilibrium emerges from the shortcomings of comparative statics in handling some of the problems related to the inclusion of the time factor in production, and was not directly aimed at solving any particular macrotheoretical problems (ibid.: 271).

In 'The rate of interest' Lindahl starts from the following Wicksellian idea: 'changes not only of relative prices but of the price level as a whole can be explained in terms of the relationship between the demand for and supply of goods' (1939: II, 245). Thus the starting point is not 'the mechanism of payment' but 'the general theory of price formation'. But the latter was developed mainly to determine relative prices for a static equilibrium, i.e. a reiterated process, while Lindahl was interested in explaining a dynamic process of change in the price level, i.e. where the immediate price determinants are changing. Therefore he had to find a method which could fulfil the following requirements:

> it must include the treatment not only of relative prices in each period, but also of the price relations between the different periods included in the dynamic process. . . . In this manner it should be possible to arrive at a theory of change in the value of money. (ibid.: 141–2)

We will show below that Lindahl developed the notion of temporary equilibrium to solve this problem. On the other hand Wicksell's analysis of price changes during the cumulative process is purely descriptive, and he did not construct a particular method to attack the problem.

The dynamic method

This section contains an analysis of intertemporal and temporary equilibrium. The two methods have an important common feature in that they both follow an equilibrium approach.

The equilibrium approach. The equilibrium approach has the following characteristic:

> an explanation of a price situation as a state of equilibrium, in the sense that there exists a *mutual* connection between supply and demand on the one hand and actual prices on the other,

and that, therefore, at existing prices exchange can continue until full satisfaction has been attained. (Lindahl, 1939: III, 339 n.)

Hence, for each individual and commodity, the anticipated price achieves a balance of demand and supply and all expectations are therefore fulfilled, though it has to be added that the assumption of perfect foresight for the period ahead is 'a necessary condition for an explanation of a price situation as a state of equilibrium' (ibid.)

According to Lindahl, the principal difference between dynamic and stationary conditions is that in the former case the factor determining the process, i.e. the immediate price determinants, is constantly changing (ibid.: 318). Instead of having reiteration of the same state, as in the stationary case, we have a system which is moving, which implies that the price determinants as well as the prices are changing. Hence the actors must in each period anticipate not only what is happening in the immediately following period but also what is supposed to take place in forthcoming periods.

The dynamic conditions imply in reality continuous changes in data, but for analytical reasons Lindahl assumed the following:

We imagine it [the dynamic process] to be subdivided into periods of time so short that the factors *directly* affecting prices, and therefore also the prices themselves, can be regarded as *unchanged in each period*. All such changes are therefore assumed to take place at the transition points between periods. The development of prices can then be expressed as a series of successive price situations. (Lindahl, 1939: II, 158)

It is important to note that the idea of dividing the dynamic process into periods was introduced to the Stockholm school as an heuristic device, and Lindahl gave no reason why it might be realistic as well as merely helpful to use it. The latter argument was first taken up by Hammarskjöld and then developed by Lindahl, when he put forward the concept of plan as the fundamental notion in the analysis of economic behaviour.

The notion of intertemporal equilibrium. In 'The place of capital' (1929) Lindahl's aim is to analyse dynamic conditions, that is, the primary factors are 'assumed to undergo change from one period to another. In this way a movement arises in the system' (Lindahl, 1939: III, 330). However, the mathematical formulation shows that there is no 'movement' in any meaningful sense (ibid.: 321–30), since it is a simultaneous determination of all prices, quantities, and interest rates for all periods under the assumption of equilibrium within each period, i.e. an intertemporal equilibrium. Consequently Lindahl states that 'all prices in all the periods included in the dynamic process thus become linked together [simultaneous determination] in a uniform system' (ibid.: 330).

If intertemporal equilibrium is applied to imperfect foresight the agents no longer consider their anticipations as certain, and it is assumed 'that people's ideas regarding the future have the character of probability judgments' (ibid.: 348). Hence risk and the valuation of risk are part and parcel of the problem.

It is not evident whether Lindahl considered the equilibrium method as being valid for imperfect foresight, since he stated that his comments on this case were outside the scope of the paper. At the same time, it seems likely that he thought that imperfect foresight could also be solved by his system of equations for intertemporal equilibrium, but the system had now to be made up of separate functions for each individual (ibid.: 349). However, this would still be true only for Myrdal's case with objective risk, since the anticipations would not otherwise be correct and a solution would thus not exist. It would seem that Lindahl later became aware of the fact that his formulations were valid only for objective risk, and that that was one of his reasons for giving up the intertemporal approach. Hence temporary equilibrium grew out of the shortcomings of intertemporal equilibrium as a method of attacking dynamic problems.

The notion of temporary equilibrium. In 'The rate of interest' (1930) Lindahl started from the following assumption:

> that in each of these short periods of time individuals have full knowledge of the prices ruling during the period, and that they allow their actions concerning supply and demand to be determined by these prices, which are therefore consistent with their actions. The price situations will then be equilibrium states in the sense that there will be equality between supply and demand during the period. The formation of prices can in this way be expressed in a system of equations for each period. (Lindahl, 1939: II, 159)

He later described this idea as analysing 'the dynamic process as a series of temporary equilibrium situations, by which I tried to get a connection with the ordinary static theory' (letter to Frisch, 23 October 1934; cf. Hicks, 1946: 127), which shows that 'temporary equilibrium' was developed before the publication of Hicks's *Value and Capital.*

The application of the notion of temporary equilibrium implies a restriction in the range of the demand and supply functions, since they are directly related only to the expected prices of the current period, i.e. the initial period under analysis. In intertemporal equilibrium, on the other hand, these functions are explicitly dependent on expected prices from both current and future periods, since anticipations relating to the later periods 'affect people's actions and thus constitute a determining factor in the price situation of the initial period' (ibid.: 339).

If we compare Lindahl's construction of temporary equilibrium with Hicks's formulation, the only obvious difference seems to be that Hicks assumes that 'the plans which are adopted in any given week depend not only upon current prices but also upon planners' expectations of future prices' (Hicks, 1946: 124). However, Lindahl must also include anticipations for several periods, since the equation to determine the general price level is an aggregate of the individuals' equations where the net income is a subjective and forward-looking concept. For the case of imperfect foresight this concept of income implies that the anticipations of events belonging to future periods will differ. But this will not affect the compatibility of the plans for the first period. However, in later periods certain individuals must necessarily be dissatisfied with their plans for the first period, since they will have realized that their income expectations for later periods, which influenced the subjective income for the first period, were wrong.

The Swedish critique of the equilibrium approach. Lundberg's criticism relates explicitly only to intertemporal equilibrium in 'The place of capital' but his critique is also valid for temporary equilibrium. He mainly attacked the idea that 'the accommodations to the disturbances are outside the system; they are not explained, but are looked upon as data for the next equilibrium period. The successive sequence of equilibrium points is not explained' (Lundberg, 1930: 157; cf. Myrdal, 1939: 122).

What is lacking, in Lundberg's opinion, is a method which could describe this accommodation process. Therefore Lundberg was critical of the intertemporal method as a method which is supposed to be a development of the static method, since in the case of perfect foresight there is no 'question of a *successive* determination of prices for the different equilibrium periods; instead all prices are determined simultaneously' (ibid.: 157). That is to say, there is no 'link' between the periods which amounts to the accommodation process. This method is therefore characterized 'as a typical static system where the existence of different prices under different periods only expresses an intertemporal equilibrium' (ibid.; cf.

142–3). In fact Lindahl himself later described his method as introducing 'dynamic problems within the static framework' (1939: 10), since with this method 'the entire static apparatus may be employed in the analysis of a dynamic sequence' (1939: I, 68). It is very likely that Lundberg's and Myrdal's critique of the equilibrium approach played an important role in Lindahl's development, since he had given up this approach in his 'Note on the dynamic pricing problem' (1934). The particularly important part of their critique was the fact that they showed that there was no real causation between the periods, and that Myrdal (1939) had in the meantime developed a disequilibrium approach.

The equilibrating mechanism in a cumulative process: Lindahl *v.* Keynes

For the comparison of Keynes's principle of effective demand with Lindahl's equilibrating mechanism, we will use the so-called 'saving paradox' as an illustration of Lindahl's ideas. The 'saving paradox' is described as follows: 'How can a lowering of the loan rate of interest, which is generally supposed to have a tendency to decrease (voluntary) saving, thus cause an increase in total saving?' (Lindahl, 1939: II, 174).

The mechanism is the following. The fall in the rate of interest increases the relative price of capital goods in relation to consumption goods, which leads to an increase in investment. Furthermore, total saving must equal the total value of real investment – new real capital could be formed, since it is assumed that forced saving has taken place (ibid.: 183) – there must be such a change in the price level and in the income distribution that new saving will be forthcoming to match the new investment. The income for a certain period is defined as the rate of interest on the capital value of all capital goods, including human capital (ibid.: 144). Saving for a period is then defined as the difference between income and the value of the consumed services for the period, and it is equal to the net increase or decrease in the value of capital. Hence, in this process, it is the change in income distribution due to the change in the price level which will play the role of an equilibrating mechanism (ibid.: 175).

At the beginning of the period planned and realized investment is greater than the planned saving, which depends on the money rate of interest and the expected income for the period. This will lead to such an increase in the price level that the nominal income and the distribution of income will change until saving *ex post*, which depends on the same money rate of interest but on the new level of income, will equal the increase in the total value of real investment. Therefore the mechanism is akin to effective demand, since changes in income are the active factor in bringing about the equality between saving and investment. But this similarity exists only during the disequilibrium process represented by the cumulative process. Once the new stationary state is reached, which is characterized by 'a larger amount of capital, a lower rate of interest and a higher price level' (ibid.: 181), the rate of interest will play its orthodox role by balancing saving and investment *ex ante*. Hence Lindahl's cumulative process describes in this case the traverse between two stationary states (ibid.: 180–3).

Lindahl's point with this example is to show that the idea that saving directly determines investment 'is thus, strictly speaking, not quite correct, as long as monetary policy is autonomous' (ibid.: 175). His analysis shows, namely, that, at least if free currency (i.e. no reserves and only bank money) is assumed, the direct link between saving and investment decisions is severed, and the investment demand has the upper hand. Therefore his purpose is in line with Wicksell's as well as Keynes's (1921) analysis of what happens when saving and investment differ. However, Lindahl's equilibrating mechanism is different from Keynes's principle of effective demand, since it is valid only for the cumulative process, not for the long-run equilibrium, because monetary policy can no longer be autonomous in a long-run equilibrium and the rate of interest is therefore determined as in orthodox theory.

The disequilibrium approach: *ex ante* and *ex post*

Myrdal's *Monetary Equilibrium* was an attempt at a critical reconstruction of Wicksell's notion of a normal rate of interest so it could be used for a monetary analysis, and the starting point was Lindahl's analysis in 'The rate of interest and the price level'. However, Myrdal's most important contribution to the development of dynamic method was the construction of the notions of *ex ante* and *ex post*, since with these notions it is possible to undertake a disequilibrium analysis.

The dynamic method

According to Myrdal, monetary equilibrium implies the following dynamic method: 'the concept of monetary equilibrium always concerns the tendency of a situation at a particular point of time. The quantities involved must be defined *ex ante*' (1939: 116). Myrdal denotes this method as an 'instantaneous' analysis (ibid.: 43) and it stands in the following relation to what he calls 'the real dynamic problem': 'The dynamic problem proper of the movement during a period can be discussed only if one starts with the tendencies which exist in a certain price situation, tendencies which are determined by the anticipations dominant in this situation' (ibid.: 121). Hence the instantaneous analysis has to be developed prior to the proper dynamic problem.

In this context Myrdal introduces the famous *ex ante/ex post* calculus, which has the following meaning: 'The first method of computation is "bookkeeping" about what has actually happened during a complete period, the second mode of computation is a business calculation founded on an estimation of what will happen in the future' (ibid.: 54). The *ex ante* anticipations are the driving force in the dynamic process, but the *ex post* results do still play a role, since 'as a basis for the *ex ante* calculations, the *ex post* recorded experiences may regularly be decisive' (ibid.: 55).

The dynamic method is constructed in such a way that there is always an *ex post* balance. However, from the point of view of monetary analysis, the interesting problem is to analyse 'the very changes during the period which are required to bring about this *ex post* balance' (ibid.: 121; emphasis omitted). These changes must be the result of anticipations which are mutually inconsistent, or due to exogenous changes during the period. However, this is never explicitly stated by Myrdal, since 'the intervening changes' are simply referred to as 'the deviations from earlier expectations' (ibid.: 122). The intervening disturbances lead to changes in the anticipations, which then determine the *ex post* formulations in respect of the outgoing period. Thus the analysis has first to localize the cause of the disturbance, which is to be found among the *ex ante* anticipations, and then to analyse the elements which make up the changes in the *ex post* anticipations (ibid.: 46, 116). It is important to notice that the *ex post* notions also contain anticipatory elements relating to forthcoming periods, but the results of the changes in anticipations cancel out in the *ex post* calculus. Therefore the intervening changes are only made up of realized changes during the period, and those changes are deduced from the differences between *ex ante* anticipations and *ex post* (realized) evaluations of the same phenomena.

It was precisely the insufficient analysis of these changes in Lindahl's method, without mentioning Lindahl's name in the German and English editions, that was criticized by Myrdal, since by 'dividing time into a number of short equilibrium periods during which no changes occur' (ibid.: 122) the intervening changes cannot even be comprehended. Myrdal (and Lundberg) had thereby hit upon the weak point in Lindahl's method. Hence the development of the notions of *ex ante* and *ex post*, and the concomitant analysis of the intervening changes, made it possible to come out of the straitjacket of the equilibrium approach implied by the notion of temporary equilibrium.

The saving–investment mechanism during a cumulative process

We will study a case where the saving ratio is changing during the cumulative process, in order to investigate whether the process may end up in an underemployment equilibrium. Myrdal's argument starts from the observation that 'the total purchasing power of the society which forms the demand for consumption goods, shrinks significantly less than does total income' (ibid.: 164). The effect will be a fall in the fraction saved, which will have a direct influence on the equilibrium relation for the capital market by reducing the saving. But there is also an indirect influence, since the maintenance of the demand for consumption goods will hinder a fall in the price level of those goods. This will bolster the capital values, because of the assumed relation between the prices of consumption goods and capital values. This, in its turn, will prop up real investment. Thus there are factors working in opposite directions on both sides of the equilibrium relation between saving and investment. Myrdal's conclusion is that 'the fixed consuming habits have an effect tending to maintain monetary equilibrium despite the tightening of credit conditions' (ibid.: 168).

Myrdal's exercise looks like an explanation of the factors which could stop the downward cumulative process. As a part of the cumulative process the income is falling, but a position will sooner or later be reached where the proportion of income saved has fallen even more, and this will eventually mean a stable price level.

This is not yet a Keynesian underemployment equilibrium, since it explains only a temporary resting point in a business cycle. It is interesting to notice that Keynes's analysis, in the Harris Foundation lecture of June 1931, follows the same lines as Myrdal:

> Now [after a continuing fall in output due to a fall in fixed investment] there is a reason for expecting an equilibrium point of decline to be reached.... there is eventually reached, therefore, a sufficiently low level of output which represents a kind of spurious equilibrium. (Keynes, 1973: 355–6)

But this 'spurious equilibrium' or 'equilibrium point of decline' is obviously the lower turning point in a business cycle and it does not imply a stable situation with unemployment. Hence neither Myrdal nor Keynes (1930) determines a Keynesian underemployment equilibrium, which has a long-run character, but an 'equilibrium point of decline' in a business cycle, which will inevitably be followed by an upturn in investment and output. Furthermore, in an 'equilibrium point of decline', saving *ex ante* may be equal to investment *ex ante*, using Myrdal's terms and Keynes's notions in the *Treatise on Money*, which implies monetary equilibrium as defined above. That shows that monetary equilibrium is a wider concept then underemployment equilibrium, that is to say, the latter implies necessarily the former but vice versa does not hold.

Myrdal and the principle of effective demand

We will first look àt the equilibrating mechanism in Myrdal's analysis by studying an example which shows the function of gains and losses during an upward cumulative process:

> the gains of this kind [in revenues and costs] regularly exceed the losses, and in so far as they do not bring about a change in the demand for consumption goods, they have to be calculated *ex post* as saving. Therefore this saving in the *ex post* calculation is greater than that in the *ex ante* calculation by an amount which covers the difference between free capital disposal *ex ante* and (in this case) the greater invested capital disposal *ex post*. (Myrdal, 1939: 118)

In this case changes in nominal income due to gains or losses (unless unemployed factors exist) will act as a balancing factor. The mechanism is very similar to Lindahl's analysis, and in both cases the changes in nominal income and the distribution of income will be brought about by an alteration in the price level.

In Myrdal's analysis, as in the principle of effective demand, income changes – whether they are made up of prices, or output, or a mixture of both – act as an equilibrating mechanism between saving *ex ante* and investment *ex ante*. However, Myrdal does not determine the equilibrium level income, which is a conditional equality, but at most the income changes necessary within a cumulative process, which are a bookkeeping equality which always holds. His mechanism for determining the changes in income is also different from Keynes's multiplier, though akin to the analysis in the *Treatise*, where unanticipated profit is 'the balancing figure' (Keynes, 1930: 136).

Therefore Myrdal does not aim to find the principle for determining the equilibrium level of output, but to determine the factors which constitute the *ex post* equality between saving and investment in an ongoing cumulative process. Hence Myrdal as well as Lindahl appear to be similar to Keynes only so long as we look at their analysis of the cumulative process, which is a process out of equilibrium, and where the banking system can determine the rate of interest on its own.

Profit as a link between consecutive periods

Hammarskjöld's views on dynamic method are important in the development of the Stockholm school, since he gives the first algebraic formulation of a link between consecutive periods, i.e. a continuation analysis.

Hammarskjöld's purpose

Hammarskjöld's point of departure is 'the truism' that 'every analysis of the general development of prices ... during a given period of time' (1932: 157) has to be based on the idea that total disbursements are equal to the total value of transacted goods and services.

The aim is then to construct a formula for the price level of consumer goods which would show the determinants of the price level for an expired period. Thus far Hammarskjöld's intentions are explicitly identical to Lindahl's and Keynes's formulations of the price level for consumer goods (ibid.: 157 n. 1). But Hammarskjöld now goes one step further, since his formula should also show 'the mechanism – that is, the ways and means by which given changes in prices and purchasing power are transmitted to the next period' (Lundberg, 1937: 77–8). Hence Hammarskjöld's formula should explicitly demonstrate how two consecutive periods are related to each other, and in his theory it is the profit earned in one period but transferred to the next one which will function as a link.

Hammarskjöld is thus the first of the Stockholm school to give a formal explanation of the way in which two periods are connected in a disequilibrium process. It has to be remembered that although Myrdal analysed the *ex post* equalization factors for one period where disequilibrium existed *ex ante*, he offered no formal account of how these factors influenced the plans for the coming period. However, it is obvious that both Lindahl and Myrdal held, with greater or lesser clarity, that unexpected changes in the price level and the concomitant income changes would keep the process going, but their formulas had no formal connection with plans in subsequent periods. The same is true of Keynes's fundamental equations, where, on the one hand, profits are said to be 'the mainspring of change in the existing economic system' (Keynes, 1930: 126), but, on the other, the algebraic formulation of these equations gives no account of how profits will influence the outcome in a forthcoming period.

The outline of Hammarskjöld's dynamic method

Time is divided into successive periods, as with Lindahl, and what is happening during those periods is 'afterwards registered and summed up in equations' (Hammarskjöld, 1933: 12; cf. 53). This is an *ex post* formulation which Hammarskjöld considers to be akin to Keynes (1930). It is by design that Hammarskjöld does not apply the *ex ante* analysis of Myrdal and Lindahl, since that analysis is supposed to be a causal analysis, while Hammarskjöld is only giving a mechanism which is not supposed to imply any particular causality (ibid.: 53).

Profit for a period is now defined as the difference between revenue and disbursement for the same period and it is a windfall profit. It follows that the size of the profit would be indeterminate if the profit could be spent during the period, since that would influence the amount of the revenue and thereby the size of the profit itself (ibid.: 13). Thus Hammarskjöld defines the length of the period in the following way: 'that the entrepreneurs' profits are registered at the end of the respective period – or, as it could be expressed, that each period comprises the time from one registration of profits to the next one during the next period' (ibid.). This is actually the first time in the Stockholm school that someone not only shows that the definition of the length of the period is a theoretical problem, but also hints at the relation between fixed plans and the length of the period. After Hammarskjöld, it was almost always assumed that the length of time for which the plans are unchanged determines the length of the unit period. Furthermore, without this assumption a sequence analysis is not possible, since such an analysis presumes that the development during the period, i.e. the *ex post* result, is completely determined by the *ex ante* plans, and that there is a fixed relation between the *ex post* result for the current period and the plans for the next period.

Autonomous changes in consumption demand

In this section Ohlin's contribution to macro-theory is used as a vantage point for a comparison with Keynes's principle of effective demand. The latter relation is also the subject which has been uppermost in discussion of the Stockholm school in the modern literature.

Ohlin's purpose

Ohlin wants to give a general answer to 'the question of the driving force behind price movements' (Ohlin, 1978: 384). His explanation is basically a restatement of an old Wicksellian idea: 'The necessary and sufficient condition for a process of rising is that the sum of those two kinds of demand [for consumption and investment goods] is rising relative to output' (ibid.: 373–4). Hence the 'driving force' is made up of two forces: one coming from the investment side and the other emanating from the consumption side. An explanation of price changes must look at the factors influencing the demand for and supply of consumption goods and investment goods respectively.

It is therefore not surprising that Ohlin finds the idea that the disequilibrium in the capital market represents the 'driving force', i.e. what he considers to be the hallmark of the 'neo-Wicksellian' approach, too narrow an explanation. This is particularly so when he can construct examples where a disequilibrium in the consumer goods market is the only factor behind a price movement or at least the initiating force (ibid.: 368).

Ohlin's specific extension of neo-Wicksellian macro-theory is thus his explicit treatment of autonomous changes in consumption. This seems also to have been Ohlin's own evaluation of his contribution to the development of the Stockholm school (Steiger, 1976: 356 n. 22).

The equilibrating mechanism

This section is mainly a study of Ohlin's analysis of the equilibrating mechanism, which is then compared with Keynes's principle of effective demand. We start with an example of the equilibrating mechanism.

The most formal account of the equilibrating mechanism is to be found in *Monetary Policy* (Ohlin, 1934: 27). Here Ohlin draws a straightforward analogy between the supply and demand analysis for one good and the same analysis for all goods. In his example the income anticipations are unchanged as well as the propensity to save, which means fixed plans for consumption and saving.

A decrease in the rate of interest will now lead to an increase in planned investment and as a result 'volume of production, realized demand, measured in money, and perhaps prices will rise more or less' (ibid.). If it is assumed that the supply curve is completely elastic because of spare capacity, then it is obvious that an increase in investment leads to the same increase in real income. Consequently Ohlin draws the following conclusion:

the increase of investment purchases implies that at the end of the period the incomes show themselves to be bigger than what was formerly expected, i.e. they have given a 'surplus'. As the consumption purchases have been unchanged, this increase in income has been saved. The saving [realized] has increased owing to the decrease in the rate of interest. (ibid.: 27–8)

Hence the whole increase in income is saved, and is equal to the increase in investment.

We will first discuss the nature of Ohlin's equilibrium notion before giving our view of the relation between Ohlin's equilibrating mechanism and Keynes's principle of effective demand.

Ohlin often seems to confuse an equilibrating mechanism leading to an equilibrium situation with an *ex post* identity at the end of the period during a dynamic process. His entanglement is exemplified by the statement: 'The new savings are produced by those, who for the time being have an increased cash holding' (ibid.: 110). Hence an increased cash holding of a temporary character is looked upon as savings. That is in line with his use of the latter term as income which has not been spent, without taking into consideration saving plans or saving propensities.

This is an offshoot of Ohlin's view of equilibrium as being just the *ex post* identity between bought and sold quantities (Ohlin, 1978: 357). But that shows that he has not understood the potentialities of an *ex ante* analysis as developed by Myrdal, which would define equilibrium as conditional *ex ante* equality among specific plans. From this point of view, the definitional *ex post* equality may represent a confirmation of an equilibrium if it implied that the *ex ante* anticipations had been fulfilled. Otherwise the *ex post* values will serve as a basis for changing the plans, which may or may not lead to an equilibrium for the coming period. Ohlin's main mistake is thus a confusion of *ex ante* and *ex post* notions.

We would therefore argue that Ohlin is not determining an equilibrium position via the principle of effective demand, even if his analysis of the process leading up to the *ex post* equalities has certain traits in common with Keynes's mechanism, e.g. changes in real income.

From our point of view it is more natural to look upon Ohlin's analysis as geared towards business-cycle theory, which explains the *ex post* equality between savings and investment via changes in prices and quantities, but it does not determine any particular equilibrium level – and certainly not a long-run equilibrium – of aggregate income and employment (ibid.: 379). In an analysis of a business cycle one could always describe, as a matter of fact, a situation which is characterized as 'a deep depression in which everything is temporarily "frozen"' (ibid.: 362). This 'temporary' situation might then be explained as follows:

> when prices have been falling for a while investment demand and consumption demand may stop falling and the price fall come to an end. The reason maybe that consumption demand cannot easily contract beyond a certain point, and its resilience will check the tendency to declining investment demand. (ibid.: 379)

In fact both the situation and the explanation of its existence are identical to Myrdal's analysis in *Monetary Equilibrium*. Hence Ohlin's analysis, like Myrdal's, amounts to an explanation of the depth of a business cycle rather than of an underemployment equilibrium. But it has to be remembered that the bottom will be followed by an upturn, and it is not the same as a Keynesian underemployment equilibrium.

Different interpretations of Ohlin's equilibrium mechanism

In this final section we discuss the interpretations of the relation between Ohlin's contribution and the Keynesian revolution given by Landgren, Steiger, Brems, and Patinkin.

According to Landgren, it is easy to reinterpret Ohlin's analysis of the equilibrating mechanism as a comparative static framework and then compare it with Keynes's analysis (Landgren, 1960: 171). This is the basis of his proposition 'that Ohlin carried out a "Keynesian" revolution in Swedish economics' (ibid.: 299). However, Ohlin, like Lindahl and Myrdal, analyses a dynamic process such as the cumulative process, which among other things involves changes in real income. But it is not possible without more ado to transfer propositions, e.g. the equilibrating mechanism, from this type of analysis to an equilibrium framework. In fact Lindahl is the only one who really says what he considers to be true of a stationary equilibrium. Landgren ends up in this mistaken analysis because he never looks at the dynamic methods developed for analysing dynamic processes with changes in the level of income and prices. Instead he draws a direct analogy with Keynes's equilibrium framework for determining the equilibrium level of income.

Brems has noticed the weakness in Landgren's interpretation:

195

'Landgren, no friend of dynamics, ascribes to Ohlin a rather un-Ohlinian static-equilibrium determination of income and output' (1978: 410; cf. Steiger, 1978: 441). But for Brems that means that Ohlin's analysis of a variable physical output actually goes beyond the 'static equilibrium' of the *General Theory*, since Ohlin supplies a dynamic analysis (ibid.: 398–9), which was later taken up by the followers of Keynes, e.g. Harrod and Samuelson (ibid.: 411). However, it must be considered completely unfounded to compare Ohlin's analysis of dynamic processes with Harrod's and Samuelson's formulations of equilibrium growth paths, since we have shown that Ohlin had no clear concept of equilibrium besides static equilibrium and later he even rejected the possibility of constructing a 'dynamic equilibrium' (Ohlin, 1937: 224).

Patinkin, who contributed to the same issue of *History of Political Economy* as Brems and Steiger, comes closer to our position, since he claims that Ohlin does not have the 'distinctive feature' of the Keynesian revolution, namely 'the assignment of an equilibrating role to variations in output' (Patinkin, 1978: 414). However, Patinkin's analysis is not satisfactory. For example, he mentions that even if Ohlin analysed variations in output his main concern was still changes in prices (ibid.: 414–15), which is in itself a dubious interpretation. But Patinkin misses the crucial difference between Keynes's principle of effective demand and Ohlin's analysis, that, although the latter mentioned variations in output, his analysis was not used to determine an equilibrium position.

All the above interpretations go astray either through lack of insight into the dynamic methods developed by the Stockholm school and/or a misunderstanding of the nature of the Keynesian revolution. In fact the confusion over Keynes's contribution is often linked with the view of his method, that is to say, not understanding or refusing to accept that it is a particular type of long-run equilibrium (Hansson, 1985). It is obvious that our somewhat impertinent conclusion rests on the validity of our two points of reference, the character of the Stockholm school and the Keynesian revolution respectively.

A fully developed sequence analysis

This section shows that towards the end of 1934 Lindahl had already laid the foundations of sequence analysis, in the sense that he had given the first proper algebraic formulation of a single-period analysis within a disequilibrium method plus a sketch of the problems involved in a continuation analysis.

Lindahl's vision behind the construction of a general dynamic theory

Economic theory mainly studies 'human actions or the results of human actions' (Lindahl, 1935: 10; cf. Lindahl, 1939: I, 35). But human behaviour could not be explained in the same way as events in the physical world, which implies that 'we cannot prove that certain human actions will necessarily be the result of a definite situation at a given point of time' (ibid.; cf. Lindahl, 1939: I, 35), i.e. to define a determinate dynamic sequence. However, this is a problem only for the empirical relevance of the theory; it does not show that the theory is inconsistent. The construction of a dynamic theory thus 'solves' the problem in the following way: 'We can ... assume that individuals, under given conditions, do act in a certain manner, and the use of this assumption makes it possible to determine exactly what results will develop from any given situation' (ibid.: 11; cf. Lindahl, 1939: I, 35).

To develop his general dynamic approach Lindahl needs only to rely on the following postulate:

> one basic assumption about the behaviour of the acting individuals, namely that their actions, for a shorter or a longer period, only represent *the fulfilment of certain plans*, given at the beginning of the period and determined by certain *principles* that can be stated in some way or the other. (ibid.; cf. Lindahl, 1939: I, 36)

The notion of planning had played a central role in the Stockholm school almost from its beginning, but here for the first time it is explicitly stated that this is the pivot of its dynamic method. The relevance of the dynamic method therefore hinges upon the realism of this basic assumption.

If the economic process is supposed to consist of actions derived from definite plans, then it is obvious that it takes a certain amount of time to realize these actions, i.e. a period of time is involved (ibid.: 13). As far as changes in plans are concerned, Lindahl assumes that these are 'related to definite moments, namely to those points of time at which the economic subject makes the decision to set in practice a new plan' (ibid.). Hence, it is implied, a period is defined by unchanged plans, which was already hinted at by Hammarskjöld.

Because of the fact that the plans are intermittently revised the dynamic process will have a discontinuous character:

> the dynamic process as a whole is not a continuous one, but that from a theoretical point of view, it consists of *two* types of

197

movements: first the events during a certain period of time, and, secondly, the events at the transition *points* between these periods. The determining of these latter *discontinuous* changes, that is, the alterations of the plans of production and consumption ... may be regarded as the central part of the dynamic theory. (Lindahl, 1934: 210–11; cf. Lindahl, 1935: 13)

It seems likely that the stress Lindahl puts on changing plans and the concomitant discontinuous process may be the reason why he shows no interest in using difference equations, since this tool presumes that the behaviour is unchanged, which implies 'mechanical dynamics'.

Sequence analysis

We will here discuss Lindahl's 'A note on the dynamic pricing problem' (1934), which gives the first proper sequence analysis. In this short note (four pages) Lindahl discusses most of the problems involved in a sequence analysis, and it is only his remarks on the complete dynamic process which are inadequate.

We start with the problem of single-period analysis. At an arbitrary point in time, t, the plans for production and consumption are given for a certain period of time (t to $t+1$), which means that once the prices are known the individual actions are determined and fixed for the period (Lindahl, 1934: 204). It is assumed that at the point $t+1$ the plans are changed. The problem to be solved is then the following:

the analysis of what happens during the said period, that is, the determination of the situation at the point $t+1$ as it *results* from the situation at the point t. When this problem is solved, the situation at the point $t+2$ can be explained in the same manner as it results from the situation at the point $t+1$, and so on. The solution of this problem implies, therefore ... the solution of the whole dynamic problem. (ibid.)

The solution to this problem, i.e. the single-period analysis, contributes to the 'whole dynamic problem' in the sense that the same method could also be employed for the period ($t+1$ to $t+2$) at point $t+1$. But it does not yet entail the proposition that the whole dynamic process (from t to $t+1$ and onwards) has been determined at point t, since the solution to that problem, i.e. continuation analysis, needs some further assumptions.

At the beginning of the period the expected value of the goods to be delivered during the period is by definition equal to the expected value of the production costs. This definitional relation follows from the assumption:

> that part of E that is contractual income is known by the entrepreneurs; the income expectations of the wage-earners are, for the period in question, thus equal to the sum that the entrepreneurs expect to pay as wages during this period. (ibid.: 207)

Judging by the way Lindahl proceeds in his analysis, it is implicit that all net incomes to the owners of factors of production have a contractual nature, including what we call normal profit. Lindahl has therefore taken over an assumption that was already developed by Hammarskjöld. The costs are thus known beforehand by the entrepreneurs, and any difference between net income *ex ante* and *ex post* must consequently be due to deviations from the normal profit. Hence the extra profit has a windfall character, and it is reckoned *ex post*, as in most of the works of the Stockholm school as well as in Keynes's *Treatise* (1930: 112–13).

Lindahl assumes that the supply prices are given during the period, so all changes in prices take place at the transition point between two consecutive periods, i.e. a fix-price method (1934: 204). At the end of the period the value of the goods actually sold must then necessarily be equal to realized net income and depreciation.

To solve the single-period analysis Lindahl assumes that the spending plans are realized as far as quantities are concerned (ibid.: 207). The role of this assumption is to show that the actions during the period 'can be directly deduced from the plans once the prices are given at the beginning of the period' (Lindahl, 1939: I, 92). Hence the result of the period is a necessary outcome of the *ex ante* plans for the current period.

The assumption that the purchasing plans for consumer and capital goods are realized implies that Lindahl, like the rest of the Swedish school, assumes that there are enough unemployed factors of production and sufficient stocks of consumer and capital goods (ibid.: 30, 45; cf. Hansen, 1951: 29). If, for example, $I > S$, then the following will happen:

> The result of this will be income gains for the producers... if that is not prevented by an increase of the depreciation term D^1. In that latter case, the only immediate effect of the excess of planned investment over planned saving will be a decrease in the stock of the producers. (Lindahl, 1934: 209)

Thus for the first time there is a formal example of how disequilibrium during one period, in the sense that not all plans are fulfilled, leads to an *ex post* equality via a change in income or stocks. This is basically the same argument as was put forward by Myrdal and to a certain extent by Ohlin, but it is now given a more explicit formulation. However, as was the case with Myrdal and Ohlin, there is no reason to interpret this *ex post* equality as proof that Lindahl applied the principle of effective demand.

Lindahl does not discuss the actual length of a unit period except to say that it is equal to the time for which the plans are unchanged. The point is that they will not be revised until the end of the period even if the entrepreneurs start to feel strongly during the period that the plans will not be fulfilled. Hence all adjustments during the period take place through changes in stocks, which is a characteristic of the fix-price method.

We can now proceed to Lindahl's handling of the continuation analysis. The single-period analysis could determine the *ex post* results from the given *ex ante* plans at *t*. But this does not imply that the ongoing process after *t*+1 can be determined at *t* without further assumptions, i.e. the problem of continuation analysis remains. The crucial supposition concerns the relation between *ex ante* plans for the forthcoming period and the *ex post* result for the current period: 'this problem could only be dealt with theoretically under the assumption that one makes particular postulates concerning the relation between the process of events during a period and the *ex ante* concepts for the next period' (letter from Lindahl to Ohlin, 31 December 1934).

Lindahl now makes the following assumption, namely that if the plans are fulfilled and there are no changes in the exterior events, then it is possible to postulate a simple functional relation between the *ex ante* plans for the consecutive period and the *ex post* result of the current period. By using this assumption for several periods we reach the following result: 'the whole dynamic process can be deduced from the data [the plans at *t* are part of the data], given at the beginning of the first period' (Lindahl, 1934: 210). Lindahl does not mention that if the functional relations between the periods always have the same form, then we can interpret the whole dynamic process as a case of moving equilibrium, since each single period is in equilibrium. The equilibrium character of the process would in such a case be defined in the following way: 'The existence of equilibrium through time ... presupposes the existence of an expectation function of constant form' (Hahn, 1952: 804).

However, it was left to Lundberg to make an explicit assumption of constant expectation functions. Lundberg also leaves out the 'particular postulate' that the plans have to be fulfilled within each period. We therefore distinguish between equilibrium and disequilibrium sequence analysis, where Lindahl is pursuing the former and Lundberg the latter.

Disequilibrium sequence analysis

The main aim of this section is to present the sense in which Lundberg's sequence analysis has a disequilibrium character, while at the same time it may be called an equilibrium process. It is these two characteristics which make Lundberg's analysis different from Lindahl's method of 1934.

Disequilibrium sequence analysis as an equilibrium process

Lundberg criticizes static equilibrium, but that does not imply that he discards equilibrium notions completely, since they 'may turn out useful, when used in connection with the system of relations that is intended to explain the total development' (1937: 6). That shows that the notion of equilibrium may play a role in sequence analysis, and Lundberg consequently concludes his introductory chapter by stating the following problem: 'The question is now to what extent equilibrium constructions may be used in a sequence analysis which starts with total categories' (ibid.: 25). In fact the equilibrium constructions play a fundamental role in the development of sequence analysis, since some equilibrium relations must hold, even out of equilibrium, if a sequence analysis is to be possible (ibid.: 27). Our aim is now to find out in what sense Lundberg's sequence analysis, which is a non-equilibrium dynamic model, may still be called an equilibrium process.

Lundberg constructs what he calls a 'neutrality condition for the general system', and it has a certain resemblance to Lindahl's complete equilibrium condition, which says that the purchase plans are equal to the production plans. Lundberg holds that such a condition is 'purely formal' (1937: 163), since for given plans it will only show whether profits or losses will exist for the current period, that is to say, a single-period analysis. But it is not possible to draw any conclusion concerning what is going to happen in subsequent periods, since 'no causal elements have so far been introduced' (ibid.), which implies a continuation analysis. This was already realized by Lindahl when he said that the formulation which gives the *ex post* results for one period does not yet imply the solution to the complete dynamic process. The 'causal elements' in a sequence analysis are 'the casual connections over successive periods of time of plans and decisions' (ibid.: 245). That is to say, they show how the *ex post* results for an outgoing period influence the *ex ante* plans for the subsequent period (ibid.: 49).

Lundberg now goes beyond Lindahl, in the sense that he looks more closely at these casual elements, while the latter just assumed that some functional relations between the periods had to exist if it were possible to determine the whole dynamic process. He assumes what he calls given response functions (ibid.: 172), which means that, for example, the current investment is functionally related to the profit for the outgoing period and the relation will have the same form independent of whether the expectations are fulfilled or not. This is an important difference from Lindahl's sequence analysis, since the latter considered it necessary to assume that the expectations were fulfilled. We would therefore denote Lundberg's version of the sequence analysis as a disequilibrium sequence analysis, while Lindahl (1934) pursued an equilibrium sequence analysis, though in 'The dynamic approach' Lindahl (1939: I, 57–8) has accepted Lundberg's version. This distinction is in line with Hahn's classification, which denotes a case similar to Lundberg's as belonging to non-equilibrium models (Hahn, 1952: 805). Hence the equilibrium process is represented by the fixed response function, since the latter implies routine behaviour and at the same time the sequence analysis is a non-equilibrium dynamic model in the sense that expectations are not fulfilled within each period.

The limitations of sequence analysis

Lundberg sometimes gives the impression that he is opting for 'mechanical' dynamics, since he assumes that the formation of expectations is 'endogenous' (1937: 175). That is to say, there is a functional relation between expectations and previous events, with the following results: 'a clearcut "sequence analysis" in which anticipations need not appear explicitly – formally a mechanical dynamics, with an expectional dynamics between the lines' (Hart, 1951: viii). However, Lundberg is aware of the fact that the model sequences have a restricted value, since the assumption of given response functions, which plays such a crucial role in the construction of model sequences, will only be true 'over a period of time by accident' (Lundberg, 1937: 243). Sequence analysis should therefore not be carried too far ahead in time (ibid.: 5–6). Thus Lundberg had at least some doubt about the value of mechanical dynamics, which was further vindicated by his application of sequence analysis after 1937.

Interlude

We have now analysed the first proposition, to prove the existence of a 'school'. The development of the dynamic method of the Stockholm school has been depicted as an almost teleological evolution from Myrdal's 'method of expectation' to the sequence analysis of Lindahl and Lundberg. The following exposition of the second proposition will just show that the later development of dynamic method took some of its ingredients from the earlier results of the school besides the influence coming from abroad, but that there is no longer such a close interrelation among the works. We start with a look at Lindahl's somewhat belated reaction to the *General Theory*.

Lindahl's comments on Keynes's *General Theory*

Lindahl's first response to Keynes's book came in 1953 in the form of a long article in *Ekonomisk Tidskrift* which was later published in the *Economic Record* in 1954 with the title 'On Keynes's economic system'. It should be emphasized that we confine ourselves to an analysis of his critique of Keynes's dynamic method and are not concerned with his views on Keynes's theory of effective demand.

It was obvious to Lindahl that Keynes put a lot of emphasis on the causal connections in his theory, but it is difficult to maintain this interpretation, since Keynes at the same time discusses 'an equilibrium with simultaneous interdependence of the various magnitudes' (Lindahl, 1954: 25). Our problem is therefore to study Lindahl's interpretation of the nature of a Keynesian equilibrium; this will at the same time prove that Lindahl's dynamic method has developed, compared with the earlier methods from the 1930s.

The interdependent relation between different variables in a system of simultaneous equations might easily be applied to stationary conditions, that is to say, 'when the development during one period is repeated without changes during the following periods' (ibid.: 27). The same system may as well be used for 'the case concerning the determination of the conditions for *correctly anticipated* processes' (ibid.), and the fundamental assumption for such situations is the following:

> that the individuals have such expectations of the future that they act in ways which are necessary for their expectations to be fulfilled. It follows that the interdependence between present

and future magnitudes is conditioned in this case by the fact that the latter, via correct anticipations, influence the former. (ibid.)

If this assumption is valid, then anticipated processes might be characterized as equilibrium processes, but they differ in their mathematical formulation from a stationary equilibrium, since the variables in an anticipated process have to be dated. According to Lindahl, it is impossible to understand Keynes's constructions unless they are interpreted as explanations of correctly anticipated processes. Lindahl is critical of Keynes's system, since it includes a mixture of static long-run functions, e.g. the consumption function, and static short-run functions, e.g. the liquidity preference function (ibid.: 32). The former functions are used to determine the equilibrium conditions and may be used for applications of comparative statics. Static short-run functions, which are defined in the relation to the equilibrium determined by the static long-run functions, can on the other hand be used only 'in a study of the directions of the movements initiated by an assumed change of the parameters or functions in the equilibrium situation to which the system [of static short-run functions] refers' (ibid.: 31). Both types of function can coincide in the sense that the systems of long-run functions and short-run functions have the same equilibrium situation, that is to say, 'they [the functions] have the same value at the point of equilibrium (in other words, the forms of the functions are different but the solution is the same)' (ibid.: 168). This distinction between two types of function is an innovation in relation to Lindahl's earlier treatment of dynamic methods.

Keynes analyses the conditions for different equilibrium situations, which presumes a system of only static long-run functions, at the same time as the tendencies to move in a given situation, which presumes a system of short-run functions (ibid.: 32). However, Keynes's system should consist only of static short-run functions, for the following reason:

With regard to *substance* and *purpose* the system is ... dynamic: it clarifies the actual tendencies in a certain equilibrium and can, consequently, be used for an investigation of how a movement is generated when the equilibrium is broken; furthermore, it gives material for a building of dynamic processes and for an examination of the transition from one equilibrium to another. (ibid.: 167)

At first Lindahl assumes correctly that in anticipated processes expectations do not have to be completely certain, which permits the existence of liquidity preference, since there is 'some uncertainty inasmuch as a rise in the interest level is not considered impossible' (ibid.: 29 n. 12; cf. ibid.: 164). However, later in the article Lindahl shifts to the assumption that 'the conditions are assumed to be permanent or correctly anticipated' (ibid.: 164) and the basis of liquidity preference disappears. If Lindahl had maintained that anticipated processes are not necessarily based on complete foresight, then he might have seen the possibility of determining a Keynesian long-run equilibrium (cf. Hansson, 1985: 334 f.).

The system of static short-run functions only 'gives material' to the analysis of a transition between two different equilibria, since the system must 'also contain connecting parts of a dynamic character' (Lindahl, 1954: 32; cf. Hansson, 1982: 211–13), but Lindahl never gives a more specific definition of the 'connecting parts'. Thus the static short-run functions of the system only give the *tendencies* for a few periods ahead: 'one can hardly assume that a real process can carry on for any longer period of time based on underlying conditions which are unchanged' (these 'underlying conditions' explain why the functions are static) (Lindahl, 1954: 221). It is therefore necessary 'to modify successively the premisses and thereby the models' (ibid.), which seems to imply that the parameters have to change in at least some of the static short-run functions. This short-run system is akin to Lindahl's dynamic method of 1935, and in particular Lundberg's sequence analysis of 1937, where it is accentuated that the method is only valid for an analysis over a few periods (Hansson, 1982: ch. 9, s. 4; ch. 10, s. 2).

Bent Hansen's quasi-equilibrium

We have not included Hansen in the original Stockholm school, since it is obvious that his contribution, *A Study in the Theory of Inflation*, which is a dissertation from 1951, has been influenced by foreign sources (Hansson, 1982: 9–10). Hansen describes these influences in the following way:

> The analytical equipment used is not new, but neither is it outmoded. It employs the terminology of the Stockholm School, as presented by Erik Lindahl, and some of the lines of reasoning of that school of thought whose pioneer is J. R. Hicks. (Hansen, 1951: viii)

The empirical object of Hansen's analysis is so-called suppressed inflation, which was a common fact during and after the Second World War. Hansen does not assume monopoly, but the agents' buying plans nevertheless take into consideration that their spending at existing prices might be limited (ibid.: 23–4), which recalls the development during the 1970s of price theory with rationing.

From the Stockholm school and Lindahl in particular, who was his supervisor, Hansen has taken notions such as plans and periods, which together with the assumption of fixed prices during the period are fundamental notions of their disequilibrium method. In this method prices are not equilibrating demand and supply, which, of course, is a suitable assumption for the analysis of suppressed inflation, since the latter is usually characterized by some type of price regulation (ibid.: 28). It is obvious that Hansen deviates from the usual assumption of the Stockholm school, namely that all spending plans can be realized.

Bent Hansen goes a step beyond what the Stockholm school had hitherto accomplished, since he shows how prices change between periods, and it is a stricter exposition than Lundberg's model sequences. He uses excess demand functions: the excess demand for goods – only one good is supposed to be produced – determines the rate of inflation for the consumption good, and the excess demand for labour – which is the only variable factor – determines the rate of wage increases (ibid.: 159–63). It seems likely that this construction has been influenced by Hicks's *Value and Capital* (see the quotation above), but Hansen also refers to Samuelson's *Foundation of Economic Analysis* and Lange's *Price Flexibility and Employment* (cf. ibid.: 163 n. 1). Bent Hansen has thus added to the Stockholm school what he considered their main drawback, 'laws of motion' which show how plans and anticipations are revised (Hansen, 1966: 2–3).

In the analysis above Hansen applies the notion of quasi-equilibrium, which is characterized by prices and wages rising at the same speed (1951: 164). This situation is an equilibrium in the sense that the relative price, the relation between the price of the consumer good and the wage, and excess demand in both markets are constant. But it is not a traditional static equilibrium, since prices and wages are rising all the time and excess demand is different from zero. Hence it is denominated as a quasi-equilibrium (ibid.; cf. Hansen, 1966: 92–5). Bent Hansen extends his model to include several markets, and quasi-equilibrium then signifies that all relative prices are unchanged over time and the general price level is increasing continuously (ibid.: 198). If it is assumed that the goods are gross substitutes, then it can be proved that the quasi-equilibrium is stable (ibid.: 205).

From the point of view of the Stockholm school, Bent Hansen's contribution is of great interest, since he constructs a new equilibrium notion. Furthermore, he unites the methods of the Stockholm school with the development of dynamic theory outside Sweden. The foreign influence gives his contribution a formal mathematical touch which is far ahead of anything else presented by the original members of the Stockholm school.

On recursive and interdependent models

Bentzel and Hansen's article 'On recursiveness and interdependency in economic models' (1954) intervened in the debate among econometricians as to whether recursive/consecutive or interdependent/simultaneous models should be the basis of econometric research. Herman Wold and Trygve Haavelmo represented the two different conceptions (cf. Bentzel and Hansen, 1954: 153-4). This debate sheds light on the methods of the Stockholm school, and we will not analyse the problem of econometric methodology. In this way it is possible to touch on Wold's idea of recursive systems – a term promoted by Wold in his book *Demand Analysis* (1952) – which to a great extent is influenced by the dynamic methods of the Stockholm school.

A recursive system consists solely of unidirectional relations between the variables of the model, which allows for a causal interpretation (Wold, 1952: 50-1). A simultaneous system, on the other hand, is also made up of mutual relations among the variables. Wold holds that the sequence analysis of the Stockholm school, where there is not equilibrium in each period, was thought of as a recursive system (ibid.: 66-7). Bentzel and Hansen now add the following complementary distinction to the one between recursiveness and simultaneity:

When we talk about a *basic* model, we mean a model in which complete and explicit regard is taken of each single economic subject and each single good in the society considered. It is obvious that such models can only be discussed in a very abstract way. The economic subjects are the millions of households, firms, organisations and public authorities, and from a practical point of view it is not possible to write down on paper the enormous number of equations necessary for the description of *all* actions of *all* subjects. But still it is possible to discuss some general properties of such 'perfectionistic', basic models, and this will turn out to be useful in this context. If, on the other hand, a basic model is simplified so that not all the variables and relations of the basic model are shown explicitly, we talk about a *derived* model. (Bentzel and Hansen, 1954: 155–6)

By constructing a basic model which builds on the disequilibrium method of the Stockholm school it should be possible, if a sufficiently short period is assumed, to have a model which contains only recursive relations (ibid.: 159–60).

Basic or recursive models are most suited to applications on an abstract and theoretical level, and it is not necessary that all economic theory should consist of basic models which are rooted in sequence analysis. As a matter of fact, most dynamic models are derived models and therefore contain simultaneous relations. There are three practical reasons, all due to deficiencies in the statistical material, for using derived models. First, information about plans, i.e. the *ex ante* magnitudes, are generally lacking, and it is therefore necessary to work with *ex post* magnitudes. Second, it is mostly impossible to get information about each single agent and commodity, and it is necessary to use aggregates. The third reason is also related to the problem with aggregation: the statistical material relates to longer time periods than the unit period of sequence analysis according to the Stockholm school (ibid.: 163).

Bentzel and Hansen (1954) have shown that, from a theoretical point of view, sequence analysis can be considered as an analysis of recursive relations, since the analysis is built on a basic model. This problem is, of course, analogous with the movement from micro to macro, which the Stockholm school generally thought of as a simple summation over the micro magnitudes. However, it is obvious that in their – empirical – work recursive models were applied to macro magnitudes without a basic model ever having been used as a foundation. Lundberg was aware of this problem from the beginning, and he suggested that the length of the unit period had to be chosen with respect to the aggregate magnitudes which were the variables of the model (1937: 47–50). That was one of the reasons why Lundberg restricted his analysis to one single period, which only expressed whether (for example) the government budget increased or decreased the tendency to inflation (cf. Lundberg, 1953: 336; Hansson, 1982: 233–5).

Faxén's equilibrium between strategies

Faxén's dissertation *Monetary and Fiscal Policy under Uncertainty* was the first to use the ideas of the Stockholm school for a general analysis of cases with imperfect competition (Faxén, 1957: 12–13). His interest was concentrated on the analysis of monetary and fiscal policy in a situation with oligopolistic relations among firms and between firms and trade unions. Despite Faxén's general use of game theory Ragnar Bentzel, in his review for *Ekonomisk Tidskrift*, considered the dissertation a continuation of the Stockholm school:

> What he has taken from game theory is mainly the dualistic view, certain technical methods, and the terminology. For the rest the dissertation builds to such an extent on the earlier generation of Swedish economists that the work, despite its game-theoretical dress, could almost be considered a continuation of the research tradition of the Stockholm school. (Bentzel, 1957: 221)

It should be mentioned that Lundberg and Svennilson seem to have been Faxén's supervisors, so there is also a direct personal relation with the Stockholm school.

The main problem is to study the manner in which uncertainty concerning the future is reflected in the agents' plans, which is akin to Myrdal (1927). Faxén has taken his views on uncertainty from Knight's well known distinction between risk and uncertainty, i.e. the latter notion cannot be described by objective probabilities (Faxén, 1957: 42–4). The real existence of uncertainty may, for example, manifest itself in attempts by firms to maintain a certain flexibility via assurances of a certain amount of liquidity (ibid.: 14, 58–9).

The purpose is to construct a dynamic analysis where from the beginning incomplete anticipations have been explicitly incorporated (ibid.: 10), but it should also study how the formation of anticipations may influence the rate of change of the economic variables (ibid.: 24). This problem is close to the interest of the Stockholm school in the adjustment process between two equilibrium situations, where the process itself may influence the final equilibrium, and it is different from the propositions of comparative statics (ibid.: 27; Hansson, 1982: 50). Faxén's opposite pole, within dynamic theory, is the approach which takes changes in prices and quantities as given, i.e. difference and differential equations.

Faxén takes the period analysis of the Stockholm school as a basis for the investigation of his own problem, because the method allows for an analysis of the changes in anticipations and plans between consecutive periods. At the same time, it is obvious that in its early stages the Stockholm school hardly ever discussed the formation of anticipations, which were later the subject of Svennilson's dissertation *Ekonomisk planering* of 1938 (Hansson, 1982: 9). This fact is more of an advantage to Faxén, since it facilitates the linkage between his own problem and the analytical methods of the Stockholm school:

> the framework of the model – period, plan, expectation, decision to act – which is the characteristic feature of the Stockholm school, can *per se* be combined with any theory of the origin of the expectations and any theory of motivation whatsoever.

The game-theoretical formulations are introduced via the concept of 'game uncertainty', which characterizes the uncertainty for oligopolistic relations. Game uncertainty is defined as:

> The characteristic feature of 'game uncertainty' as distinct from 'uncertainty' is that the acting person must use his knowledge of the objectives of the other acting persons in his immediate environment, of their ways of thinking when making decisions, etc., when he makes a rational analysis of his own situation in order to reduce the game uncertainty. He must also assume that the other persons are analysing his own objectives and decisions in the same way. (ibid.: 45)

Faxén relates directly to the notion of 'strategy', as it had been developed by von Neumann and Morgenstern, to analyse choices over several periods (ibid.: 76). Then it is necessary for an individual's rational choice between the alternatives for the present period that he also chooses between future possible situations, and the latter are also dependent on the original choice. A strategy which is chosen at the transition to the first period contains, then, a determinate choice for several periods:

> that an agent, in a situation with several successive opportunities to choose, does not look upon the choice at the first opportunity as a choice between the actual alternatives at *that point of time*, but as a choice between different combinations of decisions – *strategies* – at the present point of time and in the future. (Bentzel, 1957: 226)

Thus the agents choose at the initial point of time between different strategies. Equilibrium in a multi-period analysis with uncertainty can then be determined with the help of the following notion of strategy: 'each economic unit has a strategy, which is optimal for that unit, if it regards all the others' strategies as fixed' (Faxén, 1957: 100). This definition, which is taken from Nash, implies that in equilibrium there is no tendency to change strategy, and the equilibrium may be described as a point on the contract curve in an Edgeworth box.

Faxén's contribution to the Stockholm school is as an application of period analysis to oligopolistic conditions, which used game theory and then constructed the notion of strategy equilibrium.

Assessment

According to Hicks it is possible to speak of two different revolutions in the 1930s:

> To pass from one pure method to the other [flex-price to fix-price] is quite a revolution. It is a revolution that is mixed up with the so-called 'Keynesian Revolution'; but I do not think that it is accurate to identify them. Though the 'methods' that are used in the *Treatise on Money* and in the *General Theory* are different, neither of them is a pure method.... There is, however, no question that, as between his two works, Keynes was moving in the direction of the new method; and it is in the work of his interpreters and successors that the clearest examples of the new method are to be found. In their hands the method is often presented as a Keynesian method; but it is wiser, in my view, to avoid committing ourselves to taking it as such. It is better to recognize that the direction of movement is one that is very widespread in contemporary economics, both through the influence of Keynes and otherwise.... A corresponding change was occurring in Sweden. The original (1929–30) form of Lindahl's theory, which we have been discussing, was pure Temporary Equilibrium. But in Myrdal's *Monetary Equilibrium* (1933), in spite of its title, the change is beginning. In Lundberg's *Economic Expansion* (1937) it is fairly complete. In Lindahl's later work ... he also moved in the same direction. (Hicks, 1965: 77 and n. 1)

Hence one revolution was concerned with dynamic methods, and in this field the Stockholm school played a major role, while the other was the Keynesian revolution in a narrow sense, i.e. the principle of effective demand. In this perspective Keynes's contri-

bution in the *General Theory* and the contribution of the Stockholm school are complementary rather than antagonistic.

This view differs from those economists who argue that the
Stockholm school died a sudden death:

> Why were the Stockholm School and, specifically, its original
> contribution – the dynamic method – never able to reach an
> international breakthrough? The production of the Stockholm
> School culminated in, and was ended by, the dissertations of
> Erik Lundberg and Ingvar Svennilson in 1937 and 1938,
> respectively.... Why was the Stockholm School unable to make
> an international breakthrough, either on its own merit or by
> means of complementary analysis to Keynesian unemployment
> theory? (Siven, 1985: 578–9; cf. Jonung, 1987a)

It is true that the Stockholm school culminated around 1937–8,
but this chapter has shown that in Sweden there was also an
afterglow to the early, most productive period, and the school did
not complement Keynesian unemployment theory, if the latter is
supposed to be the principle of effective demand. There is another
great deficiency in this view of the defeat of the Stockholm school,
since it does not give a precise definition of the content and form
in which the Keynesian revolution conquered the minds of
professional economists, students, and politicians. It is my view
that the Keynesian revolution as the dominant theory took the
form of Hicks's IS–LM model, Hicks and Hansen's income-
expenditure diagram, and Samuelson's model of the multiplier-
accelerator. The IS–LM approach uses temporary equilibrium with
fixed prices in the markets for goods and labour, which is an
obvious link back to Lindahl. The income–expenditure model
analyses accommodations in stocks and quantities via the notions
of *ex ante* and *ex post.* Samuelson's development is related more to
Frisch, Tinbergen, and Kalecki, and there is only a tenuous
relation with Lundberg.

It is true that disequilibrium sequence analysis, the most
advanced notion of the Stockholm school, has hardly been used at
all, either in the Swedish or in the foreign contributions. The role
of this notion is discussed by Lundberg in his evaluation of the
dynamic methods developed by the Stockholm school:

> It is clearly an advantage to have theories of expansion and of
> the possible course of expansionist processes in the back of the
> mind and to use concepts that can be fitted into a dynamic
> sequence. But we have to be aware of the extremely limited

applicability of our more involved models to an ever changing economic reality, where it is precisely the *changes* in the assumed coefficients that will often be more important than the fixed relations. My experience shows me that the more modest approach to dynamics by way of the *disequilibrium method* – that is, *ex ante* discrepancies between plans made and measures taken by different groups and countries – in nearly all cases gives the necessary starting point for dynamic analysis. (Lundberg, 1937: iv; preface to the 1955 edition of *Economic Expansion*)

On the basis of his 'experience in practical research' Lundberg thus advocated a single-period analysis for practical purposes. Sequence analysis had limited practical value and should not be carried too far ahead in time, since the assumption of given response functions was only accidentally valid over a short period of time. In fact during the 1940s most of the empirical work done by the Swedes belonged to the category of single-period analysis, e.g. their analyses of the inflationary gap which was initiated by Keynes in his pamphlet *How to Pay for the War* (1940). The construction of 'probable sequences of economic development', i.e. a full-blown sequence analysis, functioned more as a tool which could be used for analytical purposes than something directly applicable to an empirical analysis. Nowadays, theoreticians are struggling to achieve a formal development of sequence analysis, or the analysis of sequence economies where there is trading at every date and which goes beyond an Arrow–Debreu economy (i.e. intertemporal equilibrium), in an attempt to construct a theory of a monetary economy (cf. Hahn, 1982: 2).

In this chapter we have shown that the Stockholm school was still influential in Sweden in the 1950s, and there was even a sequel to the original development of dynamic method. However, we cannot speak of a school in the same strict sense as was possible for the 1930s, since the foreign impulses were important in the later development. But at least some of the material of the Stockholm school was flexible enough either to be included in other methods or to incorporate extraneous ideas. In this sense there is no reason to say that the Stockholm school was killed off by the Keynesian revolution, since some of the dynamic methods developed by the Swedes became part and parcel of the presentation of the Keynesian message.

Chapter eight

Beyond the Stockholm school

Bo Sandelin

After the Stockholm school there are only stray signs of anything that could be called a Swedish way of economic thinking. Swedish economists, with a few notable exceptions, have taken the Anglo-American mainstream economics as an ideal, and become a part of it.

That is not to say that it is a bad ideal, or that the evolution is unique to Sweden.[1] Nor is it to say that Swedish economics earlier was devoid of ideas from abroad. It is merely a reflection of general cultural influences, and of a tendency for sciences – probably even stronger for natural sciences than for humanities and social sciences – towards less nation-bound and more uniform approaches. National traits tend to become a matter of emphasis rather than of kind.

Having said this, we should add that in recent decades, too, it has been possible to distinguish unique approaches or even schools in sufficiently self-confident cultures. One example is the Latin American thinking on economic dependence.[2] Another is economic thinking in the socialist countries, which is almost unknown to Western mainstream economists.[3] A third example is the thinking of the French regulation theorists.[4]

Some of the Stockholm school economists have won their reputation at least as much for their achievements in other fields of economics. Before concluding this book we shall therefore enlarge upon the most important contributions by Ohlin and Myrdal. We shall also touch upon the works of two economists, internationally less well known but domestically important, who more or less opposed the Stockholm school: Gösta Bagge and Johan Åkerman. Finally, we mention the political impact of the theories of two economists outside university circles, Rudolf Meidner and Gösta Rehn.

Ohlin on trade

Bertil Ohlin (with James Meade) was awarded the Nobel Prize in 1977 for 'pathbreaking contributions to the theory of international trade and international capital movements', as the official explanation of the Royal Academy of Sciences reads.[5] Ohlin's most important contributions to international economics are his doctoral dissertation *Handelns teori* (The Theory of Trade) from 1924, *Interregional and International Trade* (1933), and his dispute with Keynes in the *Economic Journal* (1929) on the transfer problem connected with Germany's reparation payments in compliance with the Versailles treaty.

His dissertation and his book of 1933 present a general equilibrium approach to the theory of international trade. He evidently himself considered the general equilibrium characteristic as his most important contribution. Ohlin was one of Cassel's students, and that made him aware of the Walrasian way of apprehending the economy as a system of interdependent relations. Within that framework, and inspired also by an article by his other teacher, Heckscher (1919), he deduced a weak form of the so-called Heckscher–Ohlin theorem which appears his most commemorated result.

The old theory of international trade which was formulated by Ricardo, and which is still taught as a first approximation on introductory courses, was essentially built on the simplest variant of the labour theory of value.

Heckscher and Ohlin increased the number of factors of production taken into account explicitly. Heckscher is given the credit for what has later been called the strong form of the Heckscher–Ohlin theorem. It says that if the demand structure is similar in different countries, a country tends to export those goods which are produced with relatively large quantities of its relatively abundant factors, and import those goods which it would produce with relatively large amounts of its relatively scarce factors. Ohlin's weak form of the theorem says that a country tends to export those goods which would be relatively cheap within the country in the absence of trade. Relative cheapness and expensiveness must not necessarily depend on the quantities of available factors of production, as in the strong form of the theorem; it may also depend on demand factors.

According to Heckscher, under certain conditions factor prices could be completely equalized between the trading countries, while Ohlin maintained that generally there would only be a tendency in that direction; factor prices would not be completely equalized.

The effect on income distribution has since been further specified within the so-called Stolper–Samuelson theorem, while the Rybezynski theorem states the effects of factor growth within a Heckscher–Ohlin framework.

Myrdal as an institutionalist

Like Ohlin, Gunnar Myrdal has made his most important contributions outside the Stockholm school. His Nobel Prize in 1974 (with Friedrich von Hayek) was awarded not only for 'pioneering work in the theory of money and economic fluctuations' but also for 'penetrating analysis of the interdependence of economic, social and institutional phenomena'. 'In addition to their contributions to economic theory, Myrdal and von Hayek have carried out interdisciplinary research so successfully that their combined contributions should be awarded the Prize for Economic Science,' says the Royal Academy of Sciences in its official announcement.[6]

Myrdal may be considered a pure theorist for a short period at the beginning of his career, although even as early as the end of the 1920s he was writing papers on social policy. Soon he became rather heterodox, emphasizing the importance of institutions much more than conventional economists did. 'Myrdal – at least since *An American Dilemma* [1944] – regards himself mainly as an "institutional economist" – and is proud of it!' says Erik Lundberg.

Myrdal's critical attitude towards traditional economic theorizing manifested itself quite early. In 1930 he published *Vetenskap och politik i nationalekonomin* (English edition, *The Political Element in the Development of Economic Theory*, 1953). This book was originally planned as a frontal attack on the 'very uncompromising *laissez-faire* doctrine' which, under Cassel, Heckscher, and others, dominated Swedish economics after the death of Wicksell. But in the course of the work Myrdal found that these ideas were much more clearly 'found further back in the history of economic thought and in other countries. Above all, they were founded on more consistent and more elaborate theories and, ultimately, on the great philosophies of natural law and utilitarianism,' he says in the preface to the English edition (p. vi). The book became a critical historical study of economic doctrines in which Myrdal tries to reveal the normative elements. In a concluding chapter he emphasizes that the economist should present his value premises explicitly before making recommendations on economic policy. Furthermore, 'only if economists are modest in their claims and renounce all pretensions to postulate universal laws and norms can they promote effectively their practical objectives, viz., to keep political arguments rational, that is to say, to base them on as complete and as correct a knowledge of the facts as possible' (p. 206).

Myrdal gained a worldwide reputation through *An American Dilemma: the Negro Problem and Modern Democracy* (1944), which book was the result of a major project for the Carnegie Corporation. In this monumental work of over a thousand tightly packed pages he sought to combine economic, social, demographic, and institutional analysis. This broad approach was to characterize almost all his subsequent writings.

His analytical framework in *An American Dilemma* consists of three bundles of interdependent causative factors: (1) the economic level; (2) standards of intelligence, ambition, health, education, decency, manners, and morals; and (3) discrimination by whites. The system of these interrelated factors may be in equilibrium, but it may also be in disequilibrium, subject to dynamic forces. The later case is the more interesting. The system will then be changing by what Myrdal calls 'cumulative causation' which may be considered a variant of a multiplier effect where the multiplier process, due to a feedback, may continue indefinitely. If, for instance, white discrimination is for some reason increased, the income of black people will decrease. This will lead to a deterioration in health, education, etc., which will cause still more white discrimination, and so forth, in a 'vicious circle'. In a similar way, an initial decrease in white discrimination may cause a cumulative improvement in the position of black people.

The principle of a cumulative causation – which goes back at least to Wicksell's cumulative process of inflation, to which Myrdal refers – is fundamental also in Myrdal's last major work – written in co-operation with a large number of researchers – the three-volume *Asian Drama: an Inquiry into the Power of Nations* (1968). Most economists have overemphasized the role of capital accumulation in the process of economic development, according to Myrdal. He regards the social system in south Asia as consisting of a number of conditions which are causally interrelated. Myrdal (1968: 1860) classifies those conditions into six broad categories: (1) output and incomes, (2) conditions of production, (3) standard of living, (4) attitudes towards life and work, (5) institutions, (6) policies.

The conditions in categories 1–5 in south Asia are in different degrees 'undesirable' from the point of view of development:

Over a period of time a change in any one of the conditions will tend to change other conditions.... If initially the system was in balance, the circular interdependence of the conditions in the social system would thus give rise to a cumulative process of change of that entire system, proceeding in the same direction as the primary change and affecting most or all conditions in the system. If, as is more probable, the system is not in balance but already changing in one direction or another, and if there is not one primary change but a number of simultaneous changes, the causal interdependence within the system would also make this more complex process cumulative. (ibid.: 1870)

In *Asian Drama* Myrdal keeps to his old principle of making his value premises explicit, dedicating twenty pages to a presentation of his own value premises and another fifty to other valuations, especially those prevailing in south Asia. His 'modernization ideals' imply that 'rationality', 'development and planning for development', 'rise of productivity', 'rise of levels of living', 'social and economic equalization', 'improved institutions and attitudes', 'national consolidation', 'national independence', 'political democracy in a narrow sense', 'democracy at the grass roots', and some other things are desirable. When at the end of the 1960s I read the chapter on his value premises, I found it rather vacant. His value premises seemed indisputable and therefore harmless. I am less sure now.

While Ohlin's contribution to the theory of trade can be considered an achievement within the neoclassical paradigm – a result of 'normal science', to use Kuhn's term – Myrdal was fundamentally an economic heretic. As such he seems to have exerted more influence on development researchers in other disciplines than on mainstream economists. (Admittedly, development economists are often not mainstream economists.)

Gösta Bagge

Some of the twentieth-century figures were domestically important, although they were in some respects odd and scarcely achieved an international reputation. One such is Gösta Bagge (1882–1951). As an economist he dedicated his genius mainly to wage formation and unemployment problems.[7] In 1917 he published his main work, the doctoral dissertation *Arbetslönens reglering genom sammanslutningar* (*The Regulation of Wages by Unions*). It deals with the effects of wage determination through collective agreements and legislation. Originally Bagge had intended to use an inductive approach, but he found that it was not appropriate. He became critical of this kind of approach – and of

American institutional research on trade unions – and presented a theoretical analysis whose results he confronted with a comprehensive empirical material.

Inter alia Bagge analysed exhaustively some problems which have been subject to more technical treatment in the last few decades, such as costs of information, risk aversion, and the relationship between wages and efficiency. His dissertation was very favourably received by Gustav Cassel, among others. For Bagge doing his own research was not enough. He established an Institute of Social Studies in Stockholm, whose head he became in 1920. He combined that position with a professorship at the University of Stockholm from 1921.

In 1924 Bagge went for a lengthy stay in Canada and the United States, where, *inter alia*, he met representatives of the Laura Spellman Rockefeller Memorial, later incorporated into the Rockefeller Foundation. The contact was maintained, and in 1925 he received an initial grant of $75,000 for a research programme based on his dissertation. In 1931 he was granted $300,000, of which $100,000 were intended for a new building. At the time such sums were really large.

The studies under the programme concentrated more on national income and long-term economic growth in Sweden than on the problems raised in Bagge's dissertation. The results were published in the new series Stockholm Economic Studies. Most of the economists who were later considered as of the Stockholm school were engaged in the programme: Erik Lindahl, Gunnar Myrdal, Erik Lundberg, Ingvar Svennilson, and Alf Johansson.

There is hardly any analysis characteristic of the Stockholm school at this early stage. Such an analysis is, however, found in the contributions from much the same group, with the addition of Hammarskjöld and Ohlin, when the group was engaged on a government committee on unemployment, set up in 1927. The four reports, by Hammarskjöld, Johansson, Myrdal, and Ohlin, were important contributions to the Stockholm school, and conduced to the weakening of Bagge's position compared with that of his subordinates. Furthermore Bagge had been considered sceptical of the ideas of the Stockholm school and of Keynesianism, a fact that did not strengthen his position.

Bagge has been more neglected than some of his contemporaries. Wadensjö (1988) suggests four reasons. First, for a decade Bagge left scientific research for politics. In 1932 he was elected a member of parliament, and in 1935 he became leader of the Conservative Party. When in 1944 he returned to Stockholm University he was a tired man. Second, he analysed trade unions and unemployment under equilibrium assumptions which in the Stockholm milieu were out of date. Third, his method, consisting of detailed accounts of different cases, was not very attractive. Fourth, his personal relations with several of the Stockholm economists became strained as time went by.

Johan Åkerman

Even more distant from the dominant view is Johan Åkerman (1896–1982), a younger brother of Gustaf Åkerman.[8] His often provocative works fitted neither into domestic nor into Anglo-American mainstream economics, but rather into the French social science tradition. An honorary degree at the Sorbonne was in line with this.

Johan Åkerman defended his doctor's thesis Om det ekonomiska livets rytmik (On the Rhythmics of Economic Life) in November 1928. Ragnar Frisch was the first opponent. Like many others, Åkerman revealed in his thesis the things that would always interest him. There is a scrupulous comparison with the statements of earlier business cycle theorists, there is a distrust of the predominant, highly aggregated equilibrium models where cyclical changes were treated as exogenous disturbances, there are considerable elements of econometrics, and there are attempts to broaden the approach, taking account also of factors other than those which are usually found in economists' analyses.

In his later writings his attempts to find connections between various social phenomena may sometimes seem overambitious and unfruitful. We may illustrate this by an example from Åkerman's review of a dissertation about communism in Sweden, written under his aegis. The author had found that the percentage of communists in the province of Blekinge was higher than expected when a 'law' of an inverse relationship between population density and communism was taken into account. This result stood even when the extent of industrialization was considered. Åkerman (1954: 75) proposes an explanation: the modest standard of the railway through the province. 'Maybe changing Blekinge's coast line to broad gauge would lower the percentage of communists so that it coincided with the "law".'

In 1939 and 1944 Åkerman published two large volumes on economic theory. The first, on economic calculations, dealt with models of rational behaviour among economic actors. But he scarcely regarded such models, based on classical and neoclassical thinking, as scientific. They did not really explain macroeconomic processes but were only schematic models of rational principles of calculation. However, causal analysis, the theme of the second volume, reconstructs actual macroeconomic courses of events. It cannot be restricted to purely economic factors but has to include sociological, political, institutional, and other factors as well.

During the last decades of his career Åkerman was especially interested in methodological problems. This study convinced him that economics needed, and would undergo, a new transformation. 'The lack of discussion about fundamental epistemological questions – in general, the lack of scientific polemic – is an omen' (1970: 131).

It is tempting to compare Åkerman with Myrdal. Both were eagerly writing on methodological issues, Myrdal emphasizing the significance of values and Åkerman focusing on epistemological problems. Both were discontented with mainstream economics and spoke for a broader socio-economic approach. They did not both, however, win the same international reputation. This is evidently a consequence of the fact that Myrdal addressed a more international audience after his Stockholm school period, and that he wrote two major works on real social and economic problems. Åkerman wrote almost exclusively in Swedish and was often quite abstruse.

Trade union economists: Meidner and Rehn

Åkerman was a purely academic economist. At the other extreme are those economists whose reputation is based on practical economic work in administration or in labour organizations. At least two such economists, Rudolf Meidner (1914–) and Gösta Rehn (1913–), have had an influence not only on actual economic policy but also to some extent on theoretical thinking about labour market policy. Their most important contribution is probably their reasoning on unemployment and inflation, which influenced Swedish economic policy for several decades, and whose traces can still be perceived. The point of their original theory was that if general economic means are to provide an acceptable level of employment even in the weakest sectors of the economy, the general level of demand has to be so high that an unacceptably high inflation is the result. They proposed a general policy of restraint combined with selective measures applied to those parts of the economy which would encounter problems.[9] In practice a deflationary policy was not achieved to that extent that Meidner and Rehn recommended. Nevertheless, discretionary means have been used until our own day. During the 1960s those means were to a large extent designed to stimulate movement from depressed areas and regions to prosperous ones. The repertoire of means has been widened as time has gone by so that those aimed at promoting migration have become less important.

In 1975 Meidner presented a far-reaching proposal for employees as a group to become owners of a substantial part of the economy by means of 'employees' funds' which should be built up from part of the profit of businesses. A considerably changed version was introduced by a law of 1983.

Lastly

We have soon reached the end of this exposition of the history of Swedish economic thought. Concluding the book, we notice that a few individual economists have played a dominant role in particular periods. As Sandmo (1988) remarks, this is a consequence of the small size of the Scandinavian countries. Those few economists are, of course, influenced by foreign currents of opinion. This makes the demarcation of Swedish economics questionable, a problem which we have solved – or, rather, run away from – by referring to the place of residence in combination with some degree of originality. However, confinement to one country is not solely problematic: it probably makes it easier for the student to consider economic theory, economic institutions, and actual economic policy simultaneously.

Another consequence of Sweden being a small country is that the academic economists not only know one another, they also know the members of the political establishment. This is evidently one reason why the leading economists – Davidson, Wicksell, Cassel, Heckscher, Myrdal, Ohlin, etc. – have been extensively involved in government committees or political work.

The specialist in the history of ideas who has read thus far may have an idea of how the evolution of economic thought in Sweden relates to the international evolution with which he is acquainted. The general reader has, we hope, been reminded of the relativity and time-boundedness of much economic thought. We are often prone to consider the state of economics in our own generation as representative of truth and wisdom, in contrast to the obsolete or confused thinking of our predecessors. Maybe the most important effect of intellectual history is that it makes the student aware, first, that things are never simple and, second, that there will be future Stiglers who claim that the economics of our time is as interesting to them as our weather forecasts.[10]

222

Notes

1 Portes (1987) even found it 'reasonable to ask whether there is now any economics outside and independent of the United States', which provoked a vehement protest from Kolm (1988).
2 An excellent survey is given by Blomström and Hettne (1984).
3 The lodestar of this thinking is, of course, the work of Marx, Engels, and Lenin. The Western historian of thought who wants an idea of how the history of economic thought can be taught in a socialist country may consult the textbooks by Fabiunke (1985) and Fabiunke and Thal (1976). A critical review, from the same camp, of contemporary Western mainstream economics (more precisely, of Samuelson's *Economics*) is presented by Sieber *et al.* (1985). What the recent political changes in Eastern Europe will mean for economic theory in those countries remains to be seen.
4 As a group French economists seem to differ from US economists especially. Frey *et al.* (1983) have examined the consensus on different statements among economists in six countries. They found that 'American economists seem to have the highest degree of consensus, followed by the German and the Swiss. More dissension was found for the French and the Belgians.' Furthermore, on several of the statements the proportion of plain agreements differed considerably between the French and the Americans. For instance, the percentage answering 'yes' without qualification on the following statements was in France and the US respectively: 'Tariffs and import quotas reduce general economic welfare', 27, 81; 'Flexible exchange rates offer an effective international monetary arrangement', 12, 61; 'Effluent taxes represent a better approach to pollution control than imposition of pollution ceilings', 28, 50; 'Consumer protection laws generally reduce economic efficiency', 5, 24. Overall the belief in economic liberalism seems to be more pronounced among US economists.
5 The text of the official announcement of the Royal Academy of Sciences is to be found in the *Scandinavian Journal of Economics* 80 (1978), 62–3. The following section on Ohlin is based mainly on Caves (1978) and Blomqvist and Siven (1988).
6 The text of the official announcement is to be found in the

Scandinavian Journal of Economics 76 (1974), 469–71. The following section is based largely on Lundberg (1974) and Reynolds (1974).

7 The section on Bagge draws mainly on Wadensjö (1988).

8 This section draws partly on Dahmén (1987), who is probably Åkerman's most interesting student. Dahmén has, *inter alia*, in the spirit of Schumpeter undertaken significant studies of economic evolution. As he is still highly active, he is not scrutinized in this historical survey.

9 One of several documents in which this policy is presented is the report from the Swedish Confederation of Trade Unions (LO), *Fackföreningsrörelsen och den fulla sysselsättningen* (Malmö, 1951).

10 According to Stigler's original statement, as quoted by Anderson and Tollison (1986), 'the economics of 1800, like the weather forecasts of 1800, is mostly out of date'. That is not to say that Stigler is uninterested in the history of thought, but that he feels that valuable older contributions are internalized in the modern literature.

References

Agardh, C.A. (1829) *Granskning av stats-ekonomiens grundläror*, Lund
Åkerman, J. (1939) *Ekonomisk teori* I, *De ekonomiska kalkylerna*, Lunds Universitets Årsskrift 36, Lund: Gleerup
—— (1944) *Ekonomisk teori* II, *Kausalanalys av det ekonomiska skeendet*, Lunds Universitets Årsskrift 39, Lund: Gleerup
—— (1954) *Politik och ekonomi i atomålderns värld*, Stockholm: Natur och Kultur
—— (1970) *Internationell politik och samhällsekonomi*, Malmö: Studentlitteratur
Anderson, G.M., and Tollison, R.D. (1986) 'Dead men tell no tales', *History of Economics Society Bulletin* 1: 59–68
Andréen, P.G. (1958) *Politik och finansväsen från 1815 års riksdag till 1830 års realisationsbeslut*, Stockholm: Almqvist & Wiksell
Arnberg, J.W. (1864) *Om arbetets och bytets frihet*, Stockholm: Norstedt
—— (1868) *Anteckningar om Frihetstidens politiska ekonomi*, Uppsala: Schultz
Bäckström, K. (1972) *Götrek och manifestet*, Stockholm: Gidlunds
Bentzel, R. (1957) Review of Faxén, *Ekonomisk Tidskrift* 59: 311–14
—— and Hansen, B. (1954) 'On recursiveness and interdependency in economic models', *Review of Economic Studies* 22: 153–68
Berch, A. (1747) *Inledning till allmänna hushållningen*, Stockholm
Bergström, V. (1969) *Den ekonomiska politiken i Sverige och dess verkningar*, Stockholm: Almqvist & Wiksell
Björkqvist, H. (1986) *Den nationalekonomiska vetenskapens utveckling i Finland intill år 1918*, Publications of the Research Institute of the Åbo Akademi Foundation 109, Åbo: Åbo Akademi
Black, D. (1955) 'Wicksell's principle in the distribution of taxation', in J.K. Eastham (ed.) *Economic Essays in Commemoration of the Dundee School of Economics, 1931–55*, London: Economists' Bookshop, for LSE
Blaug, M. (1985) *Economic Theory in Retrospect*, fourth edition, Cambridge: Cambridge University Press
Blomqvist, S., and Siven, C.H. (1988) 'Bertil Ohlin', *Ekonomisk Debatt* 4: 307–15
Blomström, M., and Hettne, B. (1984) *Development Theory in Transition:*

References

the Dependency Debate and Beyond: Third World Responses, London: Zed

Bloor, D. (1981) 'The strengths of the strong program', Philosophy of the Social Sciences 11: 199–213

Böhm-Bawerk, E. (1889) Positive Theorie des Kapitales, Innsbruck

Brahe, P. (1971) Oeconomia eller Hushållsbok för ungt Adelsfolk, ed. J. Granlund and G. Holm, Nordiska Museets Handlingar 78, Stockholm: Nordic Museum (Written in the late 1580s)

Brannigan, A. (1981) The Social Basis of Scientific Discoveries, Cambridge: Cambridge University Press

Branting, H. (1892) Socialismen, Studentföreningen Verdandis Småskrifter 45; second edition 1906, Stockholm: Bonniers

—— (1926) Tal och skrifter, ed. Z. Höglund et al., Stockholm: Tiden

Brems, H. (1978) 'What was new in Ohlin's 1933–34 macroeconomics?', History of Political Economy 10: 398–412

—— (1986) Pioneering Economic Theory, 1630–1980: a Mathematical Restatement, Baltimore, Md, and London: Johns Hopkins University Press

Buchanan, J.M. (1951) 'Knut Wicksell on marginal cost pricing', Southern Economic Journal 2: 173–8

Carlsson, S., and Rosén, J. (1980) Svensk historia II, fourth edition, Lund: Scandinavian University Books

Cassel, G. (1899a) 'Grundriss einer elementaren Preislehre', Zeitschrift für die gesamte Staatswissenschaft 55: 395–458

—— (1899b) 'Vetenskapen och det "socialistiska samhället"', Ekonomisk Tidskrift 1: 551–71

—— (1900) Das Recht auf den vollen Arbeiterstrag, Göttingen: Vandenhoeck & Ruprecht

—— (1901a) 'Die Produktionskostentheorie Ricardos und die ersten Aufgaben der theoretischen Volkwirtschaftslehre', Zeitschrift für die gesamte Staatswissenschaft 57: 68–100

—— (1901b) 'Kapitalbildningen och den socialistiska delningstanken', Ekonomisk Tidskrift 3: 129–78

—— (1902) Socialpolitik, Stockholm: Geber

—— (1903) The Nature and Necessity of Interest, London: Macmillan

—— (1908) Riksbanken under krisen, 1907–8, Stockholm: Geber

—— (1917) Dyrtid och sedelöverflöd, Stockholm: Norstedt

—— (1918) Theoretische Sozialökonomie, Leipzig: Wintersche; translated as Cassel (1923)

—— (1921) The World's Monetary Problems, London: Constable

—— (1922) Money and Foreign Exchange after 1914, London: Constable

—— (1923) The Theory of Social Economy, London: Unwin; revised edition Benn, 1929

—— (1925) Fundamental Thoughts in Economics, London: Unwin

—— (1932) The Theory of Social Economy, London: Benn

—— (1934) Teoretisk socialekonomi, Stockholm: Kooperativa Förbundet

—— (1935) *On Quantitative Thinking in Economics*, Oxford: Clarendon

—— (1936) *The Downfall of the Gold Standard*, Oxford: Clarendon

—— (1940) *I förnuftets tjänst* I, Stockholm: Natur och Kultur

—— (1941) *I förnuftets tjänst* II, Stockholm: Natur och Kultur

Caves, R.E. (1978) 'Bertil Ohlin's contribution to economics', *Scandinavian Journal of Economics* 80: 86–99

Christiernin, P.N. (1971) *The Swedish Bullionist Controversy: P.N. Christiernin's Lectures on the High Price of Foreign Exchange in Sweden*, ed. Robert V. Eagly, Philadelphia, Pa.: American Philosophical Society. (First published 1761)

Chydenius, A. (1765a) *Källan till rikets vanmakt*, Stockholm

—— (1765b) *The National Gain*, ed. G. Schauman, London: Benn, 1931

Clark, J.B. (1899) *The Distribution of Wealth*, London

Coats, A.W. (1985) 'The sociology of knowledge and the history of economics', in W. Samuels (ed.) *Research in the History of Economic Thought and Methodology*, Boston, Mass.: Jai

Dahmén, E. (1987) 'Johan Åkerman', *Ekonomisk Debatt* 6: 507–13

Davidson, D. (1878) 'Bidrag till läran om de ekonomiska lagarna för kapitalbildningen', dissertation, University of Uppsala

—— (1880) *Bidrag till jordränteteoriens historia*, Uppsala

—— (1886) *Europas centralbanker*, Uppsala

—— (1889a) *Kommentar till bevillningsförordningen*, Uppsala

—— (1889b) *Om beskattningsnormen vid inkomstskatten*, Uppsala

—— (1913) Lectures transcribed by Dr P. Jacobsson

—— (1917) Lectures transcribed by Dr P. Jacobsson

Deane, P. (1983) 'The scope and method of economic science', *Economic Journal* 93: 1–12

Fabiunke, G. (1985) *Geschichte der politischen Ökonomie. Die klassische politische Ökonomie des Bürgertums und ihre Vorläufer*, Berlin: Die Wirtschaft

Fabiunke, G., and Thal, P. (1976) *Geschichte der politischen Ökonomie. Leitfaden*, Berlin: Die Wirtschaft

Faxén, K.O. (1957) *Monetary and Fiscal Policy under Uncertainty*, Uppsala: Almqvist & Wiksell

Fisher, I. (1911) *The Purchasing Power of Money*, New York: Macmillan

—— (1935) *Stabilized Money: a History of the Movement*, London: Allen & Unwin

Frängsmyr, T. (1971–2) 'The divine economy: on religion and economy in eighteenth-century Sweden', *Lychnos* yearbook, Stockholm and Uppsala: Almqvist & Wiksell

Frey, B.S., Ginsburgh, V., Pestieau, P., Pommerehne, W.W., and Schneider, F. (1983) 'Consensus, dissension and ideology among economists in various European countries and in the United States', *European Economic Review* 23: 59–69

Frisch, R. (1951) *Knut Wicksell: a Cornerstone in Modern Economic Theory*, Oslo: Socialøkonomisk Institutt, University of Oslo

References

Gårdlund, T. (1956) *Knut Wicksell: rebell i det nya riket*, Stockholm: Bonniers
—— (1958) *The Life of Knut Wicksell*, Stockholm Economic Studies, new series 2, Stockholm: Almqvist & Wiksell
Gasslander, O. (1949) *J.A. Gripenstedt, statsman och företagare*, Lund: Gleerups
Geijer, E.G. (1836) *Svenska folkets historia* III, Örebro
—— (1980) *Historiska skrifter i urval*, ed. T. Nybom, Stockholm: Tiden
Giöbel-Lilja, I. (1948) *Gustav Cassel: en livsskildring*, Stockholm: Natur och Kultur
Hahn, F.H. (1952) 'Expectations and equilibrium', *Economic Journal* 62: 802–19
—— (1973) *On the Notion of Equilibrium in Economics*, Cambridge: Cambridge University Press
—— (1982) *Money and Inflation*, Oxford: Blackwell
Hamilton, G.K. (1858) *Om politiska ekonomiens utveckling och begrepp*, Uppsala
—— (1865) *Om arbetsklassen och arbetare-föreningar*, Lund
Hammarskjöld, D. (1932) 'Utkast till en algebraisk metod för dynamisk prisanalys', *Ekonomisk Tidskrift* 34: 157–76
—— (1933) *Konjunkturspridningen: en teoretisk och historisk undersökning*, Stockholm: Norstedt
Hansen, B. (1951) *A Study in the Theory of Inflation*, London: Allen & Unwin
—— (1966) *Lectures in Economic Theory* I, Lund: Studentlitteratur
Hansson, B.A. (1982) *The Stockholm School and the Development of Dynamic Method*, London: Croom Helm
—— (1985) 'Keynes's notion of equilibrium in the *General Theory*', *Journal of Post-Keynesian Economics* 7: 332–41
Harcourt, G.C. (1972) *Some Cambridge Controversies in the Theory of Capital*, Cambridge: Cambridge University Press
Hart, A.G. (1940) *Anticipations, Uncertainty, and Dynamic Planning*, reprinted New York: Kelley, 1965
Hatta, T. (1987) 'Capital perversities', in J. Eatwell, M. Milgate, and P. Newman (eds.) *The New Palgrave: a Dictionary of Economics*, London: Macmillan; New York: Stockton; Tokyo: Maruzen
Hayek, F.A. (1928) 'Das intertemporale Gleichgewichtssystem der Preise und die Bewegungen des Geldwertes', *Weltwirtschaftliches Archiv* 28: 3–76
—— (1941) *The Pure Theory of Capital*, London: Routledge
Heckscher, E.F. (1904) 'Ekonomisk historia: några antydningar', *Historisk Tidskrift* 24: 167–98
—— (1907) 'Till belysning av järnvägarnas betydelse för Sveriges ekonomiska utveckling', dissertation, University of Uppsala
—— (1908a) 'Betydelsen av nationalekonomisk utbildning för statsförvaltning och näringslivets korporationer', *Nationalekonomiska Föreningens Förhandlingar* 1–29
—— (1908b) 'Produktplakatet och dess förutsättningar: bidrag till

merkantilsystemets historia i Sverige', in *Historiska studier tillägnade professor Harald Hjärne*, revised edition 1922, Uppsala and Stockholm: Almqvist & Wiksell, 593–784

—— (1908c) *Socialismens grundvalar: en diskussion å Folkets Hus*, Stockholm: Socialdemokratiska Arbetarepartiets Bok- och Broschyrförlag

—— (1915) *Världskrigets ekonomi*, Stockholm: Norstedt

—— (1918a) *Kontinentalsystemet*, Stockholm: Norstedt; translated as Heckscher (1923)

—— (1918b) *Svenska produktionsproblem*, Stockholm: Bonniers

—— (1919) 'Utrikeshandelns verkan på inkomstfördelningen', *Ekonomisk Tidskrift* 21 (II, Nationalekonomiska studier tillägnade professor David Davidson): 1–32; translated as Heckscher (1949)

—— (1921a) *Gammal och ny ekonomisk liberalism*, Stockholm: Norstedt

—— (1921b) 'Verkan av för låg räntefot', *Ekonomisk Tidskrift* 23 (Nationalekonomiska studier tillägnade Knut Wicksell): 49–56

—— (1922) *Ekonomi och historia*, Stockholm: Bonniers

—— (1923) *The Continental System: an Economic Interpretation*, Oxford: Clarendon

—— (1924a) 'Intermittent fria nyttigheter', *Ekonomisk Tidskrift* 26: 41–54

—— (1924b) 'Skyddstullsystemets teoretiska grunder', *Tull- och Traktatkommitténs betänkanden* 36: 1, SOU 1924: 37, Stockholm, 22–53

—— (1926) 'Penningväsende och penningpolitik från krigsutbrottet till den internationella guldmyntfotens återställelse, 1914–25', in E.F. Heckscher (ed.) *Bidrag till Sveriges ekonomiska och sociala historia under och efter världskriget* II, Stockholm: Norstedt, 1–175; translated in Heckscher, 1930b

—— (1928) 'Den ekonomiska innebörden av offentliga åtgärder mot arbetslöshetens verkningar', in *Arbetslöshetssakkunnigas betänkande*, Bilaga 1, SOU 1928: 9, Stockholm, 393–414

—— (1929) 'A plea for theory in economic history', *Economic Journal* 38: supplement, 525–34; also in F.C. Lane and I.C. Riemersma (eds.) *Enterprise and Secular Change*, Homewood, Ill.: Irwin, 1953, 421–30

—— (1930a) 'Den ekonomiska historiens aspekter', *Ekonomisk Tidskrift* 32: 1–85; English summary in K. Kock (ed.) *Economic Essays in Honour of Gustav Cassel*, London: Allen & Unwin, 1933, 705–20

—— (1930b) 'Monetary history from 1914 to 1925 in its relations with foreign trade and shipping', in K. Bergendal, E.F. Heckscher, *et al.* (eds.) *Sweden, Norway, Denmark, and Iceland in the World War* III, New Haven, Conn., and London: Carnegie Endowment for International Peace, 127–268

—— (1931a) *Merkantilismen*, second edition 1953, Stockholm: Norstedt; translated as Heckscher (1935)

—— (1931b) *Industrialismen: den ekonomiska utvecklingen sedan 1750*, fifth edition 1953, Stockholm: Rabén & Sjörgen

—— (1931c) *Sveriges penningpolitik*, Stockholm: Norstedt

References

—— (1934) *Tvångshushållning och planhushållning*, Stockholm: Kooperativa Förbundet

—— (1935) *Mercantilism*, second edition 1955, London: Allen & Unwin

—— (1935–6) *Sveriges ekonomiska historia från Gustav Vasa* I, *Före Frihetstiden*, Stockholm; Bonniers

—— (1936a) 'Industrins historiska förutsättningar och allmänna karaktär', in *Sveriges industri*, Stockholm: Sveriges Industriförbund, 3–96; translated in Heckscher and Söderlund (1953b)

—— (1936b) *Ekonomisk-historiska studer*, Stockholm: Bonniers

—— (1939) 'Quantitative measurement in economic history', *Quarterly Journal of Economics* 53: 167–93

—— (1941) *Svenskt arbete och liv från medeltiden till nutiden*, Stockholm: Bonniers; translated as Heckscher (1954)

—— (1944) *Historieuppfattning, materialistisk och annan*, Stockholm: Bonniers

—— (1947) 'Ekonomisk historia och dess gränsvetenskaper', *Historisk Tidskrift* 67: 1–17

—— (1949) 'The effect of foreign trade on the distribution of income', *Readings in the Theory of International Trade*, Philadelphia, Pa.: AEA, 272–300

—— (1950a) *Sveriges ekonomiska historia från Gustav Vasa* II, *Det moderna Sveriges grundläggning*, Stockholm: Bonniers

—— (1950b) *Eli F. Heckschers bibliografi*, Stockholm: Ekonomiskhistoriska Institutet

—— (1951) *Studium och undervisning i ekonomisk historia*, Stockholm: Gleerup

—— (1952) 'David Davidson', *International Economic Papers* 2, London and New York: Macmillan, 111 ff.

—— (1953a) 'A survey of economic thought in Sweden, 1875–1950', *Scandinavian Economic History Review* 1: 105–25

—— and E. Söderlund (1953b) 'The rise of industry', in G. Howard Smith (ed.) *The Development and Present Scope of Industry in Sweden*, Stockholm: Svenska Industriförlaget, 17–75

—— (1954) *An Economic History of Sweden*, New Haven, Conn.: Harvard University Press. (A short version of *Sveriges ekonomiska historia*)

Henriksson, R.G.H. (1979) 'Eli F. Heckscher och svensk nationalekonomi', *Ekonomisk Debatt* 7: 510–20

—— (1987a) 'Arthur Montgomery', *Svenskt biografiskt lexikon* 25: 709–14

—— ed. (1987b) *Konjunkturinstitutet under Erik Lundbergs tid*, Stockholm: Norstedt

—— (1989) 'The institutional base of the Stockholm school: the Political Economy Club (1917–51)', *History of Economics Society Bulletin* 11, 1: 59–97

Herlitz, L. (1964) 'The concept of mercantilism', *Scandinavian Economic History Review* 12: 101–20

—— (1976) 'Härtappad fysiokratism', *Scandia* 1: 92–114
Hermann, F. (1832) *Staatswirtschaftliche Untersuchungen,* Munich
Hettne, B. (1980) 'Ekonomisk historia i Sverige under femtio år', *Historisk Tidskrift* 100: 140–75
Hicks, J.R. (1946) *Value and Capital,* second edition, Oxford: Clarendon; first edition 1939
—— (1956) 'Methods of dynamic analysis', in *25 Economic Essays in Honour of Erik Lindahl,* Stockholm: Svenska Tryckeri
—— (1965) *Capital and Growth,* Oxford: Clarendon
—— (1973) 'Recollections and documents', *Economica* 40: 2–11; reprinted in J. R. Hicks, *Economic Perspectives,* Oxford: Clarendon, 1977
Järta, H. (1823) *Om spannmålspris och spannmålshandeln,* Falun
Johannisson, K. (1988) *Det mätbara samhället,* Stockholm: Norstedt
Johansson, A. (1934) *Löneutvecklingen och arbetslösheten,* Stockholm: Norstedt
Jonung, L. (1977) 'Knut Wicksells prisstabiliseringsnorm och penningpolitiken på 1930-talet', in J. Herin and L. Werin (eds.) *Ekonomisk debatt och ekonomisk politik: nationalekonomiska föreningen 100 år,* Stockholm: Norstedt
—— (1979a) 'Konjunkturteorin och 30-talskrisen', *Ekonomisk Debatt* 4: 267–79
—— (1979b) 'Cassel, Davidsson and Heckscher on Swedish monetary policy: a confidential report to the Riksbank in 1931', *Economy and History* 22: 85–101
—— (1987a) 'The Stockholm School after Fifty Years: an attempt at appraisal', paper presented at the History of Economics Society annual meeting, Boston, Mass.
—— (1987b) 'Stockholmsskolan: vart tog den vägen', *Ekonomisk Debatt* 15: 318–26
Keynes, J.M. (1921) *A Treatise on Probability,* reprinted in *The Collected Writings of John Maynard Keynes* VIII, London: Macmillan, 1973
—— (1930) *A Treatise on Money,* reprinted in *The Collected Writings* V–VI, London: Macmillan, 1971
—— (1936) *The General Theory of Employment, Interest and Money,* reprinted in *The Collected Writings* VII, London: Macmillan, 1973
—— (1973) *The* General Theory *and After,* in *The Collected Writings* XIII–XIV, London: Macmillan, 1973
—— (1979) *The* General Theory *and After: a Supplement, The Collected Writings* XXIX, London: Macmillan, 1979
Klammer, A. (1984) 'Levels of discourse in classical economics', *History of Political Economy* 16: 263–90
Knies, K. (1873–9) *Geld und Kredit,* Berlin
Knight, F. (1921) *Risk, Uncertainty and Profit,* reprinted New York: Kelley, 1964
Knorr-Cetina, K. (1981) *The Manufacture of Knowledge: an Essay on the Constructivist and the Contextual Nature of Science,* Oxford: Pergamon
Kolm, S.C. (1988) 'Economics in Europe and in the US', *European Economic Review* 32: 207–12

References

Kuhn, T.S. (1970) *The Structure of Scientific Revolutions*, second edition, Chicago: University of Chicago Press

Landgren, K.G. (1957) *Economics in Modern Sweden*, Washington, D.C.: Library of Congress

—— (1960) *Den 'nya ekonomien' i Sverige*, Stockholm: Almqvist & Wiksell

Liedman, S.E. (1986) *Den synliga handen: Anders Berch och ekonomiämnena vid 1700-talets svenska universitet*, Stockholm: Arbetarkultur

Lindahl, E. (1929a) 'Prisbildningsproblemet från kapitalteoretisk synpunkt', *Ekonomisk Tidskrift* 31: 31–81

—— (1929b) *Penningpolitikens mål*, Malmö: Försäkringsaktiebolaget

—— (1930) *Penningpolitikens medel*, Malmö: Försäkringsaktiebolaget

—— (1934) 'A note on the dynamic pricing problem', mimeo, Göteborg, 23 October; reprinted in Steiger (1971) and Keynes (1979)

—— (1935) 'Introduction to the theory of price movements in a closed community', chapter 1 (the only surviving) of 'Monetary Policy and its Theoretical Basis', unpublished manuscript of early 1935

—— (1939) *Studies in the Theory of Money and Capital* I, 'The dynamic approach to economic theory'; II, 'The rate of interest and the price level' (translation of Lindahl, 1930); III, 'The place of capital in the theory of price' (translation of Lindahl, 1929a), London: Allen & Unwin

—— (1942) 'Metodfrågor inom den dynamiska teorien', *Ekonomisk Tidskrift* 44: 159–71

—— (1954) 'On Keynes's economic system', *Economic Record* 30

—— ed. (1958) *Knut Wicksell: Selected Papers on Economic Theory*, London: Allen & Unwin

Lindroth, S. (1975) *Svensk lärdomshistoria: medeltiden, Reformationstiden*, Stockholm: Norstedt

—— (1978) *Svensk lärdomshistoria: Frihetstiden*, Stockholm: Norstedt

Lönnroth, E. (1940) *Statsmakt och statsfinans i det medeltida Sverige*, Göteborgs Högskolas Årsskrift XLV, Göteborg; Göteborgs Högskola

Lönnroth, J. (1987) 'Ekonomporträttet: Johan Risingh', *Ekonomisk Debatt* 5: 407–12

—— (1989) 'Ekonomporträttet: Gustaf Steffen', *Ekonomisk Debatt* 3: 222–35

Lowry, S.T., ed. (1987) *Pre-classical Economic Thought*, Boston, Mass., Dordrecht, and Lancaster: Kluwer

Lundberg, E. (1930) 'Om begreppet ekonomisk jämvikt', *Ekonomisk Tidskrift* 32: 133–60

—— (1937) *Studies in the Theory of Economic Expansion*, reprinted New York: Kelley & Millman, 1955

—— (1953) *Konjunkturer och ekonomisk politik*, Stockholm: Norstedt

—— (1974) 'Gunnar Myrdal's contribution to economic theory', *Scandinavian Journal of Economics* 4: 472–8

Magnusson, L. (1977) 'Economic thought and group interests: Adam Smith, Christopher Polhem. Lars Salvius and classical political economy', *Scandinavian Journal of History* 2: 243–64

232

—— (1987) 'Mercantilism and "reform" mercantilism: the rise of economic discourse in Sweden during the eighteenth century', *History of Political Economy* 19: 415–33

Månsson, P. (1520) *Bondakonst*, ed. J. Granlund, Uppsala: Svenska Fornminnessällskapet, 1983

Marshall, A. (1920) *Principles of Economics*, ninth (variorum) edition, London: Macmillan, 1961

Marx, K. (1970) *Kapitalet* I, second edition, Staffanstorp: Cavefors/Clarté

—— (1971) *Critique of the Gotha programme* (1875), Moscow: Progress

—— (1981) *Capital* III, Harmondsworth: Penguin

Menger, C. (1871) *Grundsätze der Volkswirtschaftslehre*, Vienna; translated 1950 as *Principles of Economics*, Glencoe, Ill.: Free Press

Meurling, P. (1983) *Geijer och Marx*, Stockholm: Tiden

Mises, L. (1912) *The Theory of Money and Credit*, third English edition, Indianapolis, Ind.: Liberty Classics, 1981

Montgomery, A. (1946) *Svensk ekonomisk historia, 1913–39*, Stockholm: Kooperativa Forbundet

—— (1953) 'Eli F. Heckscher som vetenskapsman', *Ekonomisk Tidskrift* 55: 149–85; English translation in Joseph F. Lambie (ed.) *Architects and Craftsmen in History: Festschrift für Abbott Payson Usher*, Veröffentlichungen der List Gesellschaft 2, Tübingen: Mohr (Siebeck), 1956, 119–46

Myhrman, J. (1976) 'Experience of flexible exchange rates in earlier periods: theories, evidence and a new view', *Scandinavian Journal of Economics* 78: 169–96

Myrdal, G. (1927) *Prisbildningsproblemet och föränderligheten*, Uppsala and Stockholm: Almqvist & Wiksell

—— (1931) 'Om penningteoretisk jämvikt: en studie över den "normala räntan" i Wicksells penninglära', *Ekonomisk Tidskrift* 33: 191–308

—— (1933) 'Der Gleichgewichtsbegriff als Instrument in der geldtheoretischen Analyse', in F.A. von Hayek (ed.) *Beiträge zur Geldtheorie*, Vienna: Springer. (A development of Myrdal, 1931)

—— with A. Myrdal (1934) *Kris i befolkningsfrågan*, Stockholm: Bonniers

—— (1939) *Monetary Equilibrium*, reprinted New York: Kelley, 1965. (A development of Myrdal, 1933)

—— (1945) 'Gustav Cassel: in memoriam', *Ekonomisk Revy* 2: 3–13

—— (1953) *The Political Element in the Development of Economic Theory*, London: Routledge

—— (1968) *Asian Drama: an Inquiry into the Poverty of Nations*, New York: Pantheon

—— (1972) *Vetenskap och politik i nationalekonomin*, Stockholm: Rabén & Sjögren

Nagel, E., ed. (1950) *John Stuart Mill's Philosophy of Scientific Method*, New York: Hafner

Nordencrantz (Bachmansson), A. (1730) *Arcana Oeconomiae et Commercii*, Stockholm

References

—— (1759) 'Til riksens höglofl. ständer ...', in *Samling af skrifter* I
—— (1765) 'Bekymmerslösa stunders menlösa och owäldiga tankar ...', in *Samling af skrifter* II
Ohlin, B. (1924) *Handelns teori*, Stockholm: Centraltryckeriet
—— (1934) *Penningpolitik, offentliga arbeten, subventioner och tullar som medel mot arbetslösheten: bidrag till expansionens teori*, Stockholm: Norstedt
—— (1936) introduction to K. Wicksell, *Interest and Prices* (1936)
—— (1937) 'Some notes on the Stockholm theory of savings and investments' I–II, *Economic Journal* 47: 53–69, 221–40
—— (1959) 'The quantity theory in Swedish literature', *Economy and History* II: 3–18, University of Lund
Ohlin, G. (1968) 'Eli F. Heckscher', in David L. Sills (ed.) *International Encyclopedia of the Social Sciences* 6: 339–41, New York: Free Press
—— (1978) 'On the formulation of monetary theory', *History of Political Economy* 10: 353–88
Olausson, L. (1980) 'Marxism och socialdemokrati', in B. Lindberg (ed.) *17 uppsatser i svensk idé- och lärdomshistoria*, Uppsala: Carmina
Olson, J.E. (1983) 'Atterdag Wermelin och arbetarrörelsen: en biografi', in L. Vikström (ed.) *Marx i Sverige*, Stockholm: Arbetarkultur
Östlind, A. (1945) *Svensk samhällsekonomi 1914–22*, Stockholm: Svenska Bankföreningen
Patinkin, D. (1976) *Keynes's Monetary Thought*, Durham, N.C.: Duke University Press
—— (1978) 'Some observations on Ohlin's 1933 article', *History of Political Economy* 10: 413–19; reprinted in D. Patinkin and J.C. Leith (eds.) *Keynes, Cambridge and the General Theory*, London: Macmillan, 1977
Persson, M., and Siven, C.H. (1988) 'Ekonomporträttet: Pehr Niclas Christiernin', *Ekonomisk Debatt* 5: 389–99
Petander, K. (1912) *De nationalekonomiska åskådningarna i Sverige* I, *1718–65*, Stockholm: Norstedt
Péteri, G. (1984) 'The inflation-proof gold standard: the foreign policy of Riksbankschefen Victor Moll and the origin of the Swedish ban on gold imports in 1924', *Journal of European Economic History* 13: 635–63
Phinney, J.T. (1933) 'Gold production and the price level', *Quarterly Journal of Economics* 47: 647–79
Portes, R. (1987) 'Economics in Europe', *European Economic Review* 31, 6: 1329–40
Reynolds, L.G. (1974) 'Gunnar Myrdal's contribution to economics, 1940–70', *Scandinavian Journal of Economics* 4: 479–97
Ricardo, D. (1817) *On the Principles of Political Economy and Taxation* I, in P. Sraffa and M.H. Dobb (eds.) *Works and Correspondence of David Ricardo*, Cambridge: Cambridge University Press, 1951
Risingh, J.C. (1669) *Ett uthtogh om kiöphandelen eller commercierne ...*, Stockholm
Robbins, L. (1932) *An Essay on the Nature and Significance of Economic Science*, second edition 1935, London: Macmillan

Robinson, J.V. (1953–4) 'The production function and the theory of capital', *Review of Economic Studies* 80: 503–85

Saint-Etienne, C. (1984) *The Great Depression, 1920–38: Lessons for the 1980's*, Stanford, Cal.: Stanford University Press

Sandelin, B. (1980) 'Wicksell's missing equation, the production function and the Wicksell effect', *History of Political Economy* 12: 29–40

—— (1989) 'Knight's Crusonia plant: a short cut to the Wicksell effect', *History of Political Economy* 21: 15–26

Sandmo, A. (1988) 'History of economic thought: the Scandinavian contributions: introductory remarks', *European Economic Review* 32: 491–4

Schumpeter, J.A. (1972) *A History of Economic Analysis*, London: Allen & Unwin

Seligman, B. (1962) *Main Currents in Modern Economics*, New York: Free Press

Sieber, R., *et al.* (1985) *Wie bürgerliche Ökonomen erzogen werden. Eine Auseinandersetzung mit der 'Volkswirtschaftslehre' von Paul A. Samuelson*, Berlin: Dietz

Siven, C.H. (1985) 'The end of the Stockholm school', *Scandinavian Journal of Economics* 87: 577–93

—— (1987) 'Perspektiv på Stockholmsskolan', *Ekonomisk Debatt* 15: 287–97

Söderlund, E. (1953) 'Eli F. Heckscher', *Scandinavian Economic History Review* I: 137–40

Södersten, B. (1970) 'Per Albin och den socialistiska reformismen', in G. Fredriksson, D. Strand, and B. Södersten *Per Albin-linjen*, Stockholm: Norstedt

Sraffa, P. (1960) *The Production of Commodities by Means of Commodities*, Cambridge: Cambridge University Press

Steffen, G. (1890) 'Den nya riktningen inom Englands nationalekonomi', *Finsk Tidskrift* 2: 3–18

—— (1900) *Lönearbetaren och samhället*, Stockholm: Bonniers

—— (1914) *Utvecklingen av Karl Marx' materialistiska samhällsuppfattning*, Stockholm: Tiden

Steiger, O. (1971) *Studien zur Entstehung der neuen Witschaftslehre in Schweden. Eine Anti-kritik*, Berlin: Duncker & Humblot

—— (1976) 'Bertil Ohlin and the origins of the Keynesian revolution', *History of Political Economy* 8: 341–66

—— (1978) 'Prelude to the theory of a monetary economy: origins and significance of Ohlin's 1933 approach', *History of Political Economy* 10: 420–46

Stenkula, A. (1839) *En blick från stats-ekonomien på Sweriges handel och näringsflit*, Helsingborg

Stigler, G.J. (1982) *The Economist as Preacher*, Oxford: Blackwell

Svennilson, I. (1938) *Ekonomisk planering*, Uppsala: Almqvist & Wiksell

Swan, T.W. (1965) 'Economic growth and capital accumulation', *Economic Record* 32: 343–61

References

Temin, P. (1976) *Did Monetary Forces Cause the Depression?*, New York: Norton

Thomas, B. (1935) 'The monetary doctrines of Professor Davidson', *Economic Journal* 45: 36–50

—— (1936) *Monetary Policy and Crisis: a Study of Swedish Experience*, London: Routledge

Tooke, T. (1844) *An Inquiry into the Currency Principle*, London

—— and Newmarch, W. (1838–56) *A History of Prices and the State of Circulation, 1792–1856*, London

Uhr, C.G. (1951) 'Knut Wicksell: a centennial evaluation', *American Economic Review* 41: 829–60

—— (1960) *Economic Doctrines of Knut Wicksell*, Berkeley, Cal.: University of California Press

—— (1963) *Anders Chydenius, 1729–1803: a Finnish predecessor to Adam Smith*, Meddelanden från Nationalekonomiska Institutionen vid Handelshögskolan vid Åbo Akademi 6, Åbo: Åbo Akademi

—— (1975) *Economic Doctrines of David Davidsson*, Uppsala: Almqvist & Wiksell

—— (1977) 'Economists and policy-making, 1930–36: Sweden's experience', *History of Political Economy* 9: 89–121

—— (1979) 'Eli F. Heckscher, 1879–1952, and his treatise on mercantilism revisited', *Economy and History* 23: 3–39

—— (1987) 'Eli F. Heckscher', in J. Eatwell, M. Milgate, and P. Newman (eds.) *The New Palgrave: a Dictionary of Economics*, London: Macmillan

Unga, N. (1976) *Socialdemokratin och arbetslöshetsfrågan, 1912–34*, Arkiv Avhandlingsserie 4, Lund

Virrankoski, P. (1988) 'Anders Chydenius and the government of Gustavus III of Sweden in the 1770s', *Scandinavian Journal of History* 13: 107–19

Wadensjö, E. (1987) 'Ekonomporträttet: Carl Adolph Agardh', *Ekonomisk Debatt* 2: 139–46

—— (1988) 'Ekonomporträttet: Gösta Bagge', *Ekonomisk Debatt* 7: 569–76

Walker, D.A. (1988) 'Ten major problems in the study of the history of economic thought', *History of Economics Society Bulletin* 10: 99–115

Wallerius, B. (1975) 'Carl-Adolph Agardh: romantikern, politikern', dissertation (with English summary), University of Göteborg

Wermelin, A. (1887) *Karl Marx' värdeteori*, Stockholm: Bonniers

Whitley, R. (1984) *The Intellectual and Social Organization of the Sciences*, Oxford: Oxford University Press

Wicksell, K. (1890a) 'Tomme maver – og fulde magasiner', *Samtiden* 1: 245–57, 293–304

—— (1890b) 'Überproduktion oder Uberbevölkerung', *Zeitschrift für die gesamte Staatswissenschaft* 46: 1–12

—— (1892) 'Kapitalzins und Arbeitslohn', *Jahrbücher für Nationalökonomie und Statistik* 59: 852–74

References

—— (1893) *Über Wert, Kapital, und Rente*, Jena; translated as Wicksell (1954)

—— [Sven Trygg] (1894) *Vära skatter: hvilka betala dem och hvilka borde betala?* Stockholm

—— (1896) *Finanztheoretische Untersuchungen nebst Darstellung und Kritik des Steuerwesens Schwedens*, Jena

—— (1898) *Geldzins und Güterpreise*, Jena; translated as Wicksell (1936)

—— (1899) 'Klassisk nationalekonomi och vetenskaplig socialism', *Ekonomisk Tidskrift*: 462–9 (review of F. Linderberg, *Karl Marx og den historiske socialisme*)

—— (1901) *Föreläsningar i nationalekonomi* I, Lund: Berlingska

—— (1902) *Allianser mellan arbetare och arbetsgivare*, Stockholm: Studentföreningen Verdandis Småskrifter

—— (1904) 'Mål och medel i nationalekonomien', *Ekonomisk Tidskrift* 6: 457–74; translated as Wicksell (1958b)

—— (1905) *Socialiststaten och nutidssamhället*, Stockholm: Studentföreningen Verdandis Småskrifter

—— (1906) *Föreläsningar i nationalekonomi* II, second edition 1915, Stockholm; translated as Wicksell (1935)

—— (1907) review of E.F. Heckscher, *Järnvägarnas inflytande på Sveriges ekonomiska utveckling*, *Statsvetenskaplig Tidskrift* 10: 337–41

—— (1910) *Läran om befolkningen: dess sammansättning och föränderlighet*, Stockholm: Studentföreningen Verdandis Småskrifter

—— (1911) *Föreläsningar i nationalekonomi* I, second edition, Lund: Berlingska

—— (1919) review of Heckscher, *Svenska produktionsproblem* 1–2, *Forum* 6: 16–17, 29–31

—— (1925) 'Valutaspörsmålet i de skandinaviska länderna', *Ekonomisk Tidskrift* 27: 205–22; translated 1936 as an appendix to *Interest and Prices*, 199–219

—— (1928) *Föreläsningar i nationalekonomi* I, third edition, Lund: Gleerups; translated as Wicksell (1934)

—— (1934a) *Lectures on Political Economy* I, London: Routledge

—— (1934b) 'Real capital and interest', in *Lectures on Political Economy* I: 258–99 (from *Ekonomisk Tidskrift* 25: 145–80, 1923)

—— (1935) *Lectures on Political Economy* II, London: Routledge

—— (1936) *Interest and Prices*, trans. R.F. Kahn, London: Macmillan

—— (1952) 'The enigma of business cycles', *International Economic Papers* III, London and New York: Macmillan

—— (1954) *Value, Capital, and Rent*, London: Allen & Unwin

—— (1958a) 'A new principle of just taxation', trans. J.M. Buchanan, in R.A. Musgrave and A.T. Peacock (eds.) *Classics in the Theory of Public Finance*, London: Macmillan

—— (1958b) 'Ends and means in economics', in E. Lindahl (ed.) *Knut Wicksell: Selected Papers on Economic Theory*, London: Allen & Unwin

References

Wicksell Nordquist, L. (1985) *Anna Bugge Wicksell*, Malmö: Liber
Wicksteed, P.H. (1894) *The Co-ordination of the Laws of Distribution*, London: Macmillan
Winch, D. (1966) 'The Keynesian revolution in Sweden', *Journal of Political Economy* 74: 168–78
Wold, H. (1952) *Demand Analysis*, Uppsala: Almqvist & Wiksell
Yohe, W.P. (1959) 'An analysis of Professor Lindahl's sequence model', *L'Industria*
—— (1978) 'Ohlin's 1933 reformation of monetary theory', *History of Political Economy* 10: 447–53

Index

absolute value 55–7
academic freedom 166
accommodation process 185
Agardh, C.A. 21, 28–30
Age of Freedom 2–3, 4, 16–17
aggregate income 89, 93
aggregate product 89, 93
agio theory of interest 48
Åkerman, G. 86, 111–13
Åkerman, J. 86, 220–1
alcoholism 78
alloy and standard (*skrot och korn*)
    15, 41
amortization of public debt 70–1
Anderson, G.M. 224
Andréen, P.G. 42
anticipated processes 203–5; *see
    also* expectations
Arnberg, J.W. 18, 32–3
Asia, south 217–18
Association of National
    Economists
    (Nationalekonomiska
    Föreningen) 33
Austrian school 8
autonomous changes in
    consumption 192–6

Bachmansson, A. *see*
    Nordencrantz
Bäckström, K. 42
Bagge, G. 142, 159, 218–20;
    Heckscher and 146, 148–9, 164
bank credit *see* credit
bank crisis 31

Bank of Sweden: Cassel and
    138–40; gold invasion 96;
    Heckscher 158; price stability
    138
bank transport notes 22
banknotes 22–3, 160
banks 41
Bastiat, F. 31–2
Bentzel, R. 209, 210; recursive
    systems 171, 207–8
Berch, A. 3, 18–21, 33
Bergström, V. 136, 138
Bernadotte, J. 27, 28
Bernstein, E. 38
Björkqvist, H. 1, 3, 42
Black, D. 119
blasphemy 85
Blaug, M. 114
Blekinge 220
Blomqvist, S. 223
Blomström, M. 223
Bloor, D. 123
Böhm-Bawerk, E. 75, 125; capital
    theory 48–9; theory of interest
    48; Cassel and 125, 128, 130;
    Wicksell 81, 98–9
botany 21
Brahe, P. 13
Brannigan, A. 123
Branting, H. 35, 39, 42, 43
Brask, Bishop H. 12
Brems, H. 7, 88, 195–6
Brisman, S. 139
broadening 101–2
Buchanan, J.M. 115

239

Bugge, A. *see* Wicksell, Anna
business cycles: Åkerman 220;
    Cassel 133–5; Davidson 50–2;
    Ohlin 194–6; Wicksell 89
business stabilization 98

cameralism 19, 20
capital: Arnberg 32–3; Cassel and
    53, 131; Davidson's theory 5,
    47–53; Wicksell's theory 5,
    80–1, 98–114
capitalism 36, 38–9, 43
Caps 17, 19, 23
Carnegie Foundation 151, 217
Cartesius 14, 41
Cassel, G. 4, 122–40, 222; Bagge
    219; capital formation 53;
    Davidson and 45, 64; disciples
    46; divisions in economics 147;
    economic policy 66, 94, 95, 96,
    135–40; Gustav Vasa 14;
    Heckscher and 145–6, 148,
    151, 164; influence on
    Stockholm school *see*
    Stockholm school; interest and
    steady-rate growth 130–1;
    laissez-faire 216; Lund chair
    83, 124; monetary theory
    131–3; Ohlin 215; Political
    Economy Club 152;
    professional career 124–5;
    reputation 6–7, 122–4, 142;
    socialism 37, 38; trade cycle
    theory 133–5; value 56,
    126–30; Walras 6, 10, 127–8;
    Wicksell and *see* Wicksell
causation, cumulative 217–18
Caves, R.E. 223
Chairs in political economy 2–3
change, focus on 1–2, 10
China 24
Christiernin, P.N. 21–3, 42
Chydenius, A. 24–6, 42
circuit velocity 63–4
Clark, J.B. 179
cliometrics 145
Coats, A.W. 123
Cobb–Douglas function 129

colonization 19
Columella, L. 13
commodities: classification 47;
    scarcities 55–7, 64, 95–6; values
    54–7, 65
Commodity Ordinance
    (Produktplakatet) 3, 16, 143,
    149
communism 220; *see also* socialist
    economics
Communist Manifesto 34
comparative statics 175, 181–2
companies, taxation of 69
compensated dollar proposal 63
confiscatory taxation 116–17
conscription 81
consumption, autonomous changes
    in 192–6
continuation analysis 174, 176,
    176–7, 191, 200–1
credit: Davidson 47, 48–9, 63–4;
    expansion 28; liberalization 22;
    Wicksell 91–2
cumulative causation 217–18
cumulative processes 92, 173;
    equilibrating mechanisms
    186–7; saving-interest
    mechanisms 189–91
currency crises 158

Dagens Nyheter (Daily News) 151
Dahmén, E. 224
Dalton, H. 140
Danielsson, A. 36
Davenant, C. 17, 41
Davidson, D. 2, 44–73, 143;
    capital theory 5, 47–53;
    commodity scarcities 55–7, 64,
    95–6; Heckscher and *see*
    Heckscher; history of rent 53–4;
    importance 3, 4, 142; life and
    career 44–7; marginal
    productivity theory of
    distribution 57–61; Marxism
    34–5, 42, 72; monetary policy
    64–7, 137, 138, 139, 140;
    monetary theory 61–4, 94–5;
    political work 86, 139, 222;

taxation and public finance
67–73; theory of value 54–7;
transitional figure 5, 46;
Wicksell and *see* Wicksell
Deane, P. 123
debt, public 70–1
decision-making 118–19
deflation 132; *see also* inflation
demand: autonomous changes in
consumption 192–6; effective
see effective demand
deposit credit 63–4
development, economic 217–18
direct rule 13
disequilibrium approach 176–7,
186, 187–91
disequilibrium sequence analysis
171, 177, 201–3, 212–13
distribution: Cassel and 126,
129–30; marginal productivity
theory of 57–61, 81
division of labour 18, 20
double budget 72
Drysdale, C. 79
Drysdale, G. 78
durability of capital goods 111–12
dynamic method 8, 165, 169,
212–13; development of
173–211
dynamic norm 178, 179–80

East India Company 16
economic development 217–18
economic growth 131
economic history 7, 142;
Heckscher's manifesto 144–5;
Heckscher's work on 148, 149,
150–1, 154, 156, 162–3, 164;
as independent field 163
Economic History Institute 154–5
economic literature 2
economic policy: Heckscher 158,
160–1; 1930s 135–40; *see also*
monetary policy
economic thought, history of 1–2,
10
effective demand, principle of
169–70, 211–12; Lindahl's

equilibrating mechanism and
186–7; Myrdal and 190–1
Ekonomisk Tidskrift 86, 143, 157;
Davidson 45, 46, 74, 157
employees funds 222
Engels, F. 38, 39, 223
England 16, 18
enterprise capital funds 50
equilibrating mechanism 186–7,
190, 193–6
equilibrium approach 182–6;
Faxén's strategic 208–11;
Keynesian and Lindahl 203–5;
sequence analysis and 173–4,
177, 201–2; *see also*
disequilibrium;
quasi-equilibrium
equilibrium point of decline
189–90
equitable taxation 116
ex ante/ex post calculus 187–9, 194
exchange rate 22, 23
expansionism 22–3, 27, 28
expectational disequilibrium
sequence analysis 177
expectations 174, 175; anticipated
processes and 204–5;
equilibrium between strategies
209–10; method of 178–81
expenditure decisions 118–19
exploitation 25
export prices 22, 23; *see also* trade

Fabiunke, G. 223
family relations 12
Faxén, K.O. 171, 208–11
Federal Reserve Board 140
Finland 1, 42, 162
Fisher, I. 63, 136, 153
foreign exchange reserves 158
France 16, 27, 140
Frankfurt 3
Frängsmyr, T. 21
Fredrik I, King 20
freedom: academic 166; to worship
15–16
Freedom, Age of 2–3, 4, 16–17
French economists 214, 223

Index

Frey, B.S. 223
Friedman, M. 62
Fries, E. 16
Frisch, R. 6, 220
Frölander, T. 77–8, 83
funded confiscation revenues
117–18

gains, taxation of 69, 70
game uncertainty 210–11
Gårdlund, T. 121, 129, 137
Gasslander, O. 31
Geijer, E.G. 30, 34, 42
Germany 123, 215; policies
criticised 116, 125; universities
3, 13
Giöbel-Lilja, I. 125
gods 11–12
gold invasion 96
gold standard 139, 140
gold stocks 132
goods reserved for future wants
47–9; *see also* savings
Götrek, P. 42
gradual approximation 126, 128,
129
Graunt, J. 19
Great Depression 51–2
Gripenstedt, J.A. 31
growth, economic 131
Gustav I Vasa, King 14
Gustav II Adolf, King 14
Gustav III, King 16, 20, 25–6, 27

Haavelmo, T. 207
Hahn, F.H. 174, 176, 200, 202,
213
Halle 3
Hallendorff, C. 147, 154–5
Hamilton, G.K. 4, 31–2
Hammarskjöld, D. 8, 169, 171–2,
183, 197, 199; Heckscher and
159; profit 171, 191–2;
Unemployment Commission
159, 219
Hammarskjöld, H. 149, 171
Hamrin, F. 136, 140
Hansen, B. 169, 171, 199;

quasi-equilibrium 205–7;
recursive systems 207–8
Hansson, B.A. 196, 205, 208, 209,
210
Harcourt, G. C. 114
Harrod, R. 131, 196
Hart, A.G. 202
Hats 17, 18–19, 22, 23
Hatta, T. 100
Hayek, F.A. von 8, 94, 100, 172,
216; disequilibrium methods
177; intertemporal equilibrium
176
Heckscher, E.F. 7, 31, 42, 141–66:
Cassel 137, 138, 139, 151,
Bagge's Chair 164, *docent*
under 145–6, 148, purchasing
power parity 133; Davidson, 46,
75, 144, 151, 164, *Ekonomisk
Tidskrift* 157, importance to
economics 74; early work
143–6; economic history *see*
economic history; economists
39; gold standard 140;
laissez-faire 216; legacy to
economics 164–7; 1909–29
146–54; 1929–49 156–64;
political work 147, 149, 151,
158–9, 222; Risingh 14, 41;
spectacular switch 154–6;
Wicksell 86, 150, 151–2
Heckscher–Ohlin theorem 7, 141,
150, 215
Hegel, G. 34
height expansion 100, 102–4
Henrik, Bishop 13–14
Henriksson, R.G.H. 152, 157, 158,
159, 160, 162
Herlitz, L. 26, 42
Hermann, F. 47
Hettne, B. 142, 163, 223
Hicks, J.R. 8, 177, 184, 206;
economic revolutions 211;
method of expectations 178;
temporary equilibrium 176, 185
Hiertha, H. 27
historical school 3–4, 10, 30, 42
history of thought 1–2, 10, 222

Hjärne, H. 143
Holland 16
husbandry literature 2, 12–13

immaculate conception 85
imperfect foresight 184
imports 23; *see also* trade
income: aggregate 89, 93; capital
    formation and 48
income–expenditure model 212
income tax 67–9, 70, 71, 72
induction 145
industrial revolution 154
inflation 67, 160, 221–2; Cassel
    64, 132, 138–9, 140;
    commodity scarcities 64, 95–6;
    suppressed 206
innovation 50–1, 60, 67
instantaneous analysis 187–8
institutions 216
intellectual minority 120
interdependent models 207–8
interest, theory of 48–9, 128–9
interest rates: Cassel 130–1, 133,
    138; Davidson's capital theory
    53; equilibrating mechanism
    193–4; monetary policy 66–7;
    Wicksell 88–98, Wicksell effect
    105–14
intertemporal equilibrium 170,
    175–6, 181, 182, 183–4, 185
investment: Davidson's capital
    theory 47–9; Stockholm school
    186–7, 189–91, 193–4
IS–LM approach 212

Jacobsson, P. 49, 74
Jameson, F. 41
Järta, H. 27–8, 42
Jevons, W.S. 4, 5
Johan III, King 13
Johannisson, K. 19, 41
Johansson, A. 8, 155, 160, 169,
    219; Heckscher and 161
Johansson, L. *see* Lucidor
Jonung, L. 8, 136, 137, 140, 212
Jugel, C. 13

Kahn, R.F. 87
Kalm, P. 21, 24
Karl XII, King 16
Karl XIV Johan, King 28; *see also*
    Bernadotte
Keynes, J.M. 64, 125, 215;
    Davidson and 52; Heckscher
    and 151, 153; Söderström Gold
    Medal 164; Stockholm school
    and 8, 189, 190, 199, 213,
    equilibrating mechanism and
    effective demand 193, 195–6,
    Lindahl 171, 186–7, 203–5,
    objective risk 180, profits
    191–2; Wicksell 87
Keynesian revolution 169–70,
    195–6, 211–13
Keynesian school 8
Klammer, A. 123
Knies, K. 47
Knight, F. 153, 178, 209
Knorr-Cetina, K. 123
Kolm, S.C. 223
Kreuger crash 160
Kristina, Queen 41
Kuhn, T.S. 5

labour: Davidson 54, 60–1, 66–7;
    division of 18, 20; opportunity
    cost 12; reserve army of 133;
    shortage 50, 59; value and 32,
    35–6, 37, 42, 43, 54; Wicksell's
    capital theory 99–114 *passim*
laissez-faire 216
land 99–114 *passim*, 128
Landgren, K.G. 136, 195–6
landskapslagarna (provincial laws)
    2, 12
Lange, O. 206
Lappo movement 162
Laura Spellman Rockefeller
    Memorial 219
lending rate 92–5; *see also* interest
    rates
lengthening of the production
    period 49, 50–1
Lenin, V.I. 223
liberalism 4, 24–33

Liedman, S.E. 3, 19
Lindahl, E.R. 86–7, 172, 212, 219;
  Heckscher 153, 157, 164;
  intertemporal equilibrium 170,
  176, 181–7; Keynes's *General
  Theory* 171, 203–5; Myrdal
  and 87, 188, 190–1; sequence
  analysis 196–201, 202;
  single-period analysis 171,
  174–5, 195; Stockholm school
  8, 137, 169, 206, 211; Wicksell
  46, 74, 86–7, 94, 97
Lindroth, S. 18, 41
Linné, C. von (Linnaeus) 21
liquidity preference 205
Ljungberg, C.E. 30
long-run functions 204
Lönnroth, E. 14
Lönnroth, J. 41, 43
lords 11–12
Lorén Foundation 79–80, 82
Lowry, S.T. 1, 4
Löwstedt, C.R. 42
Lucidor 25, 42
Lund University 2, 3, 83, 124
Lundberg, E.F. 168, 172, 191,
  224; Cassel 46; economic policy
  136, 137, 138; *Ekonomisk
  Tidskrift* 45; equilibrium
  approach 170, 185–6, 188;
  Myrdal 216; sequence analysis
  200–2, 208; Stockholm school
  8, 169, 209, 211, 212–13, 219
Lutheran Church 85

Magnusson, L. 2, 3, 41
Malthus, T.R. 31, 32, 85
Malynes, G. 41
Månsson, P. 12–13
marginal productivity: Cassel 126,
  129, 130; Davidson 57–61;
  Wicksell 81, 90–1, 99–100,
  115; Wicksell effect 107–11
marginal utility 55–6, 127
marginalism 4–5
market socialism 84
Marshall, A. 46, 54, 178–9
Marx, K. 34, 53–4, 127, 223; law
of value 43; wealth 42
Marxism *see* socialist economics
Meade, J. 173, 215
mechanical disequilibrium
  sequence analysis 177
mechanical dynamics 202
Meidner, R. 221–2
Menger, C. 4, 47, 80
mercantilism 3, 31; Gustav Vasa
  13–14; Heckscher 141, 144,
  148, 149, 150, 154;
  Nordencrantz 17–18
Meurling, P. 34
Mill, J.S. 32, 53, 78, 145
minorities 119–20
Mises, L. von 94, 95
Moll, V. 139
monetarism 21–3
monetary equilibrium 97–8
monetary policy: Davidson 64–7;
  Wicksell 94–7; *see also*
  economic policy
monetary theory: Cassel 131–3;
  Davidson 61–4, 94–5; Wicksell
  88–98
money: overproduction 28;
  stabilization 136–7; values 15
Montgomery, A. 139, 167
Mun, T. 17, 41
Myhrman, J. 22
Myrdal, A. 161
Myrdal, G.C. 87–8, 172, 174, 219,
  222; Åkerman compared with
  221; Cassel 10, 46, 125, 128,
  135, 164; disequilibrium
  approach 171, 187–91;
  equilibrium approach 185, 186;
  expectations 170, 178–81;
  Heckscher 152, 153, 160–1; as
  institutionalist 216–18;
  Stockholm school 8, 137, 169,
  211; Wicksell 94, 97–8

Nationalekonomiska Föreningen
  (Association of National
  Economists) 33
natural history 21
natural (real) interest rate 90–5

natural science 3, 10
nature 35–6, 42
Navigation Act (Produktplakatet) 3, 16, 143, 149
Nazism 162
Nertus 11
'New Realm' 121
Newmarch, W. 88
Njord 11
nomads 50
Nordencrantz, A. 17–18, 20, 24, 33, 41, 42
Nordic Meetings 162
norms of monetary policy 64–7

objective risk 180–1
objective value 56–7, 61–3, 65
Odin 11
Ohlin, B. 42, 167, 172–3, 222; autonomous changes in consumption demand 192–6, 200; Heckscher and 156; Political Economy Club 153, 157; Stockholm school 8, 137, 155, 168, 169, 171; unemployment 219; trade 215–16, 218; Wicksell 46, 74, 86, 88, 89, 94
Öhrvall, H. 77–8, 80, 83
Olaussen, L. 42
Östlind, A. 132, 137, 139

Palm, A. 36
Palme Fund 157
Palmstruch, J. 14, 41
paper money 22–3, 160
Patinkin, D. 196
pension law 70
periods 183, 206; profit as link between 191–2; *see also* single-period analysis
Persson, M. 42
Péteri, G. 140
Petty, W. 19, 42
Phinney, J.T. 132
physiocracy 3, 26–7
Pigou, A.C. 64
planning, central 160

plans, dynamic method and 174, 175, 197–8, 201, 206
political arithmetic 19–20
political economy, Chairs of 2–3
Political Economy Club 86, 152–3, 157, 160–1
political parties: early 17; qualified majority and 119–20
politics, science and 166
popularizers 123
population 20, 85, 120
Portes, R. 223
power, wealth and 29, 30
price Wicksell effect 114
prices: Cassel 123, 126–30, 131–2; Christiernin 23; Heckscher and Ohlin 215; stabilization 137–40; Wicksell's monetary theory 88–98
private bank 41
private economics 20
product, aggregate 89, 93–4
production period 98–9; lengthening of 49, 50–1
productivity 64–5, 66–7, 97; marginal *see* marginal productivity
Produktplakatet (Navigation Act) 3, 16, 143, 149
profit 171, 191–2
progressive taxation: Davidson 68–9, 72–3; Wicksell 71, 82, 118
property, private 20
proportional growth model 175
protectionism 33
provincial laws (*landskapslagarna*) 2, 12
Prussia 3
public debt 70–1
public finance 67–73, 114–20
public opinion 159–60
public sector 72, 115–16
public service degree 147
public works programmes 30, 51–2
Pufendorf, S. von 2, 14, 41
purchasing power 62
purchasing power parity 132–3

qualified majorities 71, 118–19
quantity theory of money 88, 132, 151–2
quasi-equilibrium 171, 205–7
Quesnay, F. 29

railways 145, 149
real (natural) interest rate 90–5
real Wicksell effect 114
recessions 112
recursive systems 171, 207–8
reform mercantilists 3
Rehn, G. 221–2
rent: Davidson's history of 53–4; Wicksell's capital theory 99–114 *passim*
reserve army of labour 133
restrictionism 27–8
Reynolds, L.G. 224
Ricardo, D. 32, 53, 60, 128; bank crisis, 31; trade 215; value theory 54–5, 127
Rinteln 3
Risingh, J.C. 14–16
risk 180–1
Robbins, L. 175
Robinson, J. 113–14
Rockefeller Foundation 219
Rodbertus, J.K. 38, 53–4
Rooth, I. 158
Rousseau, J.J. 24
Royal Swedish Academy of Science 47, 157, 164
Rybezynski theorem 216

Saint-Etienne, C. 140
Samuelson, P.A. 196, 206, 212
Sandelin, B. 41
Sandmo, A. 222
saving paradox 186–7
savings 194; Cassel 131; cumulative process 189–91; Davidson's capital theory 47–50, 52, 53; Wicksell effect 53, 59–60
Say, J.B. 29, 32, 55
Say's law 134
Scandinavian Journal of

Economics 45; *see also Ekonomisk Tidskrift*
Scandinavian Monetary Union 96
scarcity: Cassel's principle of 126, 128, 131, 138; commodity 55–7, 64, 95–6
Scheffer, F. 26–7, 42
Schumpeter, J.A. 122–3, 127, 128, 134
Schwerin, F.B. von 28
science, politics and 166
Seligman, B. 122, 128, 130, 133
sequence analysis 171, 173–4, 192, 196–201, 208, 213; disequilibrium 201–2; limitations 202
short-run functions 204–5
Sieber, R. 223
simultaneous systems 207–8
single-period analysis 171, 174, 198–200, 208, 213
Siven, C.H. 8, 42, 212, 223
skilled labour 61
skrot och korn (alloy and standard) 15, 41
Smith, A. 3, 29, 35, 144
Social Democrat party 160–1
social marginal productivity rate 107–11
social reform 78–9, 115–20
socialist economics 214, 223; Davidson 34–5, 42, 72; opponents and 34–9; Wicksell 35–7, 38–9, 84
Söderlund, E. 163, 164, 167
Södersten, B. 7
Söderström Gold Medal 164
Sommarin, E. 74, 86
Sraffa, P. 55, 114
stabilization: money 136–7; prices 137–40
State 14; Agardh 29–30; Berch 20; politics in early 17; Stenkula 31; *see also* Welfare State
static method 174–5
stationary state 174–5
Steffen, G. 37–8
Steiger, O. 136, 193, 196

Stenkula, A. 30–1
Stigler, G.J. 123, 222, 224
Stockholm school 7–9, 46, 140,
    168–213; Cassel's influence 46,
    137, 169, Myrdal's dynamic
    method 178, 180; Heckscher
    and 153, 155; Wicksell's
    influence 46, 74, 97–8, 137,
    169, 173, Lindahl 182, static
    method 174
Stockholm School of Economics
    146, 148, 155–6, 157
Stockholm University 145–6
Stolper–Samuelson theorem 216
strategic equilibrium 171, 208–11
Strindberg, A. 37
subjective risk 180–1
substitution, principle of 126, 129
suffrage, universal 71
suppressed inflation 206
Svennilson, I. 173, 209, 210;
    Ekonomisk Tidskrift 45;
    Stockholm school 8, 212, 219
Svensk Tidskrift 148, 150, 151
Swan, T.W. 114
Swedish Confederation of Trade
    Unions (LO) 224
Swedish East India Company 16
Swedish Economic Society 147,
    161–2, 165
Swedish Journal of Economics 45;
    see also Ekonomisk Tidskrift
Swedish school *see* Stockholm
    school
Swedish State Railways 145

Tabellverket 20
Tacitus 11
Tariff and Treaty Commission 151
tax prices (user fees) 70, 115–16
taxation 2; Davidson 67–73;
    physiocracy 26; Wicksell 81–2,
    114–18
technological progress 50–1, 60, 67
Tegnér, E. 28
Temin, P. 140
temporary equilibrium 170, 176,
    181, 184–5, 189

tenant farming 13
test case, Wicksell's 85, 86
Thal, P. 223
Thomas, B. 46, 136, 137, 140
Thor 11
thought, history of 1–2, 10, 222
three grounds of interest 49
Thumbshirn, A. von 13
Thünen's law 107; *see also*
    marginal productivity
Tollison, R.D. 224
Tooke, T. 88
towns, importance of 20
trade, international 22, 23;
    Heckscher 141, 143–4, 150,
    215; Ohlin 215–16; Risingh 15,
    16
trade unions 60–1
trading companies 16, 41
Trygg, Sven (pseudonym for
    Wicksell) 81, 114
Turku 3
Turvey, R. 46

Uhr, C.G. 92, 98, 100, 167; Cassel
    129; Chydenius 24; Davidson
    68, 71, 75, 138; Unemployment
    Commission 159; Wicksell 105,
    137
uncertainty 170, 209–11
underemployment 189–90
unemployment 8; Davidson 50–2;
    Heckscher 158–9; Meidner and
    Rehn 221–2
Unemployment Commission
    (1927) 159
Unemployment Committee (1926)
    158–9
Unga, N. 136
United States of America 140, 217,
    223
universities 2–3, 18
Uppsala 3, 143
user fees 70, 115–16
Usselinx, W. 14, 41
utility: arithmeticians of 16–23;
    marginal 55–6, 127

value: Arnberg 32–3; Cassel
126–30; Davidson 54–7, 61–3,
65; Marxism 36–7, 37, 39, 43
velocity, circuit 63–4
Virrankoski, P. 42

Wadensjö, E. 42, 219, 224
wages: Bagge 218–19; Davidson
50–3; 59–60; Wicksell's capital
theory 99–114 *passim*
Wagner, A. 43, 80
waiting 49; Cassel's interest theory
130; Wicksell 90–1, 99
Walker, D.A. 10
Wallenberg, M. 159
Wallerius, B. 42
Walras, L. 4, 5, 81; Cassel and 6,
10, 127–8
War Planning Commission 149,
150
Wargentin, P. 20
wealth, power and 29, 30
wealth tax 70
Welfare State 72, 84, 117, 120
Wermelin, A. 35–7
Whitley, R. 123
Wicksell, Anna (née Bugge) 80, 86
Wicksell, Axel 76
Wicksell, Finn 81, 87
Wicksell, J.G. Knut 2, 76–120,

139, 217, 222; capital theory 5,
80–1, 98–114; Cassel and 5,
6–7, 129; price stability 132,
137–8; Davidson and 5, 45, 64,
71–2, 75, 82, marginal
productivity distribution 58, 59;
Hamilton and 32; Heckscher
and 86, 150, 151–2; historical
school 10; importance 3, 4,
142; induction 145; influence
on Stockholm school *see*
Stockholm school; interest rate
53; life and career 76–88; Lund
University chair 83, 124;
Marxism 35–7, 38–9, 84;
monetary theory 87–98; public
finance and social reform
114–20; technological progress
51; value theory 56
Wicksell, Liv 121
Wicksell, Sven 81, 87
Wicksell effect 52, 53, 59–60,
105–14
Wicksteed, P. 46, 58
Wigforss, E. 136
Winch, D. 168
Wold, H. 207
worship, freedom of 15–16

Zionist movement 162